Security Automation

Leverage Ansible 2 to automate complex security tasks like application security, network security, and malware analysis

Madhu Akula
Akash Mahajan

BIRMINGHAM - MUMBAI

Security Automation with Ansible 2

Copyright © 2017 Packt Publishing

All rights reserved. No part of this book may be reproduced, stored in a retrieval system, or transmitted in any form or by any means, without the prior written permission of the publisher, except in the case of brief quotations embedded in critical articles or reviews.

Every effort has been made in the preparation of this book to ensure the accuracy of the information presented. However, the information contained in this book is sold without warranty, either express or implied. Neither the authors, nor Packt Publishing, and its dealers and distributors will be held liable for any damages caused or alleged to be caused directly or indirectly by this book.

Packt Publishing has endeavored to provide trademark information about all of the companies and products mentioned in this book by the appropriate use of capitals. However, Packt Publishing cannot guarantee the accuracy of this information.

First published: December 2017

Production reference: 1121217

Published by Packt Publishing Ltd.
Livery Place
35 Livery Street
Birmingham
B3 2PB, UK.
ISBN 978-1-78839-451-2

www.packtpub.com

Credits

Authors
Madhu Akula
Akash Mahajan

Reviewer
Samuel P Doran

Commissioning Editor
Vijin Boricha

Acquisition Editor
Rahul Nair

Content Development Editor
Nithin Varghese

Technical Editor
Komal Karne

Copy Editor
Safis Editing

Project Coordinator
Virginia Dias

Proofreader
Safis Editing

Indexer
Tejal Daruwale Soni

Graphics
Tania Dutta

Production Coordinator
Shantanu Zagade

About the Authors

Madhu Akula is a security Ninja and a security and DevOps researcher with extensive experience in the industry, ranging from client-facing assignments, building scalable and secure infrastructure, to publishing industry-leading research, to running training sessions for companies and governments alike.

Madhu's research papers are frequently selected for major security industry conferences including DEF CON 24, All Day DevOps (2016, 2017), DevSecCon (London, Singapore, Boston), DevOpsDays India, c0c0n, Serverless Summit, ToorCon, DefCamp, SkyDogCon, NolaCon, and null. Madhu was also a keynote speaker for the National Cyber Security conference at Dayananda Sagar College, Bangalore in February 2016.

When he's not working with Appsecco's clients or speaking at events, Madhu is actively involved in researching vulnerabilities in open source products/platforms such as WordPress, ntop, and OpenDocMan. He is also a contributing bug hunter at Code Vigilant (a project to secure open source software).

Madhu's research has identified many vulnerabilities in over 200 organizations including the U.S. Department of Homeland Security, Google, Microsoft, Yahoo, Adobe, LinkedIn, eBay, AT&T, Blackberry, Cisco, and Barracuda. He is also an active member of Bugcrowd, Hackerone, Synack, and more. Madhu has trained over 5000 people in information security for companies and organizations including the Indian Navy and the Ministry of e-services in a leading Gulf state.

I would like to thank my parents, who have always been a great support. Apart from my parents, I want to thank my colleagues at Appsecco for letting me work on this project without any stress.

I am grateful for the support given by the folks at Packt, especially Rahul, Nithin, and Sweeny. All of them worked hard to support and guide us throughout. Last but not least, a big thank you to my coauthor, Akash Mahajan. He guided me throughout the book and taught me great things.

Akash Mahajan is an accomplished security professional with over a decade's experience in providing specialist application and infrastructure consulting services at the highest levels to companies, governments, and organizations around the world. He has lots of experience in working with clients to provide innovative security insights that truly reflect the commercial and operational needs of the organization, from strategic advice to testing and analysis, to incident response and recovery.

Akash is an active participant in the international security community and a conference speaker both individually, as the chapter lead of the Bangalore chapter of OWASP the global organization responsible for defining the standards for web application security, and as a cofounder of null India's largest open security community.

Akash runs Appsecco, a company focused on application security. He authored the book, *Burp Suite Essentials*, published by *Packt Publishing* in November 2014, which is listed as a reference by the creators of Burp Suite.

I would like to thank my parents, who have always been a great support. I would like to thank my wife Lubaina, without her help I wouldn't have managed to get through all the writing that I did. Apart from my family, I want to thank my colleagues at Appsecco for letting me work on this project without any stress.

I am grateful for the support given by the folks at Packt, especially Rahul, Nithin, and Sweeny. All of them worked hard to support and guide us throughout. Last but not least, a big thank you to my coauthor Madhu Akula. He basically made the huge task of writing a book such a breeze.

About the Reviewer

Sam Doran is a senior software engineer at Red Hat, and he is working on Ansible Engine. Sam served in the U.S. Air Force as an aircraft mechanic and is a proud alumnus of the Virginia Tech Corps of Cadets. He worked for the US Government as well as for the private industry in jobs ranging from professional photography and graphic design to site reliability engineering, network engineering, and information security. He has used Ansible since 2013 to automate security monitoring infrastructure, cloud provisioning, application installation, and configuration. He has also helped Fortune 500 companies implement large scale deployments of Red Hat Ansible Tower. Sam loves automating anything and everything using Ansible.

www.PacktPub.com

For support files and downloads related to your book, please visit www.PacktPub.com. Did you know that Packt offers eBook versions of every book published, with PDF and ePub files available? You can upgrade to the eBook version at www.PacktPub.com and as a print book customer, you are entitled to a discount on the eBook copy. Get in touch with us at service@packtpub.com for more details.

At www.PacktPub.com, you can also read a collection of free technical articles, sign up for a range of free newsletters and receive exclusive discounts and offers on Packt books and eBooks.

https://www.packtpub.com/mapt</a>

Get the most in-demand software skills with Mapt. Mapt gives you full access to all Packt books and video courses, as well as industry-leading tools to help you plan your personal development and advance your career.

Why subscribe?

- Fully searchable across every book published by Packt
- Copy and paste, print, and bookmark content
- On demand and accessible via a web browser

Customer Feedback

Thanks for purchasing this Packt book. At Packt, quality is at the heart of our editorial process. To help us improve, please leave us an honest review on this book's Amazon page at https://www.amazon.com/dp/1788394518.

If you'd like to join our team of regular reviewers, you can email us at customerreviews@packtpub.com. We award our regular reviewers with free eBooks and videos in exchange for their valuable feedback. Help us be relentless in improving our products!

Table of Contents

Preface

IT is undergoing a massive paradigm shift. From a time where uptime was a measure of IT success, we are moving to the idea of immutable infrastructure, where, based on the requirements, we can spin up and trash a server on demand automatically. Ansible is playing a lead role in this transformation. It has become the tool of choice for companies big and small for tasks that are meant for one server to entire clusters.

This book is about security automation. We apply our knowledge of Ansible to different scenarios and workloads that revolve around security, hence the title. When boring and mundane tasks are automated, people doing those tasks can focus on solving the security problems they are dealing with. This enables a whole new way to looking at how we learn about security (trainings), how much we can store, process, and analyze log data (DFIR), how we can keep applying security updates without any interruptions (security operations), and more.

In this book, we will share our experience of the types of automation we can enable using Ansible. You may be familiar with some of these, or they may be entirely new to you. Regardless, rather than trying to prescribe how Ansible should be used, we hope that you will read and understand how you can take each of these playbooks/workflows, and make your security work faster, better, and more reliable, or simply have fun creating complex infrastructure scenarios for yourself or others.

This book would not have been possible without the excellent documentation provided by the folks at Red Hat Ansible and countless other blogs and projects already creating secure, resilient playbooks that we can all learn from and use.

The book is divided into three main sections:

- Essential Ansible you should be familiar with, for building useful playbooks
- Security automation techniques and approaches
- Extending and programming Ansible for even more security

The idea is to get you to quickly refresh your knowledge of Ansible and move on to becoming productive with it, and toward the end, you'll see how you can do even more by extending Ansible or creating your own security modules.

What this book covers

Chapter 1, *Introduction to Ansible Playbooks and Roles*, covers the terms that you would already be familiar with, in Ansible. They are explained with sample playbooks and the Ansible commands required to run those playbooks. If you feel your Ansible concepts and skills are a bit rusty, start here.

Chapter 2, *Ansible Tower, Jenkins, and Other Automation Tools*, is all about automation of automation. We cover the use of scheduling automation tools commonly used with Ansible such as Ansible Tower, Jenkins, and Rundeck. If you start using these tools the mundane and boring tasks of remembering when to schedule and execute playbooks and get notifications about the output can be delegated to the tools rather than in your head. If you haven't used any tools like these, you should read this chapter.

Chapter 3, *Setting up a Hardened WordPress with Encrypted Automated Backups*, covers the exploration of various security automation techniques and approaches. As with any technique or approach, it is possible that some of what we say doesn't apply for your use case. However, by taking an opinionated approach, we show you one way of doing this, which we think works well largely. WordPress is the most popular website creation software currently. By tackling how to secure it using playbooks (and running in an IT automation tool), we start talking about an IT/ops requirement of keeping running servers safe and making sure we can recover from failure. If you are responsible for managing websites (even if it is just your own), this chapter should be useful. If you don't use WordPress, there is enough in this chapter to get you to think about how to apply this chapter to your use case.

Chapter 4, *Log Monitoring and Serverless Automated Defense (Elastic Stack in AWS)*, covers log monitoring and security automation, which are like peanut butter and jelly. In this chapter, using Ansible we set up a log monitoring server infrastructure on a server in AWS. Based on attack notifications, we create a near real-time dynamic firewall service using AWS services such as AWS Lambda, Dynamo DB, and AWS Cloudwatch.

Chapter 5, *Automating Web Application Security Testing Using OWASP ZAP*, covers one of the most common security workflows of testing the security of a website using one of the most popular open source tools, that is, OWASP ZAP. Once we have figured out the basic workflow, we supercharge it for continuous scanning of your websites using Ansible and Jenkins. Read this chapter to see how we can work with Docker containers using Ansible, while doing continuous security scanning. A sure win-win!

Chapter 6, *Vulnerability Scanning with Nessus*, explains the use of Nessus with Ansible for vulnerability scanning. This chapter covers the approach of doing basic network scans, conducting security patch audits, and enumerating vulnerabilities.

Chapter 7, *Security Hardening for Applications and Networks*, shows that Ansible has enabled us to assert our security thinking declaratively. By utilizing the idea of what the system state should be, we can create security hardening playbooks based on standards, such as CIS and NIST, and guidance provided by the US Department of Defense's STIGs. Familiarize yourself with approaches to hardening applications and servers using existing security documentation, but most importantly, in a repeatable self-documenting way, which is under version control. If you were like us, doing all of this manually for many years, you will appreciate what a game changer this is for security automation.

Chapter 8, *Continuous Security Scanning for Docker Containers*, covers how to run security scanning tools against Docker containers. A lot of modern applications are deployed using containers, and this chapter will quickly helps you understand whether you have any vulnerable containers, and as always, coupled with Ansible Tower, how to make this a continuous process.

Chapter 9, *Automating Lab Setups for Forensics Collection, Malware Analysis*, is specially for malware researchers. If you have always wanted to use Cuckoo sandbox and MISP, and have shied away because of the complicated steps involved in setting these up, this chapter has got you covered.

Chapter 10, *Writing an Ansible Module for Security Testing*, covers how we can extend the functionality offered by Ansible and learn from other projects that are using Ansible to deliver great software solutions. This chapter and the next, bring us to the third section of our book.

Sometimes with all the amazing modules that come with Ansible, they are still not enough for us to do what we want to do. This chapter delves into creating an Ansible module, and if we may say so ourselves, it doesn't try to be very formal about the approach. Remembering that what we want to focus on is security automation, we create a module for running website security scans using a ZAP proxy. With a complete module provided, this will help you writing and using your modules in no time.

Chapter 11, *Ansible Security Best Practices, References, and Further reading*, covers how to manage secrets and credentials using Ansible Vault. It will help you in setting up your own instance of Ansible Galaxy. We also highlight other projects using Ansible playbooks for security solutions such as DebOps and Algo. We also cover AWX, which is the free and open source version of Ansible Tower and show you how to set it up and use it. We conclude with a short discussion on Ansible 2.5, which is expected to be released in the first or second quarter of 2018.

What you need for this book

Ansible is a tool written in Python2. For control machines, if Python2 is installed with the minimum version 2.6, you are good to go. Since Ansible 2.2 onwards, Python3 is supported as a tech preview.

Who this book is for

This book is for ideally anyone who understands that automation is key to repeatable, error free deployment and provisioning of infrastructure, applications, and networks. However, we really like to specify this.

If you are a system administrator who also takes care of the security of websites, servers, and networks, this book is for you.

Security consultants and analysts would gain by focusing on Chapter 3, *Setting up a Hardened WordPress with Encrypted Automated Backups*, to Chapter 10, *Writing an Ansible Module for Security Testing*. Even if some of the workloads don't apply to you, you will gain insights into how to use Ansible to provide security as a service to your teams. All the DevOps teams would love to work with someone who considers automation to be as important as the security part itself

Application developers who would like an easy way to deploy secure servers especially should look at Chapter 3, *Setting up a Hardened WordPress with Encrypted Automated Backups*, to Chapter 7, *Security Hardening for Applications and Networks*.

You will get the most out of this book if you are one of these:

- Someone who has used Ansible with basic commands before
- Someone who familiar with Linux and Windows operating systems
- Someone who has a basic idea about IP addressing, networking, and working with software installers

Conventions

In this book, you will find a number of text styles that distinguish between different kinds of information. Here are some examples of these styles and an explanation of their meaning. Code words in text, database table names, folder names, filenames, file extensions, pathnames, dummy URLs, user input, and Twitter handles are shown as follows: "The harden.yml performs hardening of MySQL server configuration" A block of code is set as follows:

```
- name: deletes anonymous mysql user
  mysql_user:
    user: ""
    state: absent
    login_password: "{{ mysql_root_password }}"
    login_user: root
```

When we wish to draw your attention to a particular part of a code block, the relevant lines or items are set in bold:

```
- name: deletes anonymous mysql user
  mysql_user:
    user: ""
    state: absent
    login_password: "{{ mysql_root_password }}"
    login_user: root
```

Any command-line input or output is written as follows:

```
ansible-playbook -i inventory playbook.yml
```

New terms and **important words** are shown in bold. Words that you see on the screen, for example, in menus or dialog boxes, appear in the text like this: "Click on **Confirm Security Exception** and continue to proceed with the installation steps"

Warnings or important notes appear like this.

 Tips and tricks appear like this.

Reader feedback

Feedback from our readers is always welcome. Let us know what you think about this book-what you liked or disliked. Reader feedback is important for us as it helps us develop titles that you will really get the most out of. To send us general feedback, simply email feedback@packtpub.com, and mention the book's title in the subject of your message. If there is a topic that you have expertise in and you are interested in either writing or contributing to a book, see our author guide at www.packtpub.com/authors.

Customer support

Now that you are the proud owner of a Packt book, we have a number of things to help you to get the most from your purchase.

Downloading the example code

You can download the example code files for this book from your account at http://www.packtpub.com. If you purchased this book elsewhere, you can visit http://www.packtpub.com/support and register to have the files emailed directly to you. You can download the code files by following these steps:

1. Log in or register to our website using your email address and password.
2. Hover the mouse pointer on the **SUPPORT** tab at the top.
3. Click on **Code Downloads & Errata**.
4. Enter the name of the book in the **Search** box.
5. Select the book for which you're looking to download the code files.
6. Choose from the drop-down menu where you purchased this book from.
7. Click on **Code Download**.

Once the file is downloaded, please make sure that you unzip or extract the folder using the latest version of:

- WinRAR / 7-Zip for Windows
- Zipeg / iZip / UnRarX for Mac
- 7-Zip / PeaZip for Linux

The code bundle for the book is also hosted on GitHub at https://github.com/PacktPublishing/Security-Automation-with-Ansible-2. We also have other code bundles from our rich catalog of books and videos available at https://github.com/PacktPublishing/. Check them out!

Downloading the color images of this book

We also provide you with a PDF file that has color images of the screenshots/diagrams used in this book. The color images will help you better understand the changes in the output. You can download this file from https://www.packtpub.com/sites/default/files/downloads/SecurityAutomationwithAnsible2_ColorImages.pdf.

Errata

Although we have taken every care to ensure the accuracy of our content, mistakes do happen. If you find a mistake in one of our books-maybe a mistake in the text or the code-we would be grateful if you could report this to us. By doing so, you can save other readers from frustration and help us improve subsequent versions of this book. If you find any errata, please report them by visiting http://www.packtpub.com/submit-errata, selecting your book, clicking on the **Errata Submission Form** link, and entering the details of your errata. Once your errata are verified, your submission will be accepted and the errata will be uploaded to our website or added to any list of existing errata under the Errata section of that title. To view the previously submitted errata, go to https://www.packtpub.com/books/content/support and enter the name of the book in the search field. The required information will appear under the **Errata** section.

Piracy

Piracy of copyrighted material on the internet is an ongoing problem across all media. At Packt, we take the protection of our copyright and licenses very seriously. If you come across any illegal copies of our works in any form on the internet, please provide us with the location address or website name immediately so that we can pursue a remedy. Please contact us at copyright@packtpub.com with a link to the suspected pirated material. We appreciate your help in protecting our authors and our ability to bring you valuable content.

Questions

If you have a problem with any aspect of this book, you can contact us at questions@packtpub.com, and we will do our best to address the problem.

1
Introduction to Ansible Playbooks and Roles

According to Wikipedia, Ansible is an open source automation engine that automates software provisioning, configuration management, and application deployment. But you already knew that. This book is about taking the idea of IT automation software and applying it to the domain of Information Security Automation.

The book will take you through the journey of *security automation* to show how Ansible is used in the real world.

In this book, we will be automating security-related tasks in a structured, modular fashion using a simple human-readable format YAML. Most importantly, what you will learn to create will be repeatable. This means once it is done, you can focus on fine-tuning, expanding the scope, and so on. The tool ensures that we can build and tear down anything, from simple application stacks to simple, but extensive, multi-application frameworks working together.

If you have been playing around with Ansible, and in this book we assume you have, you would have definitely come across some of the following terms:

- Playbook
- Ansible Modules
- YAML
- Roles
- Templates (Jinja2)

Don't worry, we will address all of the aforementioned terms in this chapter. Once you are comfortable with these topics, we will move on to covering scheduler tools, and then to building security automation playbooks.

Ansible terms to keep in mind

Like all new subjects or topics, it is a good idea to get familiar with the terminology of that subject or topic. We will go through some of the Ansible terms that we will be using throughout the book, and if at any point you are not able to follow, you might want to come back to this chapter and refresh your understanding for that particular term.

Playbooks

A playbook, in the classic sense, is about offensive and defensive plays in football. The players keep a record of the plays (plan of action) in a book, usually in the form of a diagram.

In Ansible, a playbook is a series of ordered steps or instructions for an IT process. Think of a nicely-written instruction manual that can be read and understood by humans and computers alike.

In the subsequent chapters, all the automation we will focus on regarding security will lead us toward building both simple and complex playbooks.

This is what an Ansible playbook command looks like:

```
ansible-playbook -i inventory playbook.yml
```

Ignore the -i flag for now and notice the extension of the playbook file.

As stated in http://docs.ansible.com/ansible/playbooks_intro.html:

> *"Playbooks are expressed in YAML format (see YAML syntax (*http://docs.ansible.com/ansible/YAMLSyntax.html*)) and have a minimum of syntax, which intentionally tries to not be a programming language or script, but rather a model of a configuration or a process."*

Ansible modules

Ansible ships with a number of modules (called the **module library**) that can be executed directly on remote hosts or through playbooks.Tasks in playbooks call modules to do the work.

Ansible has many modules, most of which are community contributed and maintained. Core modules are maintained by the Ansible core engineering team and will always ship with Ansible itself.

Users can also write their own modules. These modules can control system resources, like services, packages, or files (anything really), or handle executing system commands.

Here is the list of modules available by Ansible: `http://docs.ansible.com/ansible/latest/modules_by_category.html#module-index`. If you use Dash (`https://kapeli.com/dash`) or Zeal (`https://zealdocs.org/`), you can download the offline version for easy reference.

Modules can be executed via the command line as well. We will be using modules to write all the tasks inside our playbooks. All modules technically return JSON format data.

Modules should be idempotent and should avoid making any changes if they detect that the current state matches the desired final state. When using Ansible playbooks, these modules can trigger *change events* in the form of notifying *handlers* to run additional tasks.

Documentation for each module can be accessed from the command line with the `ansible-doc` tool:

```
$ ansible-doc apt
```

We can list all the modules available on our host:

```
$ ansible-doc -l
```

Start the Apache web server on all nodes grouped under `webservers` by executing the `httpd` module. Note the use of the `-m` flag:

```
$ ansible webservers -m service -a "name=httpd state=started"
```

This snippet shows the exact same command but inside a playbook in YAML syntax:

```
- name: restart webserver
  service:
    name: httpd
    state: started
```

Each module contains multiple parameters and options, get to know more about the features of the modules by looking at their documentation and examples.

YAML syntax for writing Ansible playbooks

Ansible playbooks are written in **YAML**, which stands for **YAML Ain't Markup Language**.

According to the official document (http://yaml.org/spec/current.html):

> *YAML Ain't Markup Language (abbreviated YAML) is a data serialization language designed to be human-friendly and work well with modern programming languages for everyday tasks.*

Ansible uses YAML because it is easier for humans to read and write than other common data formats, such as XML or JSON. All YAML files (regardless of their association with Ansible or not) can optionally begin with --- and end with . . . . This is part of the YAML format and indicates the start and end of a document.

 YAML files should end with .yaml or .yml. YAML is case sensitive. You can also use linters, such as www.yamllint.com, or your text editor plugins for linting YAML syntax, which help you to troubleshoot any syntax errors and so on.

Here is an example of a simple playbook to showcase YAML syntax from Ansible documentation (http://docs.ansible.com/ansible/playbooks_intro.html#playbook-language-example):

```
- hosts: webservers
  vars:
    http_port: 80
    max_clients: 200
  remote_user: root

  tasks:
  - name: Ensure apache is at the latest version
    yum:
      name: httpd
```

```
    state: latest
  - name: Write the apache config file
    template:
      src: /srv/httpd.j2
      dest: /etc/httpd.conf

    notify:
    - restart apache

  - name: Ensure apache is running (and enable it at boot)
    service:
      name: httpd
      state: started
      enabled: yes

handlers:
  - name: Restart apache
    service:
      name: httpd
      state: restarted
```

Ansible roles

While playbooks offer a great way to execute *plays* in a pre-defined order, there is a brilliant feature on Ansible that takes the whole idea to a completely different level. Roles are a convenient way to bundle tasks, supporting assets such as files and templates, coupled with an automatic set of search paths.

By using a concept most programmers would be familiar with, of *including* files and folders and ascribing what is being included, a playbook becomes infinitely more readable and understandable. Roles are basically made up of tasks, handlers, and configurations, but by adding an additional layer to how a playbook is structured, we can easily get the big picture overview as well as the low-level details.

This allows for reusable code and a division of work in a team tasked with writing playbooks. For example, the database guru writes a role (almost like a partial playbook) for setting up the database and the security guru writes one on hardening such a database.

While it is possible to write a playbook in one very large file, eventually you want to reuse files and start to organize things.

Large and complex playbooks are hard to maintain and it is very difficult to reuse sections of a large playbook. Breaking a playbook into roles allows very efficient code reuse and makes playbooks much easier to understand.

The benefits of using roles while building large playbooks include:

- Collaborating on writing playbooks
- Reusing existing roles
- Roles can be updated, improved upon independently
- Handling variables, templates, and files is easier

LAMP usually stands for **Linux, Apache, MySQL, PHP**. A popular combination of software that is used to build applications for the web. Nowadays, another common combination in the PHP world is **LEMP**, which is **Linux, NGINX, MySQL, PHP**.

This is an example of what a possible LAMP stack `site.yml` can look like:

```
- name: LAMP stack setup on ubuntu 16.04
  hosts: all
  gather_facts: False
  remote_user: "{{remote_username}}"
  become: yes

  roles:
    - common
    - web
    - db
    - php
```

Note the list of roles. Just by reading the role names we can get an idea of the kind of tasks possibly under that role.

Templates with Jinja2

Ansible uses Jinja2 templating to enable dynamic expressions and access to variables. Jinja2 variables and expressions within playbooks and tasks allow us to create roles that are very flexible. By passing variables to a role written this way, we can have the same role perform different tasks or configurations. Using a templating language, such as Jinja2, we are able to write playbooks that are succinct and easier to read.

By ensuring that all the templating takes place on the Ansible controller, Jinja2 is not required on the target machine. Only the required data is copied over, which reduces the data that needs to be transferred. As we know, less data transfer usually results in faster execution and feedback.

Jinja templating examples

A mark of a good templating language is the ability to allow control of the content without appearing to be a fully-fledged programming language. Jinja2 excels in that by providing us with the ability to do conditional output, such as iterations using loops, among other things.

Let's look at some basic examples (obviously Ansible playbook-related) to see what that looks like.

Conditional example

Execute only when the operating system family is `Debian`:

```
tasks:
  - name: "shut down Debian flavored systems"
    command: /sbin/shutdown -t now
    when: ansible_os_family == "Debian"
```

Loops example

The following task adds users using the Jinja2 templating. This allows for dynamic functionality in playbooks. We can use variables to store data when required, we just need to update the variables rather than the entire playbook:

```
  - name: add several users
    user:
      name: "{{ item.name }}"
      state: present
      groups: "{{ item.groups }}"
```

```
    with_items:
      - { name: 'testuser1', groups: 'wheel' }
      - { name: 'testuser2', groups: 'root' }
```

LAMP stack playbook example – combining all the concepts

We will look at how to write a LAMP stack playbook using the skills we have learned so far. Here is the high-level hierarchy structure of the entire playbook:

```
inventory              # inventory file
group_vars/            #
   all.yml             # variables
site.yml               # master playbook (contains list of roles)
roles/                 #
   common/             # common role
      tasks/           #
         main.yml      # installing basic tasks
   web/                # apache2 role
      tasks/           #
         main.yml      # install apache
      templates/       #
         web.conf.j2   # apache2 custom configuration
      vars/            #
         main.yml      # variables for web role
      handlers/        #
         main.yml      # start apache2
   php/                # php role
      tasks/           #
         main.yml      # installing php and restart apache2
   db/                 # db role
      tasks/           #
         main.yml      # install mysql and include harden.yml
         harden.yml    # security hardening for mysql
      handlers/        #
         main.yml      # start db and restart apache2
      vars/            #
         main.yml      # variables for db role
```

Let's start with creating an inventory file. The following inventory file is created using static manual entry. Here is a very basic static inventory file where we will define a since host and set the IP address used to connect to it.

Configure the following inventory file as required:

```
[lamp]
lampstack       ansible_host=192.168.56.10
```

The following file is `group_vars/lamp.yml`, which has the configuration of all the global variables:

```
remote_username: "hodor"
```

The following file is the `site.yml`, which is the main playbook file to start:

```
- name: LAMP stack setup on Ubuntu 16.04
  hosts: lamp
  gather_facts: False
  remote_user: "{{ remote_username }}"
  become: True

  roles:
    - common
    - web
    - db
    - php
```

The following is the `roles/common/tasks/main.yml` file, which will install `python2`, `curl`, and `git`:

```
# In ubuntu 16.04 by default there is no python2
- name: install python 2
  raw: test -e /usr/bin/python || (apt -y update && apt install -y python-minimal)

- name: install curl and git
  apt:
    name: "{{ item }}"
    state: present
    update_cache: yes

  with_items:
    - curl
    - git
```

The following task, `roles/web/tasks/main.yml`, performs multiple operations, such as installation and configuration of `apache2`. It also adds the service to the startup process:

```
- name: install apache2 server
  apt:
```

```
      name: apache2
      state: present

  - name: update the apache2 server configuration
    template:
      src: web.conf.j2
      dest: /etc/apache2/sites-available/000-default.conf
      owner: root
      group: root
      mode: 0644

  - name: enable apache2 on startup
    systemd:
      name: apache2
      enabled: yes
    notify:
      - start apache2
```

The notify **parameter will trigger the handlers found in**
roles/web/handlers/main.yml:

```
  - name: start apache2
    systemd:
      state: started
      name: apache2

  - name: stop apache2
    systemd:
      state: stopped
      name: apache2

  - name: restart apache2
    systemd:
      state: restarted
      name: apache2
      daemon_reload: yes
```

The template files will be taken from role/web/templates/web.conf.j2, **which uses**
Jinja templating, it also takes values from local variables:

```
<VirtualHost *:80><VirtualHost *:80>
    ServerAdmin {{server_admin_email}}
    DocumentRoot {{server_document_root}}

    ErrorLog ${APACHE_LOG_DIR}/error.log
    CustomLog ${APACHE_LOG_DIR}/access.log combined
</VirtualHost>
```

The local variables file is located in `roles/web/vars/main.yml`:

```
server_admin_email: hodor@localhost.local
server_document_root: /var/www/html
```

Similarly, we will write database roles as well. The following file `roles/db/tasks/main.yml` includes installation of the database server with assigned passwords when prompted. At the end of the file, we included `harden.yml`, which executes another set of tasks:

```
- name: set mysql root password
  debconf:
    name: mysql-server
    question: mysql-server/root_password
    value: "{{ mysql_root_password | quote }}"
    vtype: password

- name: confirm mysql root password
  debconf:
    name: mysql-server
    question: mysql-server/root_password_again
    value: "{{ mysql_root_password | quote }}"
    vtype: password

- name: install mysqlserver
  apt:
    name: "{{ item }}"
    state: present
  with_items:
    - mysql-server
    - mysql-client

- include: harden.yml
```

The `harden.yml` performs hardening of MySQL server configuration:

```
- name: deletes anonymous mysql user
  mysql_user:
    user: ""
    state: absent
    login_password: "{{ mysql_root_password }}"
    login_user: root

- name: secures the mysql root user
  mysql_user:
    user: root
    password: "{{ mysql_root_password }}"
```

```
    host: "{{ item }}"
    login_password: "{{mysql_root_password}}"
    login_user: root
  with_items:
    - 127.0.0.1
    - localhost
    - ::1
    - "{{ ansible_fqdn }}"

- name: removes the mysql test database
  mysql_db:
    db: test
    state: absent
    login_password: "{{ mysql_root_password }}"
    login_user: root

- name: enable mysql on startup
  systemd:
    name: mysql
    enabled: yes

  notify:
    - start mysql
```

The db server role also has `roles/db/handlers/main.yml` and local variables similar to the web role:

```
- name: start mysql
  systemd:
    state: started
    name: mysql

- name: stop mysql
  systemd:
    state: stopped
    name: mysql

- name: restart mysql
  systemd:
    state: restarted
    name: mysql
    daemon_reload: yes
```

The following file is `roles/db/vars/main.yml`, which has the `mysql_root_password` while configuring the server. We will see how we can secure these plaintext passwords using `ansible-vault` in future chapters:

```
mysql_root_password: R4nd0mP4$$w0rd
```

Now, we will install PHP and configure it to work with `apache2` by restarting the `roles/php/tasks/main.yml` service:

```
- name: install php7
  apt:
    name: "{{ item }}"
    state: present
  with_items:
    - php7.0-mysql
    - php7.0-curl
    - php7.0-json
    - php7.0-cgi
    - php7.0
    - libapache2-mod-php7

- name: restart apache2
  systemd:
    state: restarted
    name: apache2
    daemon_reload: yes
```

To run this playbook, we need to have Ansible installed in the system path. Please refer to `http://docs.ansible.com/ansible/intro_installation.html` for installation instructions.

Then execute the following command against the Ubuntu 16.04 server to set up LAMP stack. Provide the password when it prompts for system access for user `hodor`:

```
$ ansible-playbook -i inventory site.yml
```

After successful completion of the playbook execution, we will be ready to use LAMP stack in a Ubuntu 16.04 machine. You might have observed that each task or role is configurable as we need throughout the playbook. Roles give the power to generalize the playbook and customize easily using variables and templating.

Summary

We have codified a fairly decent real-world stack for development using a combination of Ansible's features. By thinking about what goes in a LAMP stack overview, we can start by creating the roles. Once we have that thrashed out, the individual tasks are mapped to modules in Ansible. Any task that requires copying of a pre-defined configuration, but with dynamically-generated output, can be done by using variables in our templates and the constructs offered by Jinja2.

We will use the same approach to various security-related setups that could do with a bit of automation for orchestration, operations, and so on. Once we have a handle on how to do this for a virtual machine running our laptop, it can be repurposed for deploying on your favorite cloud-computing instance as well. The output is human readable and in text, so that it can be added to version control, various roles can be reused as well.

Now that we have a fairly decent idea of the terms we will be using throughout this book, let's get set for one final piece of the puzzle. In the next chapter, we will learn and understand how we can use automation and scheduling tools, such as Ansible Tower, Jenkins, and Rundeck, to manage and execute playbooks based on certain event triggers or time durations.

2

Ansible Tower, Jenkins, and Other Automation Tools

Ansible is powerful. Once you realize the innumerable benefits of writing down a way to configure and provision systems, you will never want to go back. In fact, you may want to go ahead and write playbooks for complex cloud environments to deploying stacks for data scientists. The rule of thumb is if you can script it, you can create a playbook for it.

Let's assume that you have gone ahead and done just that. Build different playbooks for a variety of scenarios. If you see the advantages of codifying how infrastructure is built and provisioned, you will obviously want to put your playbooks under version control:

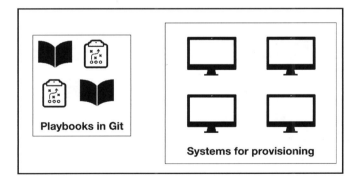

Multiple playbooks stored under version control, ready to be deployed to systems for provisioning

At this point, we have solved interesting challenges surrounding automation:

- We now have the ability to *replay* commands against multiple targets
- Remember that if the playbooks are in an idempotent manner, we can safely run them *n* number of times against our targets without any worries
- By virtue of them being text-based documents, we get versioning and all the benefits that come from doing so

What is still manual is the fact that we need someone or something to execute the `ansible-playbook` command. Not only that, this someone or something will need to do the following:

- Remember when to execute the playbooks
- Schedule them accordingly
- Store secrets safely (usually we require the SSH key to be able to login)
- Store the output or remember to rerun a playbook if something failed

We can all aspire to be that spectacular when it comes to remembering the small things, or we can accept that these detail-oriented, scheduling-based tasks are better left to competent software rather than superhumans!

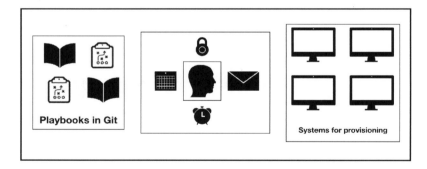

Superhumans will have the ability to remember, schedule, execute, and notify about playbooks

It turns out we don't all have to become superhumans. We can simply use scheduling and automation tools such as Ansible Tower, Jenkins, or Rundeck to do all of what we have defined previously, and more.

In this chapter, we will look at all the three tools that we mentioned to understand what do they offer so as to take our automation to the next level of abstraction of automation.

Specifically, we will cover the following topics:

- Installing and configuring Ansible Tower
- Using Ansible Tower to manage playbooks and schedule
- Installing and configuring Jenkins
- Installing and configuring Rundeck

Scheduling tools to enable the next abstraction of automation

Scheduling and automation tools enable us to automate tasks such as continuous integration and continuous delivery. They are able to do this by providing the following fairly standard services:

- A web-based UI we can use to configure them
- Usually, a REST-based API so that we can use their features programmatically
- The ability to authenticate against its local store or possibly another service (OAuth/**Security Assertion Markup Language (SAML)**)
- They all fundamentally give us a clear way to automate tasks to suit our workflow

Most security-related automation does boil down to doing a similar task over and over again and looking at the differences. This is especially true when you are in the line of doing security operations and security assessments.

 Remember that by using Ansible roles and the playbooks containing them, we are already on our way to doing security automation. Now our aim is to take away the grunt work of remembering to execute those playbooks and get going.

There are three primary contenders that are used for this kind of automation. They are listed and described here:

- Ansible Tower
- Jenkins
- Rundeck

Tools	Our take	License
Ansible Tower	Brilliant tool by the makers of Ansible so fits very well with the idea of IT automation, which we extend to our security needs.	Paid with a free trial
Jenkins	The workhorse and the mainstay of a lot of CI/CD pipelines. Has hundreds of plugins to extend its core functionality. The best option if price or license is a concern.	Free and open source
Rundeck	Great tool for job scheduling and automation.	A paid pro version is available

In this chapter, we will install and configure all three tools to get you started.

 Red Hat, who bought Ansible in the October 2015, has indicated that they plan to open source Ansible Tower. They made this announcement at AnsibleFest 2016. You can follow the progress of that at `https://www.ansible.com/open-tower`.

Getting up and running

Let's start by setting up each of the three tools we mentioned and look at some of their features.

Setting up Ansible Tower

There are multiple ways to install the Ansible Tower trial version. The simplest way to get set up is by using their existing images from `https://www.ansible.com/tower-trial`.

You can also set up manually using their bundle installation. Please have a look at the requirements before installing at `http://docs.ansible.com/ansible-tower/3.1.4/html/installandreference/index.html`.

Run the following commands to install Ansible Tower in the Ubuntu 16.04 operating
system:

```
$ sudo apt-get install software-properties-common

$ sudo apt-add-repository ppa:ansible/ansible

$ wget
https://releases.ansible.com/ansible-tower/setup/ansible-tower-setup-latest
.tar.gz

$ tar xvzf ansible-tower-setup-latest.tar.gz

$ cd ansible-tower-setup-<tower_version>
```

Then edit the inventory file for updating password and other variables and run the
setup. The inventory file contains admin_password for the tower administrator login
account, pg_host and pg_port are Postgres database it will be required if we are setting
up multi-node setup. Then finally rabbitmq details for queuing operations.

```
[tower]
localhost ansible_connection=local

[database]

[all:vars]
admin_password='strongpassword'

pg_host='' # postgres.domain.com
pg_port='' #5432

pg_database='awx'
pg_username='awx'
pg_password='postgrespasswordforuserawx'

rabbitmq_port=5672
rabbitmq_vhost=tower
rabbitmq_username=tower
rabbitmq_password='giverabitmqpasswordhere'
rabbitmq_cookie=cookiemonster

# Needs to be true for fqdns and ip addresses
rabbitmq_use_long_name=false

$ sudo ./setup.sh
```

If you have Vagrant installed, you can simply download their Vagrant box to get going.

Make sure you have Vagrant installed in your host system before running the following command:

```
$ vagrant init ansible/tower
$ vagrant up
$ vagrant ssh
```

It will prompt you to enter IP address, username, and password to login to the Ansible Tower dashboard.

Then navigate the browser to https://10.42.0.42 and accept the SSL error to proceed. This SSL error can be fixed by providing the valid certificates in the configuration at /etc/tower and need to restart the Ansible Tower service. Enter the login credentials to access the Ansible Tower dashboard:

Once you log in, it will prompt you for the Ansible Tower license:

Ansible Tower also provides **Role-Based Authentication Control (RBAC)**, which provides a granular level of control for different users and groups to manage Tower. The following screenshot shows a new user being created with the **System Administrator** privilege:

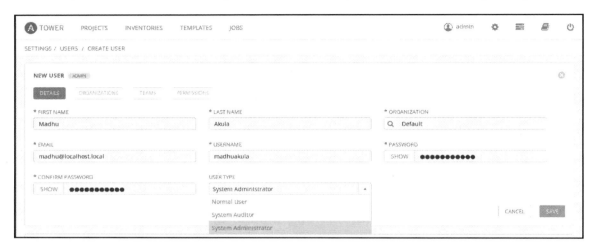

To add inventory into Ansible Tower, we can simply enter it manually, we can also use a dynamic script to gather inventory from cloud providers by providing the authentication (or) access key. The following screenshot shows how we can add the inventory into Ansible Tower, we can also provide variables for different hosts by providing it in **YAML** or **JSON** format:

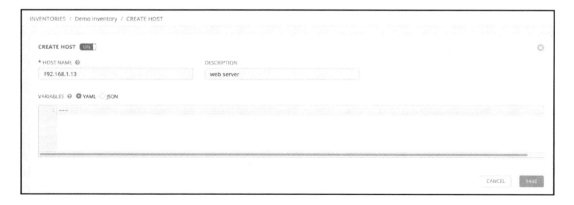

We can also add credentials (or) keys to the tower by providing them in credential management, which can be reused as well.

Secrets store in Ansible Tower are encrypted with a symmetric key unique to each Ansible Tower cluster. Once stored in the Ansible Tower database, the credentials may only be used, not viewed, in the web interface. The types of credentials that Ansible Tower can store are passwords, SSH keys, Ansible Vault keys, and cloud credentials.

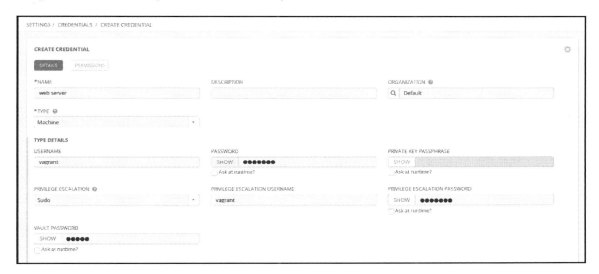

Once we have the inventory gathered, we can create jobs to perform the playbook or ad-hoc command operations:

Here we have selected the `shell` module and are running the `uname -a` command against both nodes:

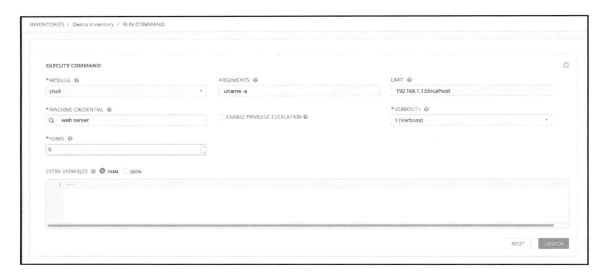

Once we launch the execution, we can see the standard output in the dashboard. We can also access this using REST API:

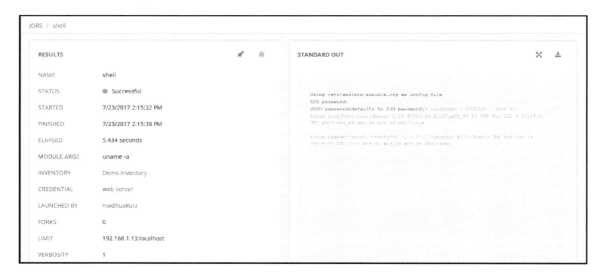

Please refer to the Ansible Tower documentation for more detailed references.

There is another way of using Ansible Tower: `tower-cli` is a command-line tool for Ansible Tower. Get started with the `pip install ansible-tower-cli` command.

The Ansible Tower REST API is a pretty powerful way to interact with the system

This basically allows you to design your playbook workflow and so on using an easy-to-follow web GUI with the added flexibility of calling this from another CI/CD tool such as Jenkins. Jenkins is, incidentally, the next software to set up and learn.

Setting up Jenkins

Let's use an Ansible playbook to install Jenkins and get started with it.

The following code snippet is a snippet of an Ansible playbook we wrote for setting up Jenkins in the Ubuntu 16.04 OS.

Once the setup has been done, playbook returns the default administrator password required to log in to the application for the first time:

```
- name: installing jenkins in ubuntu 16.04
  hosts: "192.168.1.7"
  remote_user: ubuntu
  gather_facts: False
  become: True

tasks:
  - name: install python 2
    raw: test -e /usr/bin/python || (apt -y update && apt install -y
python-minimal)

  - name: install curl and git
    apt: name={{ item }} state=present update_cache=yes

    with_items:
      - curl
      - git
```

```
  - name: adding jenkins gpg key
    apt_key:
      url: https://pkg.jenkins.io/debian/jenkins-ci.org.key
      state: present

  - name: jeknins repository to system
    apt_repository:
      repo: http://pkg.jenkins.io/debian-stable binary/
      state: present

  - name: installing jenkins
    apt:
      name: jenkins
      state: present
      update_cache: yes

  - name: adding jenkins to startup
    service:
      name: jenkins
      state: started
      enabled: yes

  - name: printing jenkins default administration password
    command: cat /var/lib/jenkins/secrets/initialAdminPassword
    register: jenkins_default_admin_password
  - debug:
      msg: "{{ jenkins_default_admin_password.stdout }}"
```

To set up Jenkins, run the following command. Where `192.168.1.7` is the server IP address where Jenkins will be installed:

```
ansible-playbook -i '192.168.1.7,' site.yml --ask-sudo-pass
```

Now we can configure Jenkins to install plugins, run scheduled jobs, and do many other things. First, we have to navigate to the Jenkins dashboard by browsing to `http://192.168.1.7:8080` and providing the auto-generated password. If the playbook runs without any errors, it will display the password at the end of the play:

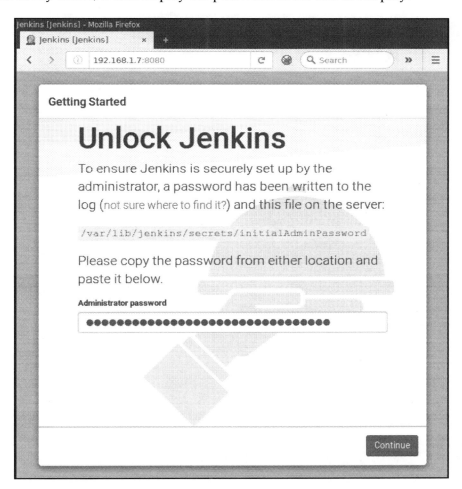

Create the new user by filling in the details and confirming to log in to the Jenkins console:

Now we can install custom plugins in Jenkins, navigate to the **Manage Jenkins** tab, select **Manage Plugins**, then navigate to the **Available** tab. In the **Filter:** enter the plugin name as `Ansible`. Then select the checkbox and click **Install without restart**:

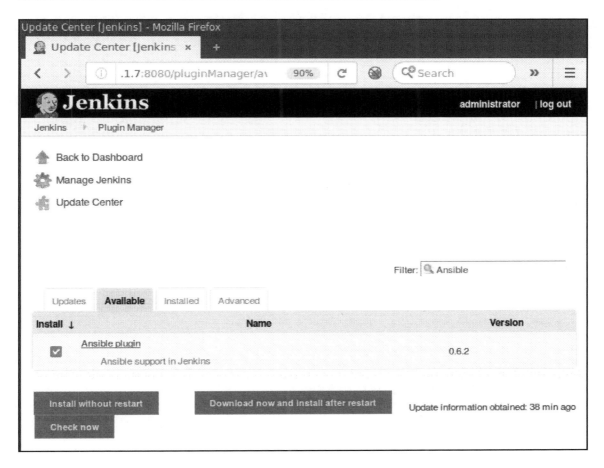

Now we are ready to work with the Ansible plugin for Jenkins. Create a new project in the main dashboard, give it a name, and select **Freestyle project** to proceed:

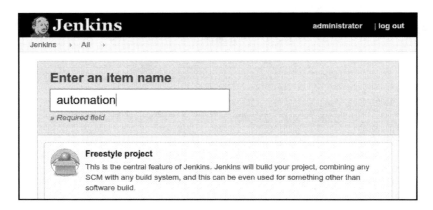

Now we can configure the build options, this is where Jenkins will give us more flexibility to define our own triggers, build instructions, and post build scripts:

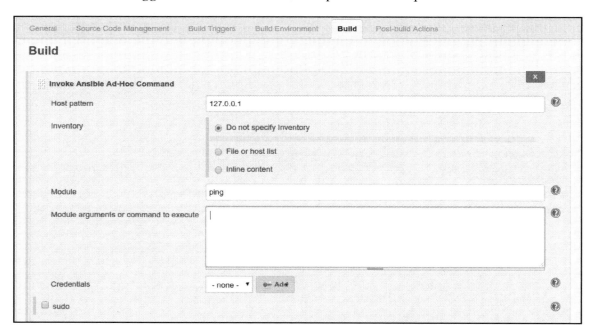

The preceding screenshot is an example of a build invoking an Ansible ad-hoc command. This can be modified to ansible-playbook or any other scripts based on certain events.

The Jenkins Ansible plugin also provides useful features such as configuring advanced commands and passing credentials, keys from Jenkins itself.

Once the build triggers based on an event, this can be sent to some artifact storage, it can also be available in the Jenkins build console output:

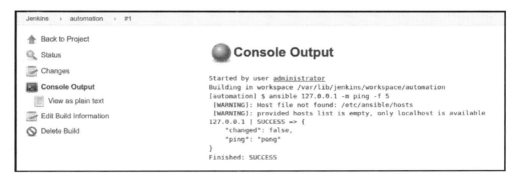

This is a really very powerful way to perform dynamic operations such as triggering automated server and stacks setup based on a code push to the repository, as well as scheduled scans and automated reporting.

Setting up Rundeck

The following Ansible playbook will set up Rundeck on the Ubuntu 16.04 OS. It also adds the Rundeck service to start up the process:

```
- name: installing rundeck on ubuntu 16.04
  hosts: "192.168.1.7"
  remote_user: ubuntu
  gather_facts: False
  become: True

  tasks:
    - name: installing python2 minimal
      raw: test -e /usr/bin/python || (apt -y update && apt install -y
python-minimal)

    - name: java and curl installation
      apt:
        name: "{{ item }}"
```

```
        state: present
        update_cache: yes

    with_items:
      - curl
      - openjdk-8-jdk

  - name: downloading and installing rundeck deb package
    apt:
      deb:
"http://dl.bintray.com/rundeck/rundeck-deb/rundeck-2.8.4-1-GA.deb"

  - name: add to startup and start rundeck
    service:
      name: rundeckd
      state: started
```

To set up Rundeck, run the following command. Where `192.168.1.7` is the server IP address where Rundeck will install:

```
ansible-playbook -i '192.168.1.7,' site.yml --ask-sudo-pass
```

Once it is successfully executed, navigate the browser to `http://192.168.1.7:4440` and you can see the login panel for the Rundeck application. The default username and password to log in to Rundeck is `admin`:

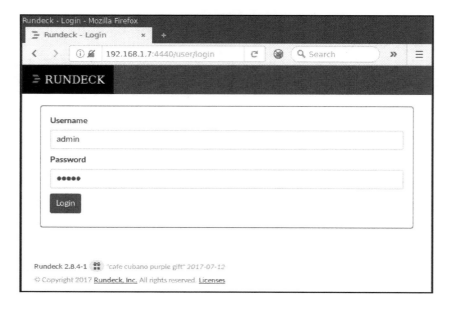

Now we can create a new project to start working on. Provide a new **Project Name** and go with the default settings for now:

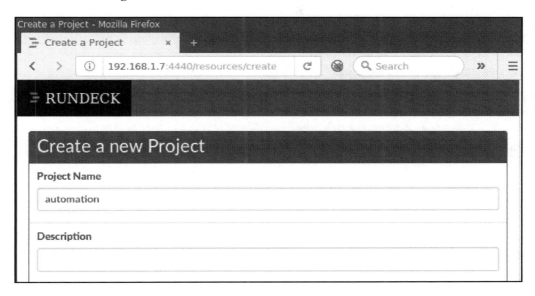

Now, we can add multiple hosts into Rundeck to perform multiple actions. The following screenshot shows an example of running the `uname -a` command across multiple nodes, which matches `osArch: amd64`, we can also create filters for different use cases:

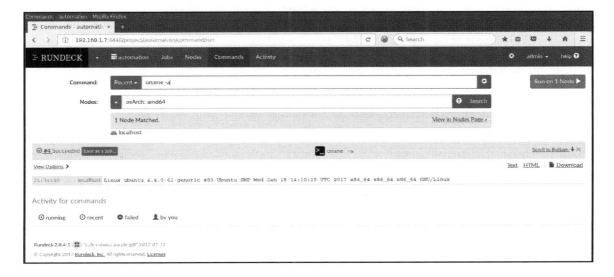

Using Rundeck, we can also schedule jobs to run at certain times and store the output in different formats. Rundeck also provides a REST API that can be integrated into the existing tool set.

Security automation use cases

Now that once we have the tools set up, let's go through some of the standard tasks that allow us to do useful things with them. In case you haven't noticed, we love lists. Here is a list of tasks that will prepare you to build layers of automation for the stuff that is important to you:

1. Adding playbooks or connecting your source code management (SCM) tools, such as GitHub/GitLab/BitBucket
2. Authentication and data security
3. Logging output and managing reports for the automation jobs
4. Job scheduling
5. Alerting, notifications, and webhooks

Adding playbooks

When starting out, either we would like to add our custom playbooks to the IT automation tools or we may be adding them to SCM tools such as GitHub, GitLab, and BitBucket. We will configure and add our playbooks to all of the three tools being discussed here.

Ansible Tower configuration

Ansible Tower has multiple features to add playbooks to perform scheduling and execution. We will see how we can add custom written playbooks (manual) and add playbooks from version control systems such as Git. Pulling playbooks from Ansible Galaxy as well. Ansible Galaxy is your hub for finding, reusing, and sharing the best Ansible content.

To add playbooks into Ansible Tower, we have to start by creating projects, then select the **SCM TYPE** as **Manual**, and add the playbooks that already exist.

Warning: There are no available playbook directories in `/var/lib/awx/projects`. Either that directory is empty, or all of the contents are already assigned to other projects. Create a new directory there and make sure the playbook files can be read by the `awx` system user, or have Tower directly retrieve your playbooks from source control using the SCM type option previously discussed.

We can choose the **SCM TYPE** set to **Git** and provide a `github.com` URL pointing to a playbook:

Git SCM to add playbooks into projects

 We can also change the `PROJECTS_ROOT` under **CONFIGURE TOWER** to change this location.

The added playbooks are executed by creating a job template. Then we can schedule these jobs (or) we can launch directly:

Following is the screenshot of a new job template creation for playbook execution:

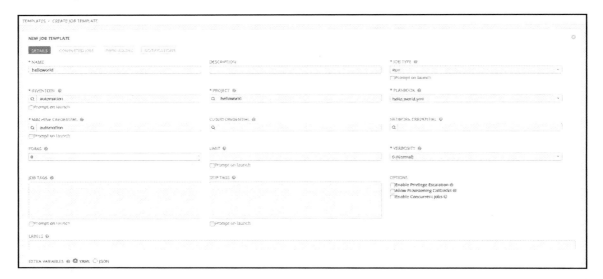

Playbook execution job template

A job run is successful with output in the following screenshot:

Playbook execution output in Ansible Tower

Jenkins Ansible integration configuration

Not surprisingly, Jenkins supports SCM to use playbooks and local directories for manual playbooks too. This can be configured with the build options. Jenkins supports both ad-hoc commands and playbooks to trigger as a build (or) post-build action.

The following screenshot shows how we can point our repository and specify a branch as well. We can also specify credentials if we want to access private repositories:

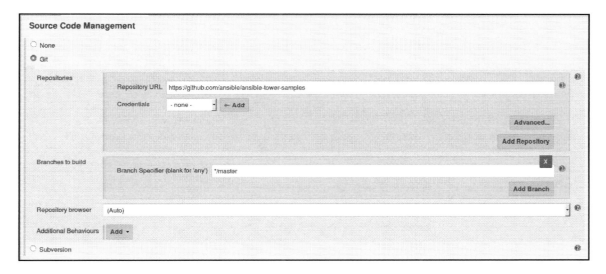

Adding Github (SCM) based playbooks for build

Then we can add the Playbook path by specifying the location of the playbook and defining inventory and variables as required:

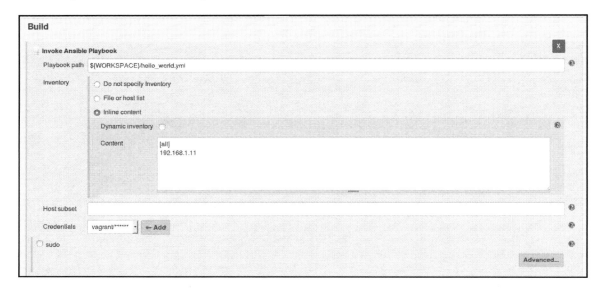

Start playbook execution when build triggers

Finally, we can execute the Jenkins job by triggering the Jenkins build (or) we can integrate this with other tools:

Jenkins build output of playbook execution

Rundeck configuration

Rundeck supports adding custom playbooks, as well as SCM and many other options. The following screenshots show different options to add playbooks and modules in Rundeck using the jobs feature.

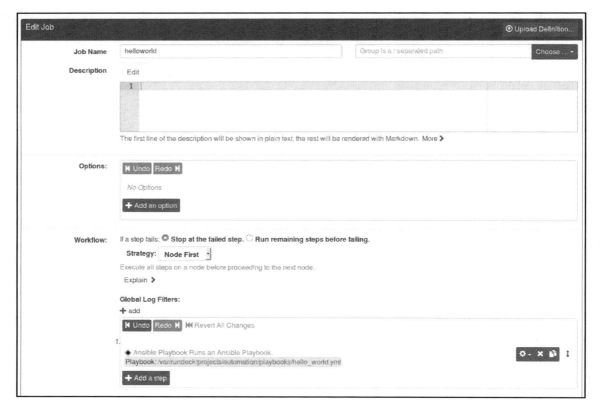

Rundeck has multiple options for us to choose from

Rundeck Ansible Playbook configuration for variables and keys

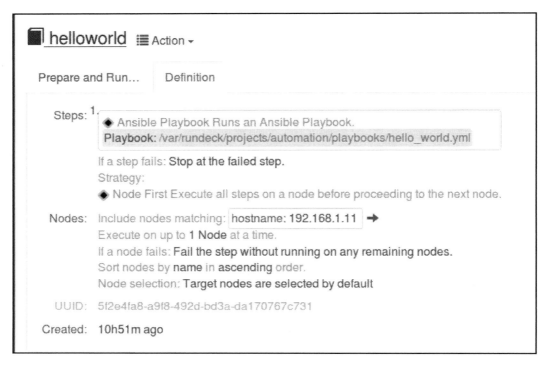

Rundeck job definition including overview of job details

Authentication and data security

When we talk about automation and working with systems, we should talk about security. We are going to keep talking about security automation as that is the title of the book.

Some of the security features the tools offer include:

- RBAC (authentication and authorization)
- Web application over TLS/SSL (security for data in motion)
- Encryption for storing secrets (security for data at rest)

RBAC for Ansible Tower

Ansible Tower supports RBAC to manage multiple users with different permissions and roles. It also supports **Lightweight Directory Access Protocol (LDAP)** integration in the enterprise version to support Active Directory. This feature allows us to create different levels of users for accessing Ansible Tower. For example:

- The operations team requires a system administrator role to perform playbook execution and other activities like monitoring
- The security team requires a system auditor role to perform audit check for compliance standards such as **Payment Card Industry Data Security Standard (PCI DSS)** or even internal policy validation
- Normal users, such as team members, might just want to see how things are going, in the form of status updates and failure (or) success of job status

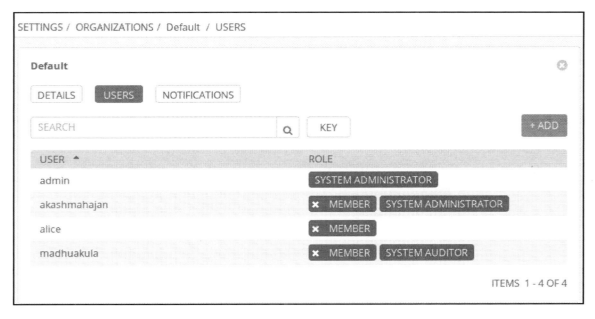

Users can be assigned to different types of roles

TLS/SSL for Ansible Tower

By default, Ansible Tower uses HTTPS using self-signed certificates at `/etc/tower/tower.cert` and `/etc/tower/tower.key`, these can be configured in the setup script. We can also update this later with the same filenames.

> For more information visit `http://docs.ansible.com/ansible-tower/latest/html/installandreference/install_notes_reqs.html#installation-notes`.

Encryption and data security for Ansible Tower

Ansible Tower has been created with built-in security for handling encryption of credentials that includes passwords and keys. It uses Ansible Vault to perform this operation. It encrypts passwords and key information in the database.

> Read more at `http://docs.ansible.com/ansible-tower/latest/html/userguide/credentials.html`.

RBAC for Jenkins

In Jenkins, which is a more generic tool, we can extend its functionality by using a plugin. The Role Strategy Plugin is a community plugin to manage roles for Jenkins. Using it, we can create different access level controls for users and groups:

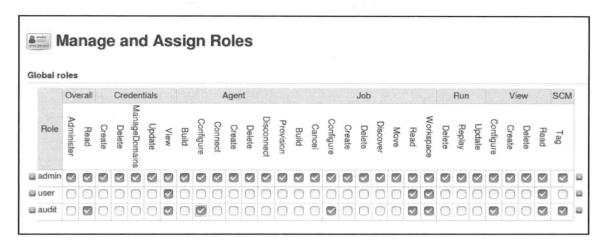

Role strategy plugin of Jenkins

Roles usually need to align with the team settings and business requirements. You may want to fine-tune this per your requirements.

Read more at `https://wiki.jenkins.io/display/JENKINS/`
`Role+Strategy+Plugin`.

TLS/SSL for Jenkins

By default, Jenkins runs as plain old HTTP. To enable HTTPS, we can use a reverse proxy, such as Nginx, in front of Jenkins to serve as HTTPS.

For reference, visit `https://www.digitalocean.com/community/`
`tutorials/how-to-configure-jenkins-with-ssl-using-an-nginx-`
`reverse-proxy`.

Encryption and data security for Jenkins

We are using Jenkins' default credential feature. This will store the keys and passwords in the local filesystem. There are also different plugins available for Jenkins to handle this, such as `https://wiki.jenkins.io/display/JENKINS/Credentials+Plugin`.

The following screenshot is a reference to show how we can add credentials in Jenkins:

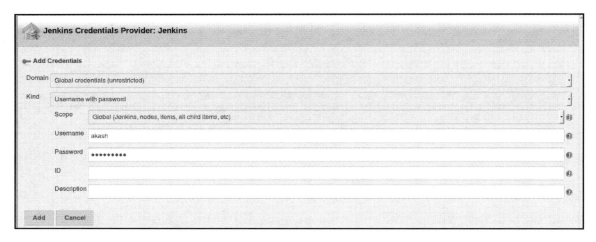

RBAC for Rundeck

Rundeck also provides RBAC as Ansible Tower. Unlike Tower, here we have to configure using the YAML configuration file in /etc/rundeck/.

The following code snippet is an example of creating an admin user policy:

```
description: Admin, all access.
context:
 application: 'rundeck'
for:
 resource:
 - allow: '*' # allow create of projects
 project:
 - allow: '*' # allow view/admin of all projects
 project_acl:
 - allow: '*' # allow all project-level ACL policies
 storage:
 - allow: '*' # allow read/create/update/delete for all /keys/* storage
content
by: group: admin
```

For more information about creating different policies, visit http://rundeck.org/docs/administration/access-control-policy.html.

HTTP/TLS for Rundeck

HTTPS can be configured for Rundeck using the `/etc/rundeck/ssl/ssl.properties` file:

```
keystore=/etc/rundeck/ssl/keystore
keystore.password=adminadmin
key.password=adminadmin
truststore=/etc/rundeck/ssl/truststore
truststore.password=adminadmin
```

 For more information, visit `http://rundeck.org/docs/administration/configuring-ssl.html`.

Encryption and data security for Rundeck

Credentials, such as password and keys, are stored in local storage and encrypted and use the Rundeck key store to encrypt and decrypt. This also supports different key store plugins to use key storage, such as the storage converter plugin. Access to the keys in the storage facilities is restricted by use of the **access control list (ACL)** policies.

Output of the playbooks

Once the automation jobs have finished, we would like to know what happened. Did they run completely, were there any errors faced, and so on. We would like to know where can we see the output of the playbooks executing and if any other logs that get created.

Report management for Ansible Tower

By default, Ansible Tower itself is a reporting platform for the status of the playbooks, job executions, and inventory collection. The Ansible Tower dashboard gives an overview of the total projects, inventories, hosts, and status of the jobs.

The output can be consumed in the dashboard, standard out, or by using the REST API and we can get this via `tower-cli` command line tool as well, which is just a pre-built command line tool for interfacing with the REST API.

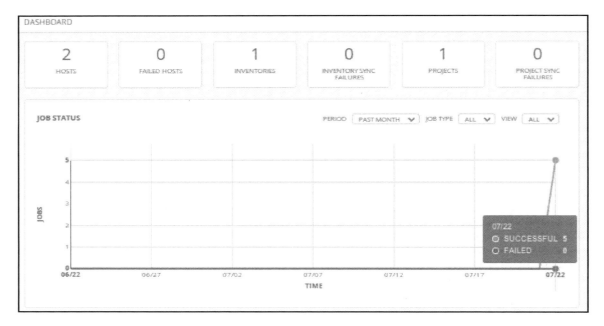

Ansible Tower dashboard

STANDARD OUT

```
    "ansible_facts": {
        "ansible_all_ipv4_addresses": [
            "192.168.1.7",
            "10.0.2.15",
            "10.42.0.42"
        ],
        "ansible_all_ipv6_addresses": [
            "fe80::a00:27ff:fe5d:a92f",
            "fe80::a00:27ff:fe57:be11"
        ],
        "ansible_apparmor": {
            "status": "disabled"
        },
        "ansible_architecture": "x86_64",
        "ansible_bios_date": "12/01/2006",
        "ansible_bios_version": "VirtualBox",
        "ansible_cmdline": {
            "BOOT_IMAGE": "/vmlinuz-3.10.0-514.26.2.el7.x86_64",
            "LANG": "en_US.UTF-8",
            "crashkernel": "auto",
            "quiet": true,
            "rd_lvm_lv": "cl/swap"
```

Ansible Tower standard output

TOWER REST API

REST API / Version 1 / Ping

Ping

OPTIONS   GET ▾

GET /api/v1/ping/

```
HTTP 200 OK
Allow: GET, HEAD, OPTIONS
Content-Type: application/json
Vary: Accept
X-API-Node: localhost
X-API-Time: 0.007s


{
    "instances": [
        {
            "node": "localhost",
            "heartbeat": "2017-08-05T05:28:42.794Z",
            "version": "3.1.4",
            "capacity": 50
        }
    ],
    "ha": false,
    "version": "3.1.4-0.git201707091350",
    "active_node": "localhost"
}
```

Ansible Tower REST API

Report management for Jenkins

Jenkins provides both standard output and REST API for managing reporting. Jenkins has a very large community and there are multiple plugins available, such as HTML Publisher Plugin and Cucumber Reports Plugin.

These plugins provide visual representation of the output:

```
Jenkins  ›  automation  ›  #7

 🚫  Delete Build                    "ansible_facts": {
                                         "ansible_all_ipv4_addresses": [
 📄  Previous Build                          "10.0.2.15",
                                             "192.168.1.9"
                                         ],
                                         "ansible_all_ipv6_addresses": [
                                             "fe80::a00:27ff:fe16:bdb0",
                                             "fe80::a00:27ff:fe58:b825"
                                         ],
                                         "ansible_architecture": "x86_64",
                                         "ansible_bios_date": "12/01/2006",
                                         "ansible_bios_version": "VirtualBox",
                                         "ansible_cmdline": {
                                             "BOOT_IMAGE": "/boot/vmlinuz-3.13.0-125-generic",
                                             "console": "ttyS0",
                                             "ro": true,
                                             "root": "UUID=1c5f6a99-2067-4876-8b63-50371af71a16"
                                         },
                                         "ansible_date_time": {
                                             "date": "2017-08-05",
                                             "day": "05",
                                             "epoch": "1501917853",
                                             "hour": "07",
                                             "iso8601": "2017-08-05T07:24:13Z",
                                             "iso8601_micro": "2017-08-05T07:24:13.575228Z",
                                             "minute": "24",
                                             "month": "08",
                                             "second": "13",
                                             "time": "07:24:13",
                                             "tz": "UTC",
                                             "tz_offset": "+0000",
                                             "year": "2017"
                                         },
                                         "ansible_default_ipv4": {
                                             "address": "10.0.2.15",
                                             "alias": "eth0",
                                             "gateway": "10.0.2.2",
                                             "interface": "eth0",
                                             "macaddress": "08:00:27:16:bd:b0",
                                             "mtu": 1500,
```

Standard output by the Jenkins job console

Report management for Rundeck

Rundeck also provides both a standard output and a REST API to query the results:

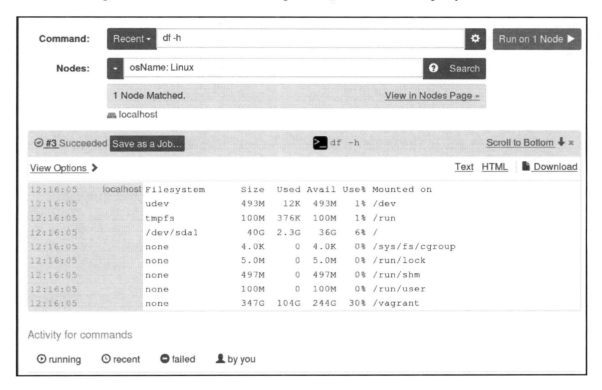

Output of a job that can be consumed via stdout, TXT, and HTML formats

Scheduling of jobs

The scheduling of jobs is simple and straightforward in Ansible Tower. For a job, you can specify a schedule and the options are mostly like cron.

For example, you can say that you have a daily scan template and would like it to be executed at 4 a.m. every day for the next three months. This kind of schedule makes our meta automation very flexible and powerful.

Alerting, notifications, and webhooks

Tower supports multiple ways of alerting and notifying users as per configuration. This can even be configured to make an HTTP POST request to a URL of your choice using a webhook:

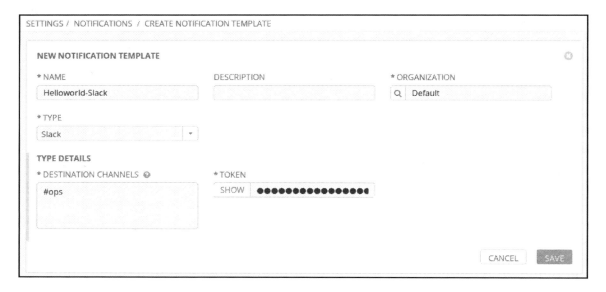

Ansible Tower notification using slack webhook

Summary

We completed a whirlwind tour of some IT automation and scheduler software. Our main aim was to introduce the software and highlight some of its common features.

These features include the following:

- Offering encryption for our secrets
- Running as per our schedule requirements
- The ability to get good reports

We already know about Ansible roles that allow us to reuse and create great playbooks. Coupled with these features, we have a complete automation system ready. Not only we will be able to run our tasks and jobs as many times as we like, we will get updates on how they ran. Also, since our tasks run on protected servers, it is important that the secrets we share for them to run are safe as well.

In the next chapter, we move away from thinking about the mechanics of Ansible automation to squarely thinking about security automation in specific situations. Automating our server's patches is the most obvious, and possibly popular, requirement. We will apply security automation techniques and approaches to set up a hardened WordPress and enable encrypted backups.

3
Setting Up a Hardened WordPress with Encrypted Automated Backups

Now that the basic setup is done, let's pick up various security automation scenarios and look at them one by one.

Everyone would agree that setting up a secure website and keeping it secured is a fairly common security requirement. And since it is so common, it would be useful for a lot of people who are tasked with building and managing websites to stay secure to look at that specific scenario.

 Are you aware that, according to Wikipedia, 27.5% of the top 10 million websites use WordPress? According to another statistic, 58.7% of all websites with known software on the entire web run WordPress.

If there are so many, an automated secure way of setting up and maintaining WordPress should be useful for some readers.

Even if WordPress is something that doesn't interest you a lot, bear in mind that the overall steps to set up and secure a LAMP/LEMP stack application are universal.

For us, setting up a hardened WordPress with encrypted automated backups can be broken down into the following steps:

1. Setting up a Linux/Windows server with security measures in place.
2. Setting up a web server (Apache/Nginx on Linux and IIS on Windows).
3. Setting up a database server (MySQL) on the same host.
4. Setting up WordPress using a command-line utility called **WP-CLI**.
5. Setting up backup for the site files and the database which is incremental, encrypted, and most importantly, automated.

In this chapter, we will do all of this using Ansible playbooks and roles. We will assume that the server that we plan to deploy our WordPress website on is already up and running and we are able to connect to it. We will store the backup in an already configured AWS S3 bucket, for which the access key and secret access key is already provisioned.

We will discuss the following topics:

- CLI for WordPress
- Why Ansible for this setup?
- A complete WordPress installation, step-by-step
- Setting up an Apache2 web server
- What if you don't want to roll your own? The Trellis stack
- Why would we use Trellis, and when is it a good idea to use it?
- Enabling TLS/SSL with Let's Encrypt
- WordPress on Windows

CLI for WordPress

We will be using a tool called WP-CLI, which allows us to do many things in WordPress that traditionally require a web browser.

 WP-CLI is the CLI for WordPress. You can update plugins, configure multisite installs, and much more, without using a web browser. For more information on WP-CLI, visit `https://WP-CLI.org/`, and for WordPress, visit `https://wordpress.org/`.

For example, the following command will download and set up a WordPress:

```
wp core install # with some options such as url, title of the website etc.
etc.
```

A complete example can be found at https://developer.WordPress.org/cli/commands/core/#examples:

```
wp core install --url=example.com --title=Example --admin_user=supervisor --admin_password=strongpassword --admin_email=info@example.com
```

This example gives us a glimpse of the power of the WP-CLI tool when invoked from an Ansible playbook.

Why Ansible for this setup?

Ansible is made for security automation and hardening. It uses YAML syntax, which helps us to codify our entire process of repeated tasks. By using this, we can automate the process of continuous delivery and deployment of infrastructure using roles and playbooks.

The modular approach enables us to perform tasks very simply. For example, the operations teams can write a playbook to set up a WordPress site and the security team can create another role which can harden the WordPress site.

It is very easy to use the modules for repeatability, and the output is idempotent, which means creating standards for the servers, applications, and infrastructure. Some use cases include creating base images for organizations using internal policy standards.

Ansible uses SSH protocol, which is by default secured with encrypted transmission and host encryption. Also, there are no dependency issues while dealing with different types of operating systems. It uses Python to perform; this can be easily extended, based on our use case.

A complete WordPress installation step-by-step

In this section, we will go ahead and do a complete setup of WordPress, the required database server, hardening, and backup. Our platform of choice is Linux (Ubuntu 16.04) with nginx web server and with PHP-FPM for PHP runtime. We will use duply to set up the backups which will get stored in AWS S3.

Setting up nginx web server

Setting up nginx is as simple as `sudo apt-get install nginx,` but configuring for our use case and managing the configuration's automated way is where Ansible gives the power. Let's look at the following snippet of nginx's role from the playbook:

```
- name: adding nginx signing key
  apt_key:
    url: http://nginx.org/keys/nginx_signing.key
    state: present

- name: adding sources.list deb url for nginx
  lineinfile:
    dest: /etc/apt/sources.list
    line: "deb http://nginx.org/packages/mainline/ubuntu/ trusty nginx"

- name: update the cache and install nginx server
  apt:
    name: nginx
    update_cache: yes
    state: present

- name: updating customized templates for nginx configuration
  template:
    src: "{{ item.src }}"
    dest: "{{ item.dst }}"

  with_items:
    - { src: "templates/defautlt.conf.j2", dst:
"/etc/nginx/conf.d/default.conf" }
  notify:
    - start nginx
    - startup nginx
```

In the preceding code snippet, we are adding the signing key, then adding the repository, then installing. This ensures that we can also perform integrity checks while downloading packages from the repositories.

Then, we are using Jinja2 templating to perform the configuration changes, which can be predefined in our configuration before updating in the server.

Setting up prerequisites

To set up WordPress CMS, we need to have a database and PHP installed, so we will be installing MySQL as a database and PHP-FPM for processing.

Setting up MySQL database

We have already seen how to set up MySQL in the previous chapter. Here, we will see how to create new users and databases for the WordPress application. Then we will apply the hardening steps via Ansible modules:

```
- name: create WordPress database
  mysql_db:
    name: "{{ WordPress_database_name }}"
    state: present
    login_user: root
    login_password: "{{ mysql_root_password }}"

- name: create WordPress database user
  mysql_user:
    name: "{{ WordPress_database_username }}"
    password: "{{ WordPress_database_password }}"
    priv: '"{{ WordPress_database_name }}".*:ALL'
    state: present
    login_user: root
    login_password: "{{ mysql_root_password }}"
```

The preceding code snippet describes creating a new database and user and assigning that user full permission to the WordPress application database using the mysql_db and mysql_user modules, respectively.

Installing PHP for WordPress setup

The following code snippet uses different modules to perform the installation of PHP and other required packages. Then it updates the PHP-FPM configuration using the `replace` module. Finally, it also updates the nginx configuration to update the PHP-FPM processing using the `template` module, and restarts the service to apply the changes:

```
- name: installing php
  apt:
    name: "{{ item }}"
    state: present
    update_cache: yes
  with_items:
    - php
    - php-curl
    - php-fpm
    - php-mysql
    - php-xmlrpc

- name: configuring php.ini for php processor
  replace:
    path: /etc/php5/fpm/php.ini
    regex: ';cgi.fix_pathinfo=1'
    replace: 'cgi.fix_pathinfo=0'
    backup: yes

- name: enable and restart the php fpm service
  service:
    name: php7.0-fpm
    enabled: yes
    state: restarted

- name: update the nginx configuration to support php-fpm
  template:
    src: "{{ item.src }}"
    dest: "{{ item.dst }}"
  with_items:
    - { src: "defautlt.conf.j2", dst: "/etc/nginx/conf.d/default.conf" }

- name: restart the nginx
  service:
    state: restarted
    name: nginx
```

Installing WordPress using WP-CLI

The following code snippet will install and set up WordPress so it is up and running:

```
- debug:
    msg: ensure you have installed lamp (or) lemp stack

- name: downloading WordPress cli aka wp-cli
  get_url:
    url:
https://raw.githubusercontent.com/wp-cli/builds/gh-pages/phar/wp-cli.phar
    dest: /usr/local/bin/wp
    mode: 0755

- name: download latest WordPress locally
  command: wp core download
  become_user: "{{ new_user_name }}"
  args:
    chdir: /var/www/html/

- name: WordPress site configuration
  command: "wp core config --dbname={{ WordPress_database_name }} --
dbuser={{ WordPress_database_username }} --dbpass={{
WordPress_database_password }}

- name: information for WordPress site
  command: "wp core install --url={{ WordPress_site_name }} --title={{
WordPress_site_title }} --admin_user={{ WordPress_admin_username }} --
admin_password={{ WordPress_admin_password }} --admin_email={{
WordPress_admin_email }}"
```

Hardening SSH service

This will be like a more traditional approach, with a modern automated method, using Ansible. Some of the items included here are:

- Disabling the root user login, and instead creating a different user, and, if required, providing the sudo privilege:

```
- name: create new user
  user:
    name: "{{ new_user_name }}"
    password: "{{ new_user_password }}"
```

```
shell: /bin/bash
groups: sudo
append: yes
```

- Using key-based authentication to log in. Unlike with password-based authentication, we can generate SSH keys and add the public key to the authorized keys:

```
- name: add ssh key for new user
  authorized_key:
    user: "{{ new_user_name }}"
    key: "{{ lookup('file', '/home/user/.ssh/id_rsa.pub') }}"
    state: present
```

- Some of the configuration tweaks using the SSH configuration file; for example, PermitRootLogin, PubkeyAuthentication, and PasswordAuthentication:

```
- name: ssh configuration tweaks
  lineinfile:
    dest: /etc/ssh/sshd_config
    state: present
    line: "{{ item }}"
    backups: yes

  with_items:
    - "PermitRootLogin no"
    - "PasswordAuthentication no"

  notify:
    - restart ssh
```

- We can also set up services like fail2ban for protecting against basic attacks.
- Also, we can enable MFA, if required to log in. For more information, visit https://www.digitalocean.com/community/tutorials/how-to-set-up-multi-factor-authentication-for-ssh-on-ubuntu-16-04.

The following playbook will provide more advanced features for SSH hardening by dev-sec team: https://github.com/dev-sec/ansible-ssh-hardening

Hardening a database service

We have seen setting up the database. The following code snippet shows how we can harden the MySQL service by binding it to localhost and the required interfaces for interacting with the application. It then removes the anonymous user and test databases:

```
- name: delete anonymous mysql user for localhost
  mysql_user:
    user: ""
    state: absent
    login_password: "{{ mysql_root_password }}"
    login_user: root

- name: secure mysql root user
  mysql_user:
    user: "root"
    password: "{{ mysql_root_password }}"
    host: "{{ item }}"
    login_password: "{{ mysql_root_password }}"
    login_user: root

  with_items:
    - 127.0.0.1
    - localhost
    - ::1
    - "{{ ansible_fqdn }}"

- name: removes mysql test database
  mysql_db:
    db: test
    state: absent
    login_password: "{{ mysql_root_password }}"
    login_user: root
```

Hardening nginx

Here, we can start looking at things like disabling server tokens to not display version information, adding headers like X-XSS-Protection, and many other configuration tweaks. Most of these changes are done via configuration changes, and Ansible allows us to version and control and automate these changes based on user requirements:

- The nginx server version information can be blocked by adding the server_tokens off; value to the configuration

- `add_header X-XSS-Protection "1; mode=block";` will enable the cross-site scripting (XSS) filter
- SSLv3 can be disabled by adding `ssl_protocols TLSv1 TLSv1.1 TLSv1.2;`
- This list can be pretty large, based on the use case and scenario:

The following code snippet contains nginx configuration template for updating the hardened nginx configuration changes:

```
- name: update the hardened nginx configuration changes
  template:
    src: "hardened-nginx-config.j2"
    dest: "/etc/nginx/sites-available/default"

  notify:
    - restart nginx
```

 Mozilla runs an updated web page on guidance for SSL/TLS at `https://wiki.mozilla.org/Security/Server_Side_TLS`. The guidance offers an opinion on what cipher suites to use, and other security measures. Additionally, if you trust their judgment, you can also use their SSL/TLS configuration generator to quickly generate a configuration for your web server configuration. For more information, visit `https://mozilla.github.io/server-side-tls/ssl-config-generator/`.

Whichever configuration you decide to use, the template needs to be named as `hardened-nginx-config.j2`.

Hardening WordPress

This includes basic checks for WordPress security misconfigurations. Some of them include:

- Directory and file permissions:

```
- name: update the file permissions
  file:
    path: "{{ WordPress_install_directory }}"
    recurse: yes
    owner: "{{ new_user_name }}"
    group: www-data

- name: updating file and directory permissions
  shell: "{{ item }}"
```

```
with_items:
  - "find {{ WordPress_install_directory }} -type d -exec chmod
    755 {} \;"
  - "find {{ WordPress_install_directory }} -type f -exec chmod
    644 {} \;"
```

- Username and attachment enumeration blocking. The following code snippet is part of nginx's configuration:

```
# Username enumeration block
if ($args ~ "^/?author=([0-9]*)"){
    return 403;
}

# Attachment enumeration block
if ($query_string ~ "attachment_id=([0-9]*)"){
    return 403;
}
```

- Disallowing file edits in the WordPress editor:

```
- name: update the WordPress configuration
  lineinfile:
    path: /var/www/html/wp-config.php
    line: "{{ item }}"
  with_items:
    - define('FS_METHOD', 'direct');
    - define('DISALLOW_FILE_EDIT', true);
```

There are many other checks we can add as the configuration changes and updates.

Hardening a host firewall service

The following code snippet is for installing and configuring the **uncomplicated firewall (UFW)** with its required services and rules. Ansible even has a module for UFW, so the following snippet starts with installing this and enabling logging. It follows this by adding default policies, like default denying all incoming and allowing outgoing.

Then it will add SSH, HTTP, and HTTPS services to allow incoming. These options are completely configurable, as required. Then it will enable and add to startup programs that apply the changes:

```
- name: installing ufw package
  apt:
    name: "ufw"
```

```
      update_cache: yes
      state: present

  - name: enable ufw logging
    ufw:
      logging: on

  - name: default ufw setting
    ufw:
      direction: "{{ item.direction }}"
      policy: "{{ item.policy }}"

    with_items:
      - { direction: 'incoming', policy: 'deny' }
      - { direction: 'outgoing', policy: 'allow' }
  - name: allow required ports to access server
    ufw:
      rule: "{{ item.policy }}"
      port: "{{ item.port }}"
      proto: "{{ item.protocol }}"

    with_items:
      - { port: "22", protocol: "tcp", policy: "allow" }
      - { port: "80", protocol: "tcp", policy: "allow" }
      - { port: "443", protocol: "tcp", policy: "allow" }

  - name: enable ufw
    ufw:
      state: enabled

  - name: restart ufw and add to start up programs
    service:
      name: ufw
      state: restarted
      enabled: yes
```

Setting up automated encrypted backups in AWS S3

Backups are always something that most of us feel should be done, but they seem quite a chore. Over the years, people have done extensive work to ensure we can have simple enough ways to back up and restore our data.

In today's day and age, a great backup solution/software should be able to do the following:

Feature	Remark
Automated	Automation allows for process around it
Incremental	While storage is cheap overall, if we want backups at five minute intervals, what has changed should be backed up
Encrypted before it leaves our server	This is to ensure that we have security of data at rest and in motion
Cheap	While we care about our data, a good back up solution will be much cheaper than the server which needs to be backed up

For our backup solution, we will pick up the following stack:

Software	Duply - A wrapper over duplicity, a Python script
Storage	While duply offers many backends, it works really well with AWS S3
Encryption	By using GPG, we can use asymmetric public and private key pairs

The following code snippet is to set up duply for encrypted automated backups from the server to AWS S3:

```
- name: installing duply
  apt:
    name: "{{ item }}"
    update_cache: yes
    state: present
  with_items:
    - python-boto
    - duply

- name: check if we already have backup directory
  stat:
    path: "/root/.duply/{{ new_backup_name }}"
  register: duply_dir_stats

- name: create backup directories
  shell: duply {{ new_backup_name }} create
  when: duply_dir_stats.stat.exists == False

- name: update the duply configuration
  template:
```

```
      src: "{{ item.src }}"
      dest: "{{ item.dest }}"
   with_items:
      - { src: conf.j2, dest: /root/.duply/{{ new_backup_name }}/conf }
      - { src: exclude.j2, dest: /root/.duply/{{ new_backup_name }}/exclude }

 - name: create cron job for automated backups
   template:
      src: duply-backup.j2
      dest: /etc/cron.hourly/duply-backup
```

Executing playbook against an Ubuntu 16.04 server using Ansible Tower

Once we are ready with the playbook and updating the variables as required, we can go ahead and execute the playbook. Before that, we have to create the template in Ansible Tower to perform this operation.

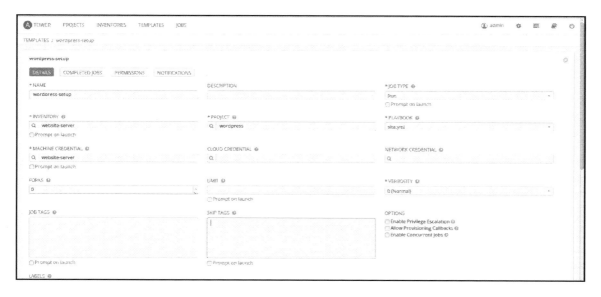

Ansible Tower job template for WordPress setup playbook

WordPress setup playbook job execution

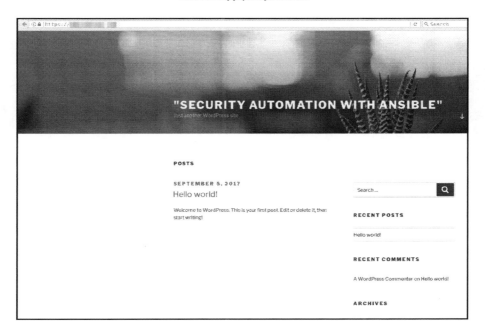

WordPress website with HTTPS

Secure automated the WordPress updates

The following code snippet is to run the backups and update WordPress core, themes, and plugins. This can be scheduled via an Ansible Tower job for every day:

```
- name: running backup using duply
  command: /etc/cron.hourly/duply-backup

- name: updating WordPress core
  command: wp core update
  register: wp_core_update_output
  ignore_errors: yes

- name: wp core update output
  debug:
    msg: "{{ wp_core_update_output.stdout }}"

- name: updating WordPress themes
  command: wp theme update --all
  register: wp_theme_update_output
  ignore_errors: yes

- name: wp themes update output
  debug:
    msg: "{{ wp_theme_update_output.stdout }}"

- name: updating WordPress plugins
  command: wp plugin update --all
  register: wp_plugin_update_output
  ignore_errors: yes

- name: wp plugins update output
  debug:
    msg: "{{ wp_plugin_update_output.stdout }}"
```

Scheduling via Ansible Tower for daily updates

Ansible Tower allows us to schedule jobs to run automatically against servers. We can configure this in templates by configuring the start date and repeat frequency to execute the playbook.

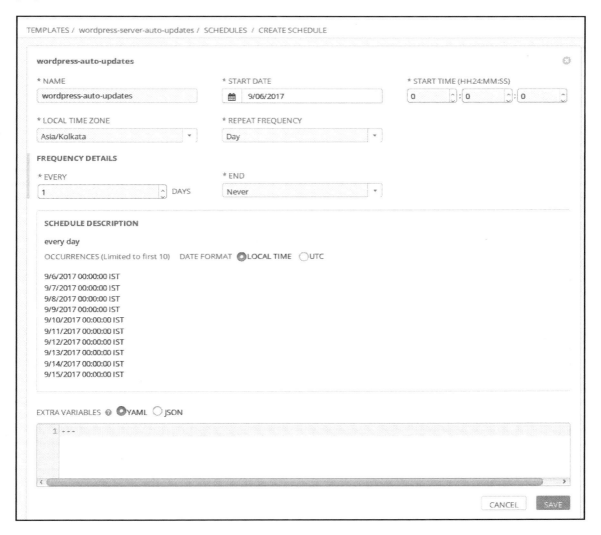

Ansible Tower job scheduling for automated WordPress updates

Otherwise, we can use the `cron` job template to perform this daily and add this template while deploying the WordPress setup:

```
#!/bin/bash

/etc/cron.hourly/duply-backup
wp core update
wp theme update --all
wp plugin update --all
```

Setting up Apache2 web server

We have already seen this in our LEMP stack setup, and it's very similar. But here, we have to use the required modules for working with WordPress. The following code snippet shows how we can use templating to perform configuration updates in the server:

```
- name: installing apache2 server
  apt:
    name: "apache2"
    update_cache: yes
    state: present

- name: updating customized templates for apache2 configuration
  template:
    src: "{{ item.src }}"
    dest: "{{ item.dst }}"
    mode: 0644
  with_tems:
    - { src: apache2.conf.j2, dst: /etc/apache2/conf.d/apache2.conf }
    - { src: 000-default.conf.j2, dst: /etc/apache2/sites-available/000-default.conf }
    - { src: default-ssl.conf.j2, dst: /etc/apache2/sites-available/default-ssl.conf }

- name: adding custom link for sites-enabled from sites-available
  file:
    src: "{{ item.src }}"
    dest: "{{ item.dest }}"
    state: link
  with_items:
    - { src: '/etc/apache2/sites-available/000-default.conf', dest: '/etc/apache2/sites-enabled/000-default.conf' }
    - { src: '/etc/apache2/sites-available/default-ssl.conf', dest: '/etc/apache2/sites-enabled/default-ssl.conf' }
```

```
notify:
  - start apache2
  - startup apache2
```

Enabling TLS/SSL with Let's Encrypt

We can use a command-line tool offered by Let's Encrypt to get free SSL/TLS certificates in an open, automated manner.

The tool is capable of reading and understanding an nginx virtual host file and generating the relevant certificates completely automatically, without any kind of manual intervention:

```
- name: adding certbot ppa
  apt_repository:
    repo: "ppa:certbot/certbot"

- name: install certbot
  apt:
    name: "{{ item }}"
    update_cache: yes
    state: present

  with_items:
    - python-certbot-nginx

- name: check if we have generated a cert already
  stat:
    path: "/etc/letsencrypt/live/{{ website_domain_name }}/fullchain.pem"
  register: cert_stats

- name: run certbot to generate the certificates
  shell: "certbot certonly --standalone -d {{ website_domain_name }} --
email {{ service_admin_email }} --non-interactive --agree-tos"
  when: cert_stats.stat.exists == False

- name: configuring site files
  template:
    src: website.conf
    dest: "/etc/nginx/sites-available/{{ website_domain_name }}"

- name: restart nginx
  service:
    name: nginx
    state: restarted
```

Let's Encrypt has become an extremely popular and secure way of enabling SSL/TLS on a website.

> By the end of June 2017, Let's Encrypt had issued over 100 million free SSL/TLS certificates in an automatic manner. For more information, visit `https://letsencrypt.org/2017/06/28/hundred-million-certs.html`.

What if you don't want to roll your own? The Trellis stack

Trellis stack is a way for development teams to have a local staging and production setup for WordPress websites.

> Trellis is an open source MIT license set of Ansible playbooks for a WordPress LEMP stack.

Why would we use Trellis, and when is it a good idea to use it?

Trellis is a full-fledged project, based on various tools held together by Ansible. In many ways, it is a better alternative to using the playbook for this chapter.

If you are expected to build/develop, deploy, and then maintain the production of a WordPress website or websites, then Trellis is a good choice.

The only caveat is that a lot of the features available are more useful if there is a team doing development and deployment. Otherwise, the stack is opinionated, and you may be saddled with some software choices that you may not like.

WordPress on Windows

This is one of the new things we are going to perform now. Until now, we have been setting up things in Linux based operating systems. Now we are going to set up IIS web server in the Windows operating system, which requires that we enable the WinRM feature in Windows services to perform Ansible playbook execution.

We need to make sure that the pywinrm module is installed in the control machine; we can install it by executing the following pip command:

```
pip install "pywinrm>=0.2.2"
```

How to enable WinRM in Windows

To simplify this process, Ansible provides a PowerShell script, which needs to be run as an administrator in the PowerShell console. Download the PowerShell script from https://raw.githubusercontent.com/ansible/ansible/devel/examples/scripts/ConfigureRemotingForAnsible.ps1.

On a Windows machine, open the command prompt as an administrator and run the following command:

```
powershell.exe -File ConfigureRemotingForAnsible.ps1 -CertValidityDays 100
```

 Make sure you opened port 5986 for the Windows machine in firewall rules. For more references, about Windows setup, visit http://docs.ansible.com/ansible/latest/intro_windows.html.

Running Ansible against a Windows server

Now, let's test by executing a simple ping module against the Windows server.

First, we need to create the inventory file, which includes the options for connecting the Windows winrm service:

```
[windows]
192.168.56.120 ansible_user=Administrator ansible_password=strongpassowrd
ansible_connection=winrm ansible_winrm_server_cert_validation=ignore
ansible_port=5986
```

To execute the Windows ping module, we can run the following Ansible command:

```
ansible -i inventory windows -m win_ping
```

```
$ ansible -i inventory winblows -m win_ping
               | SUCCESS => {
    "changed": false,
    "ping": "pong"
}
```

 To learn more about the different available modules in Windows, refer to http://docs.ansible.com/ansible/latest/list_of_windows_modules.html.

Installing IIS server using playbook

The following code snippet explains how we can install and start the IIS service in the Windows server operating system:

```
- name: Install and start IIS web server in Windows server
  hosts: winblows

  tasks:
    - name: Install IIS
      win_feature:
        name: "Web-Server"
        state: present
        restart: yes
        include_sub_features: yes
        include_management_tools: yes
```

```
$ ansible-playbook -i inventory basic-playbook-for-windows.yml

PLAY [Creating a new user in Windows server] ***********************************

TASK [Gathering Facts] *********************************************************
ok:

TASK [Install IIS] *************************************************************
changed:

PLAY RECAP *********************************************************************
                      : ok=2    changed=1    unreachable=0    failed=0
```

We will be using Chocolatey (for more information, visit `https://chocolatey.org/`), a package manager for Windows, for advanced installations and setup in Windows.

The next step is installing the Web Platform Installer.

 The Microsoft Web Platform Installer (Web PI) is a free tool that makes getting the latest components of the Microsoft Web Platform, including **Internet Information Services (IIS)**, SQL Server Express, .NET Framework, and Visual Web Developer, easy. For more information, visit `https://www.microsoft.com/web/downloads/platform.aspx`.

Once this is installed, we can install MySQL and WordPress using this:

 The following playbook runs the PowerShell script created by `https://gist.github.com/chrisloweau/8a15516d551a87b096620134c3624b73`. Please refer to `http://www.lowefamily.com.au/2017/04/11/how-to-install-wordpress-on-windows-server-2016/` for more details about the PowerShell script.

This setup requires some of the prerequirements. Which includes setting up the PowerShell execution policy and windows version supported.

- First, we need to setup the Execution Policy by running the following command:

    `Set-ExecutionPolicy RemoteSigned CurrentUser`

- This script only supports Windows Server 2016 operating system and Windows 10

The following Ansible playbook is executing PowerShell script to setup WordPress in Windows operating system.

```
- name: Windows Wordpress Setup Playbook
  hosts: winblows

  tasks:
    - name: download wordpress setup script
      win_get_url:
        url:
https://gist.githubusercontent.com/chrisloweau/8a15516d551a87b096620134c362
4b73/raw/b7a94e025b3cbf11c3f183d20e87c07de86124a3/wordpress-install.ps1
        dest: ~\Downloads\wordpress-install.ps1

    # This requires `Set-ExecutionPolicy RemoteSigned CurrentUser` to All
    - name: running windows wordpress script
```

```
    win_shell: ~\Downloads\wordpress-install.ps1
    args:
      chdir: ~\Downloads\wordpress-install.ps1
    register: output
  - debug:
      msg: "{{ output.stdout }}"
```

- After the execution it returns the output similar to the following. Then we can navigate to the IP address and follow the instructions to setup the WordPress final configuration

```
Installation Complete!

MySQL Accounts
      root = 2*Bb!o4#4T2yy/*44ngb
  wordpress = B*OGGrg{{ghr$35nGt4rU

Connect your web browser to http://192.168.56.100/ to complete this
WordPress
installation.
```

Summary

This chapter was all about WordPress. We used Ansible to create a fairly secure installation of WordPress by default. By changing the default values for the database, web server, and WordPress, we utilized the ability to codify security knowledge using Ansible playbooks. Additionally, by setting up automated, incremental, encrypted backups, we allowed for resilience and continuity in the face of the worst that could happen.

We took a brief look at how to enable Windows for working with Ansible.

In the next chapter, we will look at Elastic stack for setting up a centralized logging infrastructures. This will serve us well not only for storing all kinds of logs but will also alert and notify us in case we are attacked. We will also learn how to deploy serverless defenses to automatically block attackers.

4
Log Monitoring and Serverless Automated Defense (Elastic Stack in AWS)

Log monitoring is the perfect place to think about security automation. For monitoring to be effective, a few things need to happen. We should be able to move logs from different devices to a central location. We should be able to make sense of what a regular log entry is and what could possibly be an attack. We should be able to store the logs, and also operate on them for things such as aggregation, normalization, and eventually, analysis.

But, before diving into setting up the stack and building centralized logging and monitoring using Elastic Stack, we need to understand a little bit about why we need to use and automate the setup for defending against near real-time attacks. It's difficult to be a jack-of-all-trades. Traditional logging systems find it difficult to log for all applications, systems, and devices. The variety of time formats, log output formats, and so on, makes the task pretty complicated.

The biggest roadblock is finding a way to be able to centralize logs. This gets in the way of being able to process log entries in real time, or near real time effectively.

Some of the problematic points are as follows:

- Access is often difficult
- High expertise in mined data is required
- Logs can be difficult to find
- Log data is immense in size

In this chapter, we will discuss the following topics:

- Installing Elastic Stack for log monitoring
- Installing Beats on the server
- Setting up and configuring alerts
- Setting up an AWS Lambda endpoint to do automated defense

Introduction to Elastic Stack

Elastic Stack is a group of open source products from the Elastic company. It takes data from any type of source and in any format and searches, analyzes, and visualizes that data in real time. It consists of four major components, as follows:

- Elasticsearch
- Logstash
- Kibana
- Beats

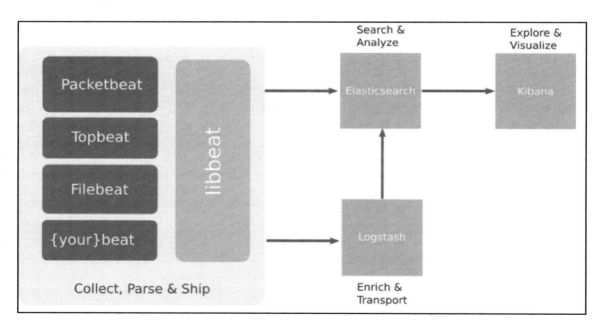

Elastic Stack architecture overview (image taken from https://www.elastic.co/blog/beats-1-0-0)

It helps users/admins to collect, analyze, and visualize data in (near) real time. Each module fits based on your use case and environment.

Elasticsearch

Elasticsearch is a distributed, RESTful search and analytics engine capable of solving a growing number of use cases. As the heart of the Elastic Stack, it centrally stores your data so you can discover the expected and uncover the unexpected

Main plus points of Elastic Stack:

- Distributed and highly available search engine, written in Java, and uses Groovy
- Built on top of Lucene
- Multi-tenant, with multi types and a set of APIs
- Document-oriented, providing (near) real-time search

Logstash

Logstash is an open source, server-side data processing pipeline that ingests data from a multitude of sources, simultaneously transforms it, and then sends it to your favorite *stash*.

Just to highlight Logstash is:

- A tool for managing events and logs written in Ruby
- Centralized data processing of all types of logs
- Consists of the following three main components:
  - **Input**: Passing logs to process them into machine-understandable format
  - **Filter**: A set of conditions to perform a specific action on an event
  - **Output**: The decision maker for processed events/logs

Kibana

Kibana lets you visualize your Elasticsearch data and navigate the Elastic Stack, so you can do anything from learning why you're getting paged at 2:00 a.m. to understanding the impact rain might have on your quarterly numbers.

Kibana's list of features:

- Powerful frontend dashboard is written in JavaScript
- Browser-based analytics and search dashboard for Elasticsearch
- A flexible analytics and visualization platform
- Provides data in the form of charts, graphs, counts, maps, and so on, in real time

Beats

Beats is the platform for single-purpose data shippers. They install as lightweight agents and send data from hundreds or thousands of machines to Logstash or Elasticsearch.

Beats are:

- Lightweight shippers for Elasticsearch and Logstash
- Capture all sorts of operational data, like logs or network packet data
- They can send logs to either Elasticsearch or Logstash

The different types of Beats are as follows:

- **Libbeat**: The Go framework for creating new Beats
- **Packetbeat**: Taps into your wire data
- **Filebeat**: Lightweight log forwarder to Logstash and Elasticsearch
- **Winlogbeat**: Sends windows event logs, and many other Beats, by community

Why should we use Elastic Stack for security monitoring and alerting?

The Elastic Stack solves most of the problems that we have discussed before, such as:

- Ability to store large amounts of data
- Ability to understand and read a variety of log formats
- Ability to ship the log information from a variety of devices in near real time to one central location
- A visualization dashboard for log analysis

Prerequisites for setting up Elastic Stack

Let's start with the prerequisites. Here, we are using `debconf` to add values for interactive inputs. Then we are installing Java, nginx, and other required packages:

```
- name: install python 2
  raw: test -e /usr/bin/python || (apt -y update && apt install -y python-
minimal)

- name: accepting oracle java license agreement
  debconf:
    name: 'oracle-java8-installer'
    question: 'shared/accepted-oracle-license-v1-1'
    value: 'true'
    vtype: 'select'

- name: adding ppa repo for oracle java by webupd8team
  apt_repository:
    repo: 'ppa:webupd8team/java'
    state: present
    update_cache: yes

- name: installing java nginx apache2-utils and git
  apt:
    name: "{{ item }}"
    state: present
    update_cache: yes

  with_items:
    - python-software-properties
    - oracle-java8-installer
    - nginx
    - apache2-utils
    - python-pip
    - python-passlib
```

Setting up the Elastic Stack

The stack is a combination of:

- The Elasticsearch service
- The Logstash service
- The Kibana service
- The Beats service on all the devices

This Elastic Stack can be set up in different ways. In this chapter, we are going to set up Elasticsearch, Logstash, and Kibana on a single machine.

This is the main log collection machine:

- It requires a minimum of 4 GB RAM, as we are using a single machine to serve three services (Elasticsearch, Logstash, and Kibana)
- It requires a minimum of 20 GB disk space, and, based on your log size, you can add the disk space

Logstash integrations

Logstash has a very large amount of integration support for the following:

- **Input**: An input plugin enables a specific source of events to be read by Logstash. The input plugin has file, lumberjack, s3, Beats, stdin, and many more.
- **Filter**: A filter plugin performs intermediary processing on an event. Filters are often applied conditionally, depending on the characteristics of the event.
- **Output**: An output plugin sends event data to a particular destination. Outputs are the final stage in the event pipeline. The output plugin has Elasticsearch, email, stdout, s3, file, HTTP, and so on.

Kibana

Kibana has different kinds of plugins and integrations by default, as well as those from the community, which can be found at `https://www.elastic.co/guide/en/kibana/current/known-plugins.html`.

ElastAlert

ElastAlert is a Python tool which also bundles with the different types of integrations to support with alerting and notifications. Some of them include Command, Email, JIRA, OpsGenie, AWS SNS, HipChat, Slack, Telegram, and so on. It also provides a modular approach to creating our own integrations.

Installing Elasticsearch

Install Elasticsearch from the repository with `gpg key` and add it to the startup programs:

```
- name: adding elastic gpg key for elasticsearch
  apt_key:
    url: "https://artifacts.elastic.co/GPG-KEY-elasticsearch"
    state: present

- name: adding the elastic repository
  apt_repository:
    repo: "deb https://artifacts.elastic.co/packages/5.x/apt stable main"
    state: present

- name: installing elasticsearch
  apt:
    name: "{{ item }}"
    state: present
    update_cache: yes

  with_items:
    - elasticsearch

- name: adding elasticsearch to the startup programs
  service:
    name: elasticsearch
    enabled: yes
  notify:
    - start elasticsearch
```

Configure the Elasticsearch cluster with the required settings. Also, set up the JVM options for the Elasticsearch cluster. Also, create a backup directory for Elasticsearch cluster backups and snapshots:

```
- name: creating elasticsearch backup repo directory at {{
  elasticsearch_backups_repo_path }}
  file:
    path: "{{ elasticsearch_backups_repo_path }}"
    state: directory
    mode: 0755
    owner: elasticsearch
    group: elasticsearch

- name: configuring elasticsearch.yml file
  template:
    src: "{{ item.src }}"
    dest: /etc/elasticsearch/"{{ item.dst }}"
```

```
    with_items:
      - { src: 'elasticsearch.yml.j2', dst: 'elasticsearch.yml' }
      - { src: 'jvm.options.j2', dst: 'jvm.options' }

    notify:
      - restart elasticsearch
```

The notify part will trigger the `restart elasticsearch` handler and the handler file will look as follows. We can use handlers anywhere in tasks once we create them in the handlers directory:

```
- name: start elasticsearch
  service:
    name: elasticsearch
    state: started

- name: restart elasticsearch
  service:
    name: elasticsearch
    state: restarted
```

Installing Logstash

Install Logstash from the repository with `gpg key` and add it to the startup programs:

```
- name: adding elastic gpg key for logstash
  apt_key:
    url: "https://artifacts.elastic.co/GPG-KEY-elasticsearch"
    state: present

- name: adding the elastic repository
  apt_repository:
    repo: "deb https://artifacts.elastic.co/packages/5.x/apt stable main"
    state: present

- name: installing logstash
  apt:
    name: "{{ item }}"
    state: present
    update_cache: yes

  with_items:
    - logstash

- name: adding logstash to the startup programs
  service:
```

```
name: logstash
enabled: yes

notify:
  - start logstash
```

Configure the Logstash service with input, output, and filter settings. This enables receiving logs, processing logs, and sending logs to the Elasticsearch cluster:

```
- name: logstash configuration files
  template:
    src: "{{ item.src }}"
    dest: /etc/logstash/conf.d/"{{ item.dst }}"
  with_items:
    - { src: '02-beats-input.conf.j2', dst: '02-beats-input.conf' }
    - { src: '10-sshlog-filter.conf.j2', dst: '10-sshlog-filter.conf' }
    - { src: '11-weblog-filter.conf.j2', dst: '11-weblog-filter.conf' }
    - { src: '30-elasticsearch-output.conf.j2', dst: '10-elasticsearch-output.conf' }

notify:
  - restart logstash
```

Logstash configuration

To receive logs from different systems, we use the Beats service from Elastic. The following configuration is to receive logs from different servers to the Logstash server. Logstash runs on port 5044 and we can use SSL certificates to ensure logs are transferred via an encrypted channel:

```
# 02-beats-input.conf.j2
input {
    beats {
        port => 5044
        ssl => true
        ssl_certificate => "/etc/pki/tls/certs/logstash-forwarder.crt"
        ssl_key => "/etc/pki/tls/private/logstash-forwarder.key"
    }
}
```

The following configuration is to parse the system SSH service logs (`auth.log`) using `grok` filters. It also applies filters like `geoip`, while providing additional information like country, location, longitude, latitude, and so on:

```
#10-sshlog-filter.conf.j2
filter {
    if [type] == "sshlog" {
        grok {
            match => [ "message", "%{SYSLOGTIMESTAMP:syslog_date}
%{SYSLOGHOST:syslog_host} %{DATA:syslog_program}(?:\[%{POSINT}\])?:
%{WORD:login} password for %{USERNAME:username} from %{IP:ip}
%{GREEDYDATA}",
            "message", "%{SYSLOGTIMESTAMP:syslog_date}
%{SYSLOGHOST:syslog_host} %{DATA:syslog_program}(?:\[%{POSINT}\])?: message
repeated 2 times: \[ %{WORD:login} password for %{USERNAME:username} from
%{IP:ip} %{GREEDYDATA}",
            "message", "%{SYSLOGTIMESTAMP:syslog_date}
%{SYSLOGHOST:syslog_host} %{DATA:syslog_program}(?:\[%{POSINT}\])?:
%{WORD:login} password for invalid user %{USERNAME:username} from %{IP:ip}
%{GREEDYDATA}",
            "message", "%{SYSLOGTIMESTAMP:syslog_date}
%{SYSLOGHOST:syslog_host} %{DATA:syslog_program}(?:\[%{POSINT}\])?:
%{WORD:login} %{WORD:auth_method} for %{USERNAME:username} from %{IP:ip}
%{GREEDYDATA}" ]
        }
        date {
            match => [ "timestamp", "dd/MMM/YYYY:HH:mm:ss Z" ]
            locale => en
        }
        geoip {
            source => "ip"
        }
    }
}
```

The following configuration is to parse web server logs (`nginx`, `apache2`). We will also apply filters for `geoip` and `useragent`. The `useragent` filter allows us to get information about the agent, OS type, version information, and so on:

```
#11-weblog-filter.conf.j2
filter {
    if [type] == "weblog" {
        grok {
            match => { "message" => '%{IPORHOST:clientip} %{USER:ident}
%{USER:auth} \[%{HTTPDATE:timestamp}\] "%{WORD:verb} %{DATA:request}
HTTP/%{NUMBER:httpversion}" %{NUMBER:response:int} (?:-
|%{NUMBER:bytes:int}) %{QS:referrer} %{QS:agent}' }
```

```
        }

        date {
        match => [ "timestamp", "dd/MMM/YYYY:HH:mm:ss Z" ]
        locale => en
        }

        geoip {
            source => "clientip"
        }
        useragent {
            source => "agent"
            target => "useragent"
        }
    }
}
```

The following configuration will send the log output into the Elasticsearch cluster with daily index formats:

```
#30-elasticsearch-output.conf.j2
output {
    elasticsearch {
        hosts => ["localhost:9200"]
        manage_template => false
        index => "%{[@metadata][beat]}-%{+YYYY.MM.dd}"
        document_type => "%{[@metadata][type]}"
    }
}
```

Installing Kibana

The following playbook will install Kibana. By default we are not making any changes in Kibana, as it works out of the box with Elasticsearch:

```
- name: adding elastic gpg key for kibana
  apt_key:
    url: "https://artifacts.elastic.co/GPG-KEY-elasticsearch"
    state: present

- name: adding the elastic repository
  apt_repository:
    repo: "deb https://artifacts.elastic.co/packages/5.x/apt stable main"
    state: present

- name: installing kibana
```

```
apt:
  name: "{{ item }}"
  state: present
  update_cache: yes

with_items:
  - kibana

- name: adding kibana to the startup programs
  service:
    name: kibana
    enabled: yes

notify:
  - start kibana
```

 By default Kibana doesn't have any authentication, X-Pack is the commercial plug-in by Elastic for RBAC (role-based access control) with security. Also, some open source options include https://readonlyrest.com/ and Search Guard (https://floragunn.com) to interact with Elasticsearch. Using TLS/SSL and custom authentication and aauthorization is highly recommended. Some of the open source options includes Oauth2 Proxy (https://github.com/bitly/oauth2_proxy) and Auth0, and so on.

Setting up nginx reverse proxy

The following configuration is to enable basic authentication for Kibana using nginx reverse proxy:

```
server {
    listen 80;
    server_name localhost;
    auth_basic "Restricted Access";
    auth_basic_user_file /etc/nginx/htpasswd.users;
    location / {
        proxy_pass http://localhost:5601;
        proxy_http_version 1.1;
        proxy_set_header Upgrade $http_upgrade;
        proxy_set_header Connection 'upgrade';
        proxy_set_header Host $host;
        proxy_cache_bypass $http_upgrade;
    }
}
```

Setting up and configuring the nginx service looks as follows:

```
#command: htpasswd -c /etc/nginx/htpasswd.users
- name: htpasswd generation
  htpasswd:
    path: "/etc/nginx/htpasswd.users"
    name: "{{ basic_auth_username }}"
    password: "{{ basic_auth_password }}"
    owner: root
    group: root
    mode: 0644

- name: nginx virtualhost configuration
  template:
    src: "templates/nginxdefault.j2"
    dest: "/etc/nginx/sites-available/default"

  notify:
    - restart nginx
```

Installing Beats to send logs to Elastic Stack

As we discussed, Beats are different types. In the following playbook, we are going to install Filebeat to send SSH and web server logs to the Elastic Stack:

```
- name: adding elastic gpg key for filebeat
  apt_key:
    url: "https://artifacts.elastic.co/GPG-KEY-elasticsearch"
    state: present

- name: adding the elastic repository
  apt_repository:
    repo: "deb https://artifacts.elastic.co/packages/5.x/apt stable main"
    state: present

- name: installing filebeat
  apt:
    name: "{{ item }}"
    state: present
    update_cache: yes

  with_items:
    - apt-transport-https
    - filebeat

- name: adding filebeat to the startup programs
```

```
    service:
      name: filebeat
      enabled: yes

    notify:
      - start filebeat
```

Now we can configure the Filebeat to send both SSH and web server logs to Elastic Stack, to process and index in near real-time:

```
filebeat:
  prospectors:
    -

      paths:
        - /var/log/auth.log
        # - /var/log/syslog
        # - /var/log/*.log
      document_type: sshlog
    -

      paths:
        - /var/log/nginx/access.log
      document_type: weblog

  registry_file: /var/lib/filebeat/registry

output:
 logstash:
   hosts: ["{{ logstash_server_ip }}:5044"]
   bulk_max_size: 1024
   ssl:
    certificate_authorities: ["/etc/pki/tls/certs/logstash-forwarder.crt"]

logging:
 files:
   rotateeverybytes: 10485760 # = 10MB
```

ElastAlert for alerting

First, we need to install the prerequisites for setting up ElastAlert. Then we will add the configuration files to perform alerting based on the rules:

```
- name: installing pre requisuites for elastalert
  apt:
    name: "{{ item }}"
    state: present
    update_cache: yes
```

```
    with_items:
      - python-pip
      - python-dev
      - libffi-dev
      - libssl-dev
      - python-setuptools
      - build-essential

  - name: installing elastalert
    pip:
      name: elastalert

  - name: creating elastalert directories
    file:
      path: "{{ item }}"
      state: directory
      mode: 0755

    with_items:
      - /opt/elastalert/rules
      - /opt/elastalert/config

  - name: creating elastalert configuration
    template:
      src: "{{ item.src }}"
      dest: "{{ item.dst }}"

    with_items:
      - { src: 'elastalert-config.j2', dst:
'/opt/elastalert/config/config.yml' }
      - { src: 'elastalert-service.j2', dst:
'/lib/systemd/system/elastalert.service' }
      - { src: 'elastalert-sshrule.j2', dst: '/opt/elastalert/rules/ssh-
bruteforce.yml' }

  - name: enable elastalert service
    service:
      name: elastalert
      state: started
      enabled: yes
```

We are also creating a simple startup script so that ElastAlert will be used as a system service:

```
[Unit]
Description=elastalert
After=multi-user.target
```

```
[Service]
Type=simple
WorkingDirectory=/opt/elastalert
ExecStart=/usr/local/bin/elastalert --config
/opt/elastalert/config/config.yml

[Install]
WantedBy=multi-user.target
```

Configuring the Let's Encrypt service

We can use a command-line tool offered by Let's Encrypt to get free SSL/TLS certificates in an open, automated manner.

The tool is capable of reading and understanding an nginx virtual host file and generating the relevant certificates completely automatically, without any kind of manual intervention:

```
- name: adding certbot ppa
  apt_repository:
    repo: "ppa:certbot/certbot"

- name: install certbot
  apt:
    name: "{{ item }}"
    update_cache: yes
    state: present

  with_items:
    - python-certbot-nginx

- name: check if we have generated a cert already
  stat:
    path: "/etc/letsencrypt/live/{{ website_domain_name }}/fullchain.pem"
    register: cert_stats

- name: run certbot to generate the certificates
  shell: "certbot certonly --standalone -d {{ website_domain_name }} --
email {{ service_admin_email }} --non-interactive --agree-tos"
  when: cert_stats.stat.exists == False

- name: configuring site files
  template:
    src: website.conf
    dest: "/etc/nginx/sites-available/{{ website_domain_name }}"
```

```
- name: restart nginx
  service:
    name: nginx
    state: restarted
```

ElastAlert rule configuration

Assuming that you already have Elastic Stack installed and logging SSH logs, use the following ElastAlert rule to trigger SSH attack IP blacklisting:

```
es_host: localhost
es_port: 9200
name: "SSH Bruteforce attack alert"
type: frequency
index: filebeat-*
num_events: 20
timeframe:
  minutes: 1
# For more info:
http://www.elasticsearch.org/guide/en/elasticsearch/reference/current/query
-dsl.html

filter:
- query:
    query_string:
      query: '_type:sshlog AND login:failed AND (username: "ubuntu" OR
username: "root")'

alert:
  - slack:
      slack_webhook_url: "https://hooks.slack.com/services/xxxxx"
      slack_username_override: "attack-bot"
      slack_emoji_override: "robot_face"
  - command: ["/usr/bin/curl",
"https://xxxxxxxxxx.execute-api.us-east-1.amazonaws.com/dev/zzzzzzzzzzzzz
/ip/inframonitor/%(ip)s"]

realert:
  minutes: 0
```

In the preceding example rule, most of the parameters are configurable, based on use case.

For more references, visit `https://elastalert.readthedocs.io/en/latest/running_elastalert.html`.

Kibana dashboards

We can import existing dashboard files (JSON format) into Kibana to view different patterns by uploading the JSON file.

Index creation in Kibana dashboard

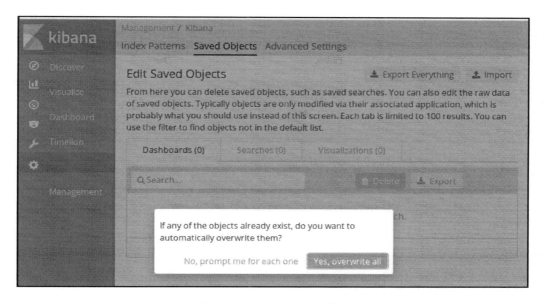

Importing existing dashboards and visualizations into Kibana dashboard

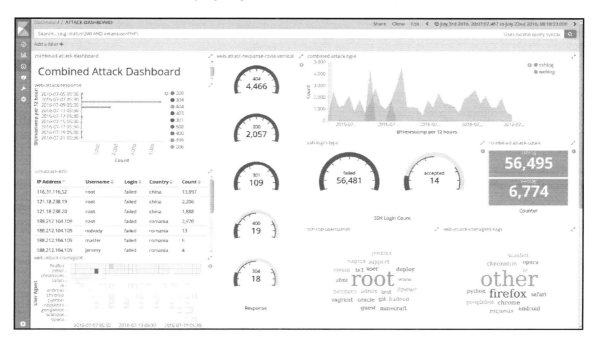

Attack dashboards from SSH and web server logs

Automated defense?

If we can get a notification for an attack, we can set up and do the following:

- Call an AWS Lambda function
- Send the attacker's IP address information to this AWS Lambda function endpoint
- Use the code deployed in the Lambda function to call the VPC network access list API and block the attacker's IP address

To ensure that we don't fill up the ACLs with attacker IPs, we can combine this approach with AWS DynamoDB to store this information for a short duration and remove it from the block list.

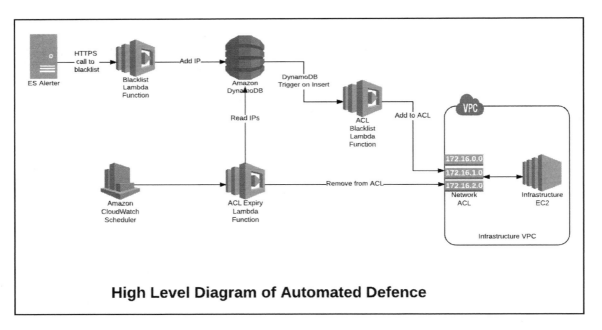

High Level Diagram of Automated Defence

AWS services used in setup

As soon as an attack is detected, the alerter sends the IP to the blacklist lambda endpoint via an HTTPS request. The IP is blocked using the network ACL and the record of it is maintained in DynamoDB. If the IP is currently blocked already, then the expiry time for the rule will be extended in the DynamoDB.

An expiry handler function is periodically triggered, which removes expired rules from DynamoDB and ACL accordingly.

DynamoDB

DynamoDB is the central database where rules are mapped to their respective ACL IDs. Rules for IP addresses are added and removed from the `blacklist_ip` table by appropriate lambda functions.

Blacklist lambda function

The Blacklist function is the only exposed endpoint from the setup. Any IP that needs to be blacklisted needs to be supplied to this function via an HTTPS request.

HandleExpiry lambda function

The HandleExpiry function is triggered every minute and removes expired rules from the ACL and DynamoDB based on the `expirymin` field.

Cloudwatch

Cloudwatch is used to trigger the HandleExpiry lambda function periodically. By default, the function is triggered every minute.

VPC Network ACL

The VPC Network ACL is where the ACL rules are added and deleted from. The ACL ID must be configured during the time of setup.

Setup

The setup involves the following steps:

- Obtain IAM credentials
- Create a table in DynamoDB
- Configure the lambda function based on requirement

- Deploy code to AWS Lambda
- Configure Cloudwatch to periodic invocation

The entire setup is automated, except for obtaining the IAM credentials and configuring the function based on requirements.

Configuration

The following parameters are configurable before deployment:

- `region`: AWS region to deploy in. This needs to be the same as the region where the VPC network resides.
- `accessToken`: The accessToken that will be used to authenticate the requests to the blacklist endpoint.
- `aclLimit`: The maximum number of rules an ACL can handle. The maximum limit in AWS is 20 by default.
- `ruleStartId`: The starting ID for rules in the ACL.
- `aclID`: The ACL ID of the network where the rules will be applied.
- `tableName`: The unique table name in DynamoDB, created for each VPC to be defended.
- `ruleValidity`: The duration for which a rule is valid, after which the IP will be unblocked.

Configure the following in the `config.js` file:

```
module.exports = {
    region: "us-east-1",                                    // AWS
Region to deploy in
    accessToken: "YOUR_R4NDOM_S3CR3T_ACCESS_TOKEN_GOES_HERE",   //
Accesstoken to make requests to blacklist
    aclLimit: 20,                                           // Maximum
number of acl rules
    ruleStartId: 10,                                        // Starting
id for acl entries
    aclId: "YOUR_ACL_ID",                                   // AclId
that you want to be managed
    tableName: "blacklist_ip",                              // DynamoDB
table that will be created
```

```
    ruleValidity: 5                                          // Validity
of Blacklist rule in minutes
}
```

Make sure to modify at least the `aclId`, `accessToken,` and `region` based on your setup. To modify the lambda deployment configuration use the `serverless.yml` file:

```
...

functions:
  blacklist:
    handler: handler.blacklistip
    events:
      - http:
          path: blacklistip
          method: get

  handleexpiry:
    handler: handler.handleexpiry
    events:
      - schedule: rate(1 minute)


...
```

For example, the rate at which the expiry function is triggered and the endpoint URL for the blacklist function can be modified using the YML file. But the defaults are already optimal.

The playbook looks as follows:

```
- name: installing node run time and npm
  apt:
    name: "{{ item }}"
    state: present
    update_cache: yes

  with_items:
    - nodejs
    - npm

- name: installing serverless package
  npm:
    name: "{{ item }}"
    global: yes
    state: present

  with_items:
    - serverless
```

```
          - aws-sdk

    - name: copy the setup files
      template:
        src: "{{ item.src }}"
        dest: "{{ item.dst }}"

      with_items:
        - { src: 'config.js.j2', dst: '/opt/serverless/config.js' }
        - { src: 'handler.js.j2', dst: '/opt/serverless/handler.js' }
        - { src: 'iamRoleStatements.json.j2', dst:
'/opt/serverless/iamRoleStatements.json' }
        - { src: 'initDb.js.j2', dst: '/opt/serverless/initDb.js' }
        - { src: 'serverless.yml.j2', dst: '/opt/serverless/serverless.yml' }
        - { src: 'aws-credentials.j2', dst: '~/.aws/credentials' }

    - name: create dynamo db table
      command: node initDb.js
      args:
        chdir: /opt/serverless/

    - name: deploy the serverless
      command: serverless deploy
      args:
        chdir: /opt/serverless/
```

The current setup for AWS Lambda is to block the IP address against network ACL. This can be reused with other API endpoints, like a firewall dynamic block list and other security devices.

 As per the AWS documentation, the VPC network ACL rule limit is set to 20: http://docs.aws.amazon.com/AmazonVPC/latest/UserGuide/VPC_Appendix_Limits.html#vpc-limits-nacls

Usage - block an IP address

The blacklist endpoint is responsible for blocking an IP address.

Request

The URL looks like the
following: `https://lambda_url/blacklistipaccessToken=ACCESS_TOKEN&ip=IP_A`
`DDRESS`

The query parameters are as follows:

- `IP_ADDRESS`: This is the IP address to be blocked
- `ACCESS_TOKEN`: The `accessToken` to authenticate the request

Response

Responses are standard HTTP status codes, which are explained as follows:

Status code	Body	Explanation
200	Blocked	The IP has been added to the blacklist
200	Expiryextended	The blacklist rule validity has been extended
400	Bad Request	Required fields are missing
401	Unauthorized	The accessToken is invalid or missing
500	Rulelimitreached	The ACL rule limit has been reached

Automated defense lambda in action

When the ElastAlert detects an SSH brute force attack, it will trigger a request to lambda endpoint by providing the attacker's IP address. Then our automated defense platform will trigger a network ACL blocklist rule. This can be configurable to say for how much time it should be blocked.

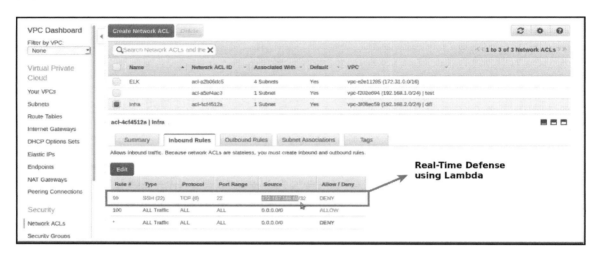

Summary

That is a lot of information to take in. Also, we have made many assumptions about the scenario. But if this spurs you into thinking about combining the various logs of your devices and servers into one central location and enabling automated alerting and defenses, we have done our job well.

As this chapter demonstrates, security automation is a bit like plumbing. As long as we can understand how a bunch of disparate systems can be made to communicate together, we can add them to our playbooks. In many cases, Ansible will already have a module in place for us to use and get going.

Now that we have whet your appetite for logging and attack detection, in the next chapter, let's dive into what it takes to set up an automated web security testing setup. We will pick the incredibly powerful and versatile OWASP ZAP scanner and intercepting proxy and use it to scan and test websites and APIs.

5
Automating Web Application Security Testing Using OWASP ZAP

The OWASP **Zed Attack Proxy** (commonly known as **ZAP**) is one of the most popular web application security testing tools. It has many features that allow it to be used for manual security testing; it also fits nicely into **continuous integration/continuous delivery (CI/CD)** environments after some tweaking and configuration.

More details about the project can be found at `https://www.owasp.org/index.php/OWASP_Zed_Attack_Proxy_Project`.

 Open Web Application Security Project (OWASP) is a worldwide not-for-profit charitable organization focused on improving the security of software. Read more about OWASP projects and resources at `https://www.owasp.org`.

OWASP ZAP includes many different tools and features in one package. For a pentester tasked with doing the security testing of web applications, the following features are invaluable:

Feature	Use case
Intercepting proxy	This allows us to intercept requests and responses in the browser
Active scanner	Automatically run web security scans against targets
Passive scanner	Glean information about security issues from pages that get downloaded using spider tools and so on
Spiders	Before ZAP can attack an application, it creates a site map of the application by crawling all the possible web pages on it
REST API	Allows ZAP to be run in headless mode and to be controlled for running automated scanner, spider, and get the results

As you may have guessed, in this chapter, for security automation we will invoke ZAP in headless mode and use the API interfaces provided by it to do the scanning and security testing.

ZAP is a Java-based software. The typical way of using it will involve the following:

- **Java Runtime Environment** (**JRE**) 7 or more recent installed in the operating system of your choice (macOS, Windows, Linux)
- Install ZAP using package managers, installers from the official downloads page

 You can find the latest updated stable links here: `https://github.com/zaproxy/zaproxy/wiki/Downloads`.

While we can build a playbook to do exactly that, the developer world is moving toward concepts of CI/CD and continuous security. An approach in which we can bootstrap a stable version of ZAP as and when required would be ideal.

The best way to achieve that is to use OWASP ZAP as a container. In fact, this is the kind of setup Mozilla uses ZAP in a CI/CD pipeline to verify the baseline security controls at every release.

If you are wondering about the connection between Mozilla and OWASP ZAP, Simon Bennetts leads the OWASP ZAP project and works at Mozilla. Read his blog post about ZAP baseline scans at `https://blog.mozilla. org/security/2017/01/25/setting-a-baseline-for-web-security- controls/`.

Installing OWASP ZAP

We are going to use OWASP ZAP as a container in this chapter, which requires container runtime in the host operating system. The team behind OWASP ZAP releases ZAP Docker images on a weekly basis via Docker Hub. The approach of pulling Docker images based on tags is popular in modern DevOps environments and it makes sense that we talk about automation with respect to that.

Official ZAP is now available with stable and weekly releases via the Docker container at Docker Hub: `https://github.com/zaproxy/zaproxy/ wiki/Docker`.

Installing Docker runtime

Docker is an open platform for developers and system administrators to build, ship, and run distributed applications whether on laptops, data center VMs, or the cloud. To learn more about Docker, refer to `https://www.docker.com/what-docker`.

The following playbook will install Docker Community Edition software in Ubuntu 16.04:

```
- name: installing docker on ubuntu
  hosts: zap
  remote_user: "{{ remote_user_name }}"
  gather_facts: no
  become: yes
  vars:
    remote_user_name: ubuntu
    apt_repo_data: "deb [arch=amd64]
https://download.docker.com/linux/ubuntu xenial stable"
    apt_gpg_key: https://download.docker.com/linux/ubuntu/gpg

  tasks:
    - name: adding docker gpg key
      apt_key:
```

```
        url: "{{ apt_gpg_key }}"
        state: present
 - name: add docker repository
   apt_repository:
        repo: "{{ apt_repo_data }}"
        state: present
 - name: installing docker-ce
   apt:
        name: docker-ce
        state: present
        update_cache: yes
 - name: install python-pip
   apt:
        name: python-pip
        state: present
 - name: install docker-py
   pip:
        name: "{{ item }}"
        state: present

   with_items:
        - docker-py
```

Docker requires a 64-bit version OS and a Linux kernel version equal to or greater than 3.10. Docker runtime is available for Windows and macOS as well. For the purposes of this chapter, the containers we will use are Linux-based. So the runtime can be in Windows, but the container running in that will be a Linux-based one. These are the standard OWASP ZAP containers available for use.

OWASP ZAP Docker container setup

The two new modules to deal with Docker containers that we will be using here are docker_image and docker_container.

These modules require you to be using a 2.1 and higher version of Ansible. Right now would be a good time to check your version of Ansible using the —version flag.

If you need to get the latest stable version using `pip`, run the following command:

```
pip install ansible --upgrade
```

The following playbook will take some time to complete as it has to download about 1 GB of data from the internet:

```
- name: setting up owasp zap container
  hosts: zap
  remote_user: "{{ remote_user_name }}"
  gather_facts: no
  become: yes
  vars:
    remote_user_name: ubuntu
    owasp_zap_image_name: owasp/zap2docker-weekly

  tasks:
    - name: pulling {{ owasp_zap_image_name }} container
      docker_image:
        name: "{{ owasp_zap_image_name }}"

    - name: running owasp zap container
      docker_container:
        name: owasp-zap
        image: "{{ owasp_zap_image_name }}"
        interactive: yes
        state: started
        user: zap
        command: zap.sh -daemon -host 0.0.0.0 -port 8090 -config
api.disablekey=true -config api.addrs.addr.name=.* -config
api.addrs.addr.regex=true
        ports:
          - "8090:8090"
</span>
```

In the following configuration, we are saying `api.disablekey=true`, which means we are not using any API key. This can be overwritten by giving the specific API key. `api.addrs.addr.name=.*` and `api.addrs.addr.regex=true` will allow all IP addresses to connect to the ZAP API. More information about ZAP API key settings can be found at `https://github.com/zaproxy/zaproxy/wiki/FAQapikey`.

You can access the ZAP API interface by navigating
to `http://ZAPSERVERIPADDRESS:8090`:

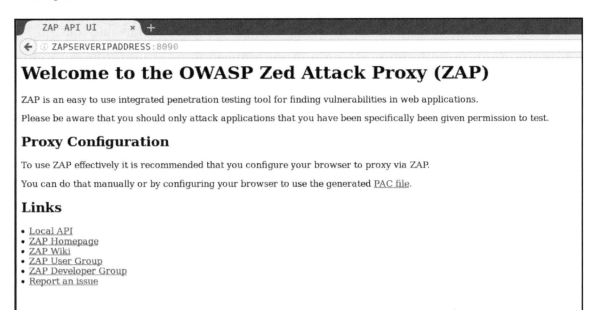

OWASP ZAP API Web UI

A specialized tool for working with Containers - Ansible Container

Currently, we are using Docker modules to perform container operations. A new
tool, `ansible-container`, provides an Ansible-centric workflow for building, running,
testing, and deploying containers.

This allows us to build, push, and run containers using existing playbooks. Dockerfiles are
like writing shell scripts, therefore, `ansible-container` will allow us to codify those
Dockerfiles and build them using existing playbooks rather writing complex scripts.

The `ansible-container` supports various orchestration tools, such as Kubernetes and
OpenShift. It can also be used to push the build images to private registries such as Google
Container Registry and Docker Hub.

Read more about `ansible-container` at `https://docs.ansible.com/ansible-container`.

Configuring ZAP Baseline scan

The ZAP Baseline scan is a script that is available in the ZAP Docker images.

More details about OWASP ZAP Baseline scan can be found at `https://github.com/zaproxy/zaproxy/wiki/ZAP-Baseline-Scan`.

This is what the script does:

- Runs ZAP spider against the specified target for one minute and then does a passive scan
- By default, reports all alerts as warnings
- This script is intended to be ideal to run in a CI/CD environment, even against production sites

Before setting up and running the ZAP Baseline scan, we want to run a simple vulnerable application so that all scans and testing using ZAP are running against that application, rather than running the scans against real-world applications, which is illegal without permission.

Running a vulnerable application container

We will be using the **Damn Vulnerable Web Services (DVWS)** application (for more information, you can visit `https://github.com/snoopysecurity/dvws`). It is an insecure web application with multiple vulnerable web service components that can be used to learn real-world web service vulnerabilities.

The following playbook will set up the Docker container for running the DVWS application:

```
- name: setting up DVWS container
  hosts: dvws
  remote_user: "{{ remote_user_name }}"
  gather_facts: no
  become: yes
```

```
vars:
  remote_user_name: ubuntu
  dvws_image_name: cyrivs89/web-dvws

tasks:
  - name: pulling {{ dvws_image_name }} container
    docker_image:
      name: "{{ dvws_image_name }}"

  - name: running dvws container
    docker_container:
      name: dvws
      image: "{{ dvws_image_name }}"
      interactive: yes
      state: started
      ports:
        - "80:80"
```

Once the playbook is successfully executed, we can navigate to `http://DVWSSERVERIP`:

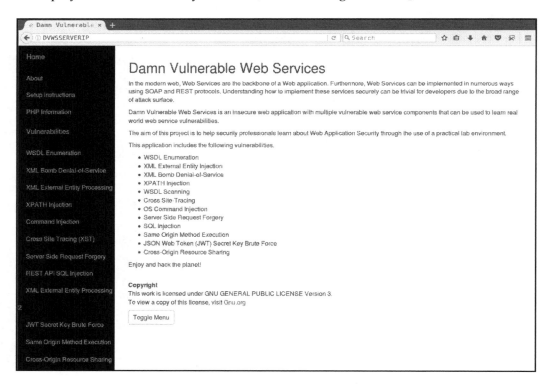

DVWS application home page

Now, we are ready to perform our OWASP ZAP Baseline scan against the DVWS application, by running the Baseline scan playbook.

Running an OWASP ZAP Baseline scan

The following playbook runs the Docker Baseline scan against a given website URL. It also stores the output of the Baseline's scan in the host system in HTML, Markdown, and XML formats:

```
- name: Running OWASP ZAP Baseline Scan
  hosts: zap
  remote_user: "{{ remote_user_name }}"
  gather_facts: no
  become: yes
  vars:
    remote_user_name: ubuntu
    owasp_zap_image_name: owasp/zap2docker-weekly
    website_url: {{ website_url }}
    reports_location: /zapdata/
    scan_name: owasp-zap-base-line-scan-dvws

  tasks:
    - name: adding write permissions to reports directory
      file:
        path: "{{ reports_location }}"
        state: directory
        owner: root
        group: root
        recurse: yes
        mode: 0770

    - name: running owasp zap baseline scan container against "{{
website_url }}"
      docker_container:
        name: "{{ scan_name }}"
        image: "{{ owasp_zap_image_name }}"
        interactive: yes
        auto_remove: yes
        state: started
        volumes: "{{ reports_location }}:/zap/wrk:rw"
        command: "zap-baseline.py -t {{ website_url }} -r {{ scan_name
}}_report.html"

    - name: getting raw output of the scan
      command: "docker logs -f {{ scan_name }}"
      register: scan_output
```

```
- debug:
    msg: "{{ scan_output }}"
```

Let's explore the parameters of the preceding playbook:

- `website_url` is the domain (or) URL that you want to perform the Baseline scan, we can pass this via `--extra-vars "website_url:` `http://192.168.33.111"` from the `ansible-playbook` command
- `reports_location` is the path to ZAP host machine where reports get stored

The following screenshot is the scanning report output from OWASP ZAP:

⬤ ZAP Scanning Report

Summary of Alerts

Risk Level	Number of Alerts
High	0
Medium	3
Low	5
Informational	2

Alert Detail

Medium (Medium)	X-Frame-Options Header Not Set
Description	X-Frame-Options header is not included in the HTTP response to protect against 'ClickJacking' attacks.
URL	http://192.168.33.111/dvws/vulnerabilities/cors/?C=S;O=A
Method	GET
Parameter	X-Frame-Options
URL	http://192.168.33.111/dvws/about.php
Method	GET
Parameter	X-Frame-Options
URL	http://192.168.33.111/dvws/vulnerabilities/xst/?C=M;O=D
Method	GET
Parameter	X-Frame-Options
URL	http://192.168.33.111/dvws/vulnerabilities/xxe2/
Method	GET
Parameter	X-Frame-Options
URL	http://192.168.33.111/dvws/vulnerabilities/?C=N;O=A
Method	GET
Parameter	X-Frame-Options
URL	http://192.168.33.111/dvws/vulnerabilities/hiddendir/?C=M;O=A
Method	GET

OWASP ZAP Baseline scan HTML report

To generate reports in the Markdown and XML formats, add `-w report.md` and `-x report.xml`, respectively, to command.

Security testing against web applications and websites

Until now, we have seen how to run a Baseline scan using the OWASP ZAP container. Now we will see how we can perform active scans against web applications. An active scan may cause the vulnerability to be exploited in the application. Also, this type of scan requires extra configuration, which includes authentication and sensitive functionalities.

Running ZAP full scan against DVWS

The following playbook will run the full scan against the DVWS application. Now we can see that the playbook looks almost similar, except the flags sent to command:

```
- name: Running OWASP ZAP Full Scan
  hosts: zap
  remote_user: "{{ remote_user_name }}"
  gather_facts: no
  become: yes
  vars:
    remote_user_name: ubuntu
    owasp_zap_image_name: owasp/zap2docker-weekly
    website_url: {{ website_url }}
    reports_location: /zapdata/
    scan_name: owasp-zap-full-scan-dvws

  tasks:
    - name: adding write permissions to reports directory
      file:
```

```
            path: "{{ reports_location }}"
            state: directory
            owner: root
            group: root
            recurse: yes
            mode: 0777

    - name: running owasp zap full scan container against "{{ website_url
}}"
        docker_container:
            name: "{{ scan_name }}"
            image: "{{ owasp_zap_image_name }}"
            interactive: yes
            auto_remove: yes
            state: started
            volumes: "{{ reports_location }}:/zap/wrk:rw"
            command: "zap-full-scan.py -t {{ website_url }} -r {{ scan_name
}}_report.html"

    - name: getting raw output of the scan
        raw: "docker logs -f {{ scan_name }}"
        register: scan_output

    - debug:
        msg: "{{ scan_output }}"
```

The OWASP ZAP full scan checks for a lot of vulnerabilities, which includes OWASP TOP 10 (for more information visit `https://www.owasp.org/index.php/Category:OWASP_Top_Ten_Project`) and many others. This can be intrusive to the application and it sends active requests to the application. It may cause damage to the functionality based on the vulnerability that exists in the application:

🔍 ZAP Scanning Report

Summary of Alerts

Risk Level	Number of Alerts
High	5
Medium	5
Low	5
Informational	2

Alert Detail

High (Medium)	Anti CSRF Tokens Scanner
	A cross-site request forgery is an attack that involves forcing a victim to send an HTTP request to a target destination without their knowledge or intent in order to perform an action as the victim. The underlying cause is application functionality using predictable URL/form actions in a repeatable way. The nature of the attack is that CSRF exploits the trust that a web site has for a user. By contrast, cross-site scripting (XSS) exploits the trust that a user has for a web site. Like XSS, CSRF attacks are not necessarily cross-site, but they can be. Cross-site request forgery is also known as CSRF, XSRF, one-click attack, session riding, confused deputy, and sea surf.
	CSRF attacks are effective in a number of situations, including:
Description	* The victim has an active session on the target site.
	* The victim is authenticated via HTTP auth on the target site.
	* The victim is on the same local network as the target site.
	CSRF has primarily been used to perform an action against a target site using the victim's privileges, but recent techniques have been discovered to disclose information by gaining access to the response. The risk of information disclosure is dramatically increased when the target site is vulnerable to XSS, because XSS can be used as a platform for CSRF, allowing the attack to operate within the bounds of the same-origin policy.
URL	http://192.168.33.111/dvws/vulnerabilities/jwt/api.php
Method	POST
Evidence	<form method="post" action="">
URL	http://192.168.33.111/dvws/vulnerabilities/jwt/login.php
Method	GET

OWASP ZAP full scan for DVWS application report

The preceding screenshot is the report from the OWASP ZAP full scan for the DVWS application. We can clearly see the difference between the Baseline scan and the full scan, based on the number of vulnerabilities, different types of vulnerabilities, and risk rating.

Testing web APIs

Similar to the ZAP Baseline scan, the fine folks behind ZAP provide a script as part of their live and weekly Docker images. We can use it to run scans against API endpoints defined either by OpenAPI specification or **Simple Object Access Protocol (SOAP)**.

The script can understand the API specifications and import all the definitions. Based on this, it runs an active scan against all the URLs found:

```
- name: Running OWASP ZAP API Scan
  hosts: zap
  remote_user: "{{ remote_user_name }}"
  gather_facts: no
  become: yes
  vars:
    remote_user_name: ubuntu
    owasp_zap_image_name: owasp/zap2docker-weekly
    website_url: {{ website_url }}
    reports_location: /zapdata/
    scan_name: owasp-zap-api-scan-dvws
    api_type: openapi
>
  tasks:
    - name: adding write permissions to reports directory
      file:
        path: "{{ reports_location }}"
        state: directory
        owner: root
        group: root
        recurse: yes
        mode: 0777

    - name: running owasp zap api scan container against "{{ website_url
}}"
      docker_container:
        name: "{{ scan_name }}"
        image: "{{ owasp_zap_image_name }}"
        interactive: yes
        auto_remove: yes
        state: started
        volumes: "{{ reports_location }}:/zap/wrk:rw"
        command: "zap-api-scan.py -t {{ website_url }} -f {{ api_type }} -r
{{ scan_name }}_report.html"

    - name: getting raw output of the scan
      raw: "docker logs -f {{ scan_name }}"
      register: scan_output
```

```
- debug:
    msg: "{{ scan_output }}"
```

Continuous scanning workflow using ZAP and Jenkins

Jenkins is an open source automation server. It is used extensively in CI/CD pipelines. These pipelines usually refer to a series of automated steps that occur based on triggers, such as code commits to version control software or a new release being created.

We already saw the example of ZAP Baseline's scans being part of the Mozilla release cycle. We can integrate ZAP with Jenkins. While there are many ways we can do this, a useful set of steps will be the following:

1. Based on a trigger, a new ZAP instance is ready for scanning
2. The ZAP instance runs against an automatically deployed application
3. The results of the scan are captured and stored in some format
4. If we choose, the results can also create tickets in bug tracking systems such as Atlassian Jira

For this, we will set up our pipeline infrastructure first:

1. Set up Jenkins using a playbook
2. Add the official OWASP ZAP Jenkins plugin
3. Trigger the workflow using another playbook

> The official OWASP ZAP Jenkins plugin can be found at `https://wiki.jenkins.io/display/JENKINS/zap+plugin`.

Setting up Jenkins

Set up Jenkins on the server to be used as a CI/CD platform for OWASP ZAP. This will return the Jenkins administrator password and once it has been done, we can install the Ansible plugin:

```
- name: installing jenkins in ubuntu 16.04
  hosts: jenkins
  remote_user: {{ remote_user_name }}
```

```
gather_facts: False
become: yes
vars:
  remote_user_name: ubuntu

tasks:
  - name: adding jenkins gpg key
    apt_key:
      url: 'https://pkg.jenkins.io/debian/jenkins-ci.org.key'
      state: present

  - name: jeknins repository to system
    apt_repository:
      repo: 'deb http://pkg.jenkins.io/debian-stable binary/'
      state: present
  - name: installing jenkins
    apt:
      name: jenkins
      state: present
      update_cache: yes

  - name: adding jenkins to startup
    service:
      name: jenkins
      state: started
      enabled: yes

  - name: printing jenkins default administration password
    command: cat "/var/lib/jenkins/secrets/initialAdminPassword"
    register: jenkins_default_admin_password

  - debug:
      msg: "{{ jenkins_default_admin_password.stdout }}"
```

Then, we can add the playbook to the project. When the new trigger happens in the Jenkins build, the playbook will start to scan the website to perform the Baseline scan:

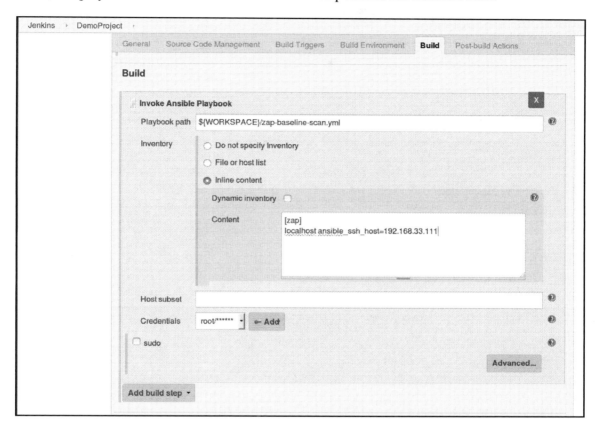

Once the playbook triggers, it will execute the playbook against the URL and return the ZAP Baseline scan output:

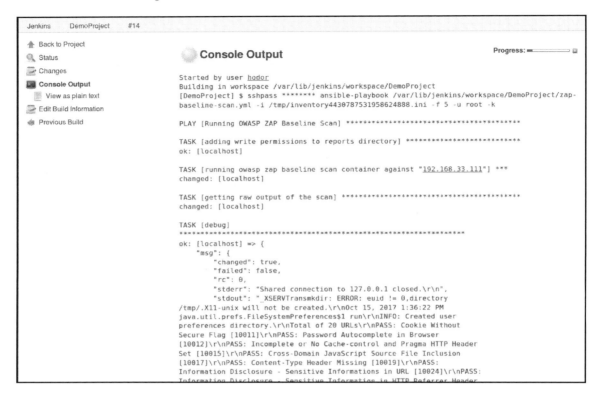

Setting up the OWASP ZAP Jenkins plugin

OWASP ZAP working in tandem with Jenkins is a fairly well-known setup. We already know how to set up Jenkins. We can install the official ZAP Jenkins plugin using our playbook.

Once the playbook is ready, a bit of manual configuration is required. We start after our playbook has installed Jenkins and restarted the server so that the plugin is available for our build jobs.

Let's create a new build job and call it ZAP-Jenkins, as shown in the following screenshot:

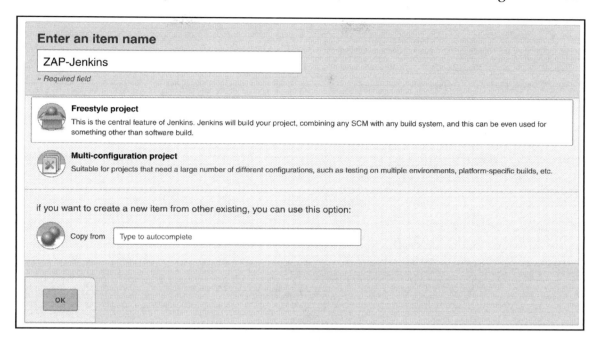

This will be a freestyle project for us. Now we will add the magic of ZAP to this:

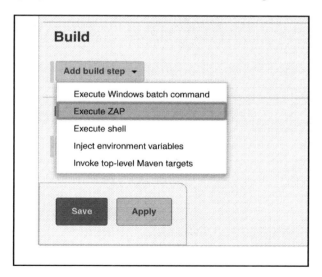

We are following the instructions as given on the Jenkins page for the official plugin: `https://wiki.jenkins.io/display/JENKINS/zap+plugin`.

Some assembly required

Specify the interface's IP address and the port number on which ZAP should be listening. Usually, this port is `8080`, but since Jenkins is listening on that, we choose `8090`:

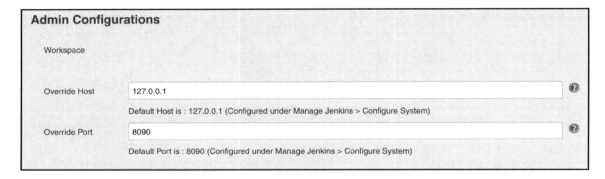

For JDK, we choose the only available option, **InheritFromJob**:

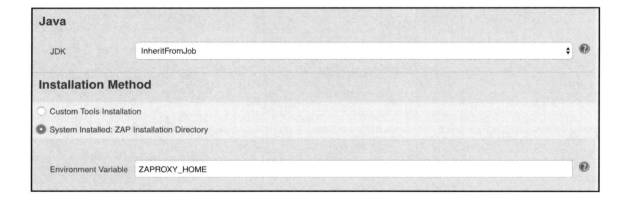

For the installation method, we select the ZAP that is already installed on `/usr/share/owasp-zap`. We add this value to a `ZAPROXY_HOME` environment variable in `/etc/environment`.

By doing this, we have ensured that the environment variable values will survive a system reboot as well:

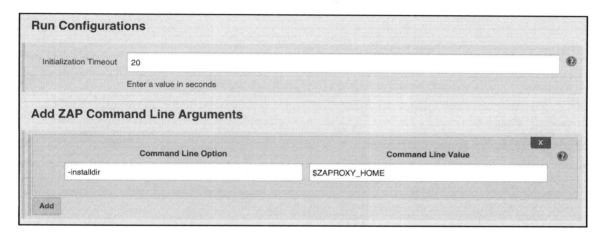

We specify a fairly small value for a timeout to ensure that in case something goes wrong, we don't have to wait long to see that the build failed or ZAP isn't responding.

We also specify a command-line option to tell Jenkins what the install directory for ZAP is.

 You may need to click on the **Advanced** button to see these options.

We specify the path to the ZAP home directory:

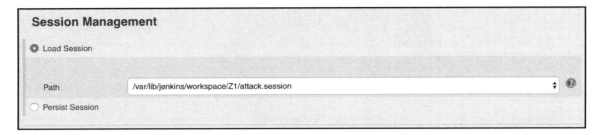

Then we configure where we plan to load the ZAP session from:

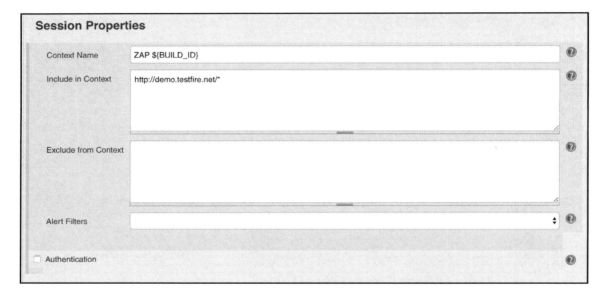

The context name, scope, and exclusions are shown here:

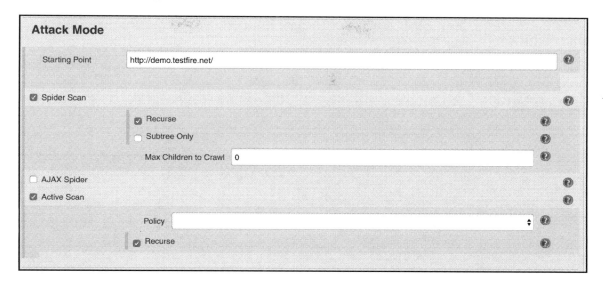

This is the starting point of the URL to test. The kind of test we are planning to do is **Spider Scan**, default **Active Scan**:

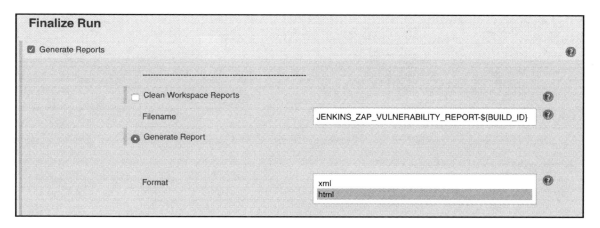

Finally, we specify the filename for the report that will be generated. We are adding the BUILD_ID variable to ensure that we don't have to worry about overwriting the reports.

Triggering the build (ZAP scan)

Once the job is configured, we are ready to trigger the build. Of course, you can manually click **Build now** and get going.

But we will configure the build job to be triggered remotely, and at the same time pass the necessary target information.

Under **General** check **This project is parameterized**:

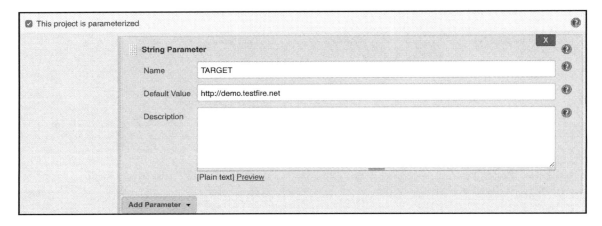

Inside that, we add a TARGET parameter with a default value.

Under **Build Triggers**, we specify an authentication token to be passed as a parameter while remotely triggering a build:

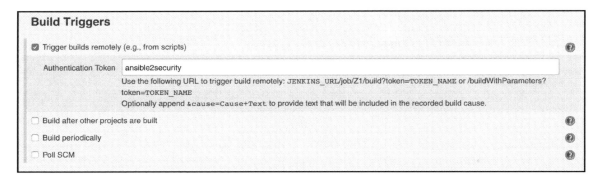

Try to ensure that this token is sufficiently lengthy and random, and not the simple word we have used as an example.

> A great way to generate sufficiently random strings in Linux/macOS is to use the OpenSSL command. For the hex output (20 is the length of the output), use **openssl rand —hex 20**. For the base64 output (24 is the length of the output), use **openssl rand —base64 24**.

At this point, all we have to do is note the **API Token** of the logged in user (from `http://JENKINS-URL/user/admin/configure`):

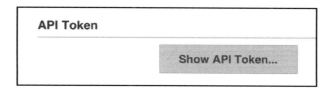

Clicking **Show API Token** will show the token:

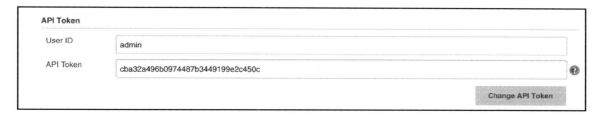

We can now use a command-line tool, such as `curl`, to see if this works.

The format of the link is `curl "http://username:API-TOKEN@JENKINS-URL/job/ZAP-Jenkins/buildWithParameters?TARGET=http://demo.testfire.net&token=ansible2security"`.

This will trigger the build and the application will get scanned for security issues.

Playbook to do this with automation

To perform the preceding trigger, we can use the following Ansible playbook. This can be used in our Ansible Tower to schedule the scan as well.

The following playbook can store the the API Token key using Ansible Vault, feature to store secret data in an encrypted format in playbooks. We will learn more about Ansible Vault usage in `Chapter 11`, *Ansible Security Best Practices, References and Further Reading*.

To create an Ansible Vault encrypted variable, run the following command. When it prompts for a password, give a password to encrypt this variable and it requires while executing the playbook

```
echo 'YOURTOKENGOESHERE' | ansible-vault encrypt_string --stdin-name
'jenkins_api_token'
```

After executing, it returns the encrypted variable which we can use in the playbook it self directly as a variable:

```
- name: jenkins build job trigger
  hosts: localhost
  connection: local
  vars:
    jenkins_username: username
    jenkins_api_token: !vault |
        $ANSIBLE_VAULT;1.1;AES256
36636563313932313366313030623232623338333638363465343339636362353534363563
66161
30626665366137643964393265346632376534386163356340a613564643666234626663616
33763
31326161303666653366343931366265333238383937656435663061363665643431336638
53436
35326464343765533390a646332646639653161341653638326162333332323231306230343
13032
666435373366346332633463633134376662623230643865396163336461323533363
    jenkins_host: 192.168.11.111
    jenkins_target_url: 'http://demo.testfire.net'
    jenkins_token: ansible2security
>
  tasks:
    - name: trigger jenkins build
      uri:
        url: "http://{{ jenkins_username }}:{{ jenkins_api_token }}@{{
jenkins_host }}/job/ZAP-Jenkins/buildWithParameters?TARGET={{
jenkins_target_url }}&token={{ jenkins_token }}"
        method: GET
      register: results
    - debug:
        msg: "{{ results.stdout }}"
```

To perform the `ansible-vault` decryption while executing the playbook, the playbook execution command looks like this:

```
$ ansible-playbook --ask-vault-pass main.yml
```

ZAP Docker and Jenkins

There is a great blog series by the folks at Mozilla about configuring the ZAP Docker with Jenkins. Rather than repeating what they have to say, we thought it made sense to point you to the first post in that series.

 For further reading, you can check out the interesting blog *Dockerized, OWASP-ZAP security scanning, in Jenkins, part one at* `https://blog.mozilla.org/webqa/2016/05/11/docker-owasp-zap-part-one/`.

Summary

OWASP ZAP is a great addition to any security team's arsenal of tools. It provides complete flexibility in terms of what we can do with it and how it can fit into our setup. By combining ZAP with Jenkins, we can quickly set up a decent production-worthy continuous scanning workflow and align our process around it. Ansible allows us to install and configure all of these great tools using playbooks. This is great as it is mostly a one-time effort and then we can start seeing the results and the reports for ZAP.

Now that we are on our way to automating security tools, next we shall see the most popular vulnerability assessment tool, Nessus, and how we can build a similar workflow for vulnerability assessment for software and networks.

6
Vulnerability Scanning with Nessus

Scanning for vulnerabilities is one of the best understood periodic activities security teams take up on their computers. There are well-documented strategies and best practices for doing regular scanning for vulnerabilities in computers, networks, operating system software, and application software:

- Basic network scans
- Credentials patch audit
- Correlating system information with known vulnerabilities

With networked systems, this type of scanning is usually executed from a connected host that has the right kind of permissions to scan for security issues.

One of the most popular vulnerability scanning tools is Nessus. Nessus started as a network vulnerability scanning tool, but now incorporates features such as the following:

- Port scanning
- Network vulnerability scanning
- Web application-specific scanning
- Host-based vulnerability scanning

Introduction to Nessus

The vulnerability database that Nessus has is its main advantage. While the techniques to understanding which service is running and what version of the software is running the service are known to us, answering the question, "Does this service have a known vulnerability" is the important one. Apart from a regularly updated vulnerability database, Nessus also has information on default credentials found in applications, default paths, and locations. All of this fine-tuned in an easy way to use CLI or web-based tool.

Before diving into how we are going to set up Nessus to perform vulnerability scanning and network scanning against our infrastructure, let's see why we have to set it up and what it will give us in return.

In this chapter, we will focus on doing vulnerability scanning using Nessus. We will try out the standard activities required for that and see what steps are needed to automate them using Ansible:

1. Installing Nessus using a playbook.
2. Configuring Nessus.
3. Running a scan.
4. Running a scan using AutoNessus.
5. Installing the Nessus REST API Python client.
6. Downloading a report using the API.

Installing Nessus for vulnerability assessments

First, get the URL to download the Nessus from `https://www.tenable.com/products/nessus/select-your-operating-system`, then select the Ubuntu operating system, and then run the following playbook role against the server on which you want to set up Nessus:

```
- name: installing nessus server
  hosts: nessus
  remote_user: "{{ remote_user_name }}"
  gather_facts: no
  vars:
    remote_user_name: ubuntu
    nessus_download_url:
"http://downloads.nessus.org/nessus3dl.php?file=Nessus-6.11.2-ubuntu1110_amd64.deb&licence_accept=yes&t=84ed6ee87f926f3d17a218b2e52b61f0"
```

```
tasks:
  - name: install python 2
    raw: test -e /usr/bin/python || (apt -y update && apt install -y
python-minimal)

  - name: downloading the package and installing
    apt:
      deb: "{{ nessus_download_url }}"

  - name: start the nessus daemon
    service:
      name: "nessusd"
      enabled: yes
      state: started
```

Configuring Nessus for vulnerability scanning

Perform the following steps to configure Nessus for vulnerability scanning:

1. We have to navigate to `https://NESSUSSERVERIP:8834` to confirm and start the service:

2. As we can see it returns with an SSL error and we need to accept the SSL error and confirm the security exception and continue with the installation:

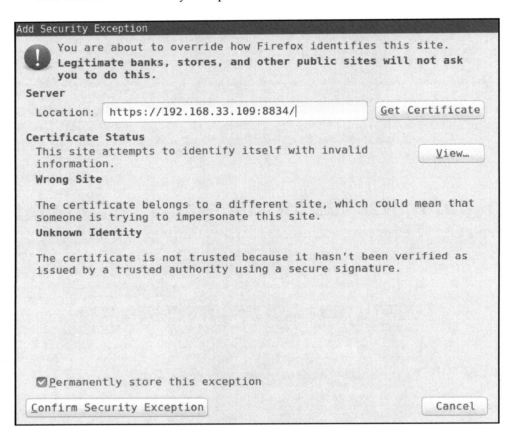

3. Click on **Confirm Security Exception** and continue to proceed with the installation steps:

Welcome to Nessus

Nessus

Thank you for installing Nessus, the industry leader in vulnerability scanning. This application allows you to:

- Run high-speed vulnerability and discovery scans on your network
- Conduct agentless auditing on hosts to confirm they are running up-to-date software
- Perform compliance checks on hosts to verify they are adhering to your security policy
- Schedule scans to launch automatically at the frequency you select
- And much more!

Press continue to perform account setup, register or link this scanner, and download the latest plugins.

Continue

© 2017 Tenable Network Security®

4. Click on **Continue** and provide the details of the user, this user has full administrator access:

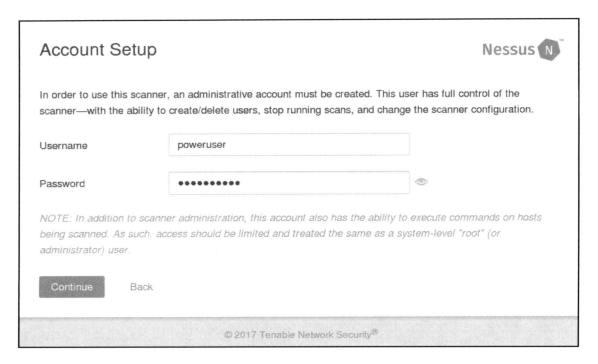

5. Then finally, we have to provide the registration code (**Activation Code**), which can be obtained from registering at `https://www.tenable.com/products/ nessus-home`:

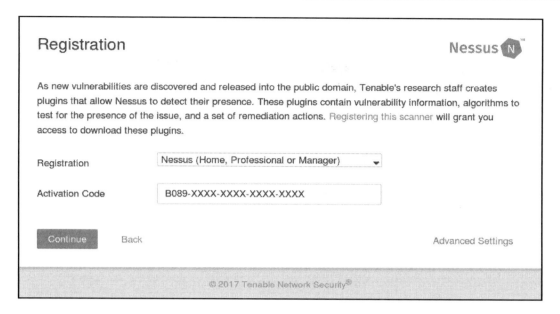

6. Now it will install the required plugins. It will take a while to install, and once it is done we can log in to use the application:

7. Now, we have successfully set up the Nessus vulnerability scanner:

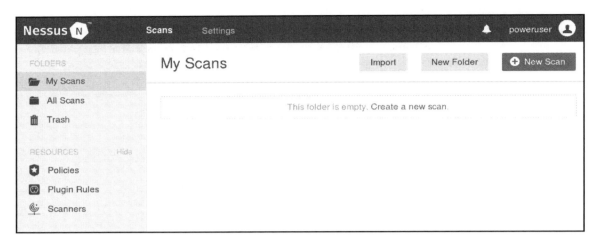

Executing scans against a network

Now, it's time to perform some vulnerability scanning using Nessus.

Basic network scanning

Nessus has a wide variety of scans, some of them are free and some of them will be available only in a paid version. So, we can also customize the scanning if required.

The following are the list of templates currently available:

1. We can start with a basic network scan to see what's happening in the network. This scan will perform a basic full system scan for the given hosts:

2. As you can see in the preceding screenshot, we have to mention the scan name and targets. Targets are just the hosts we want.

Targets can be given in different formats, such as 192.168.33.1 for a single host, 192.168.33.1-10 for a range of hosts, and also we can upload the target file from our computer.

Choosing the **New Scan / Basic Network Scan** for analysis using Nessus:

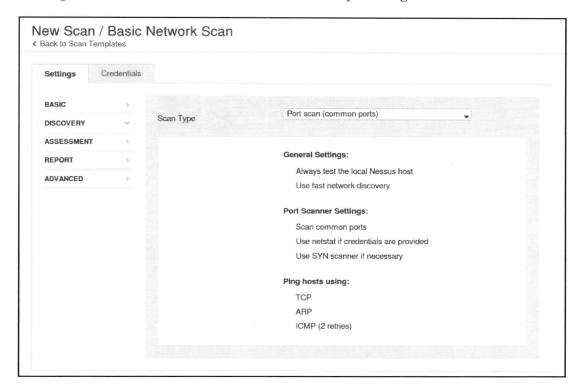

3. We can also customize the scan type. For example, we can perform a common ports scan which will scan known ports, we can also perform a full port scan if required:

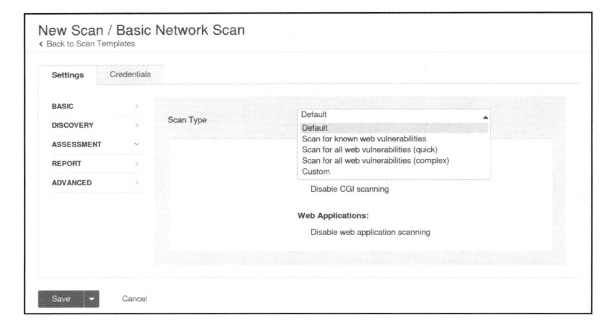

4. Then, similarly, we can specify to perform a different type of web application scan, as mentioned previously:

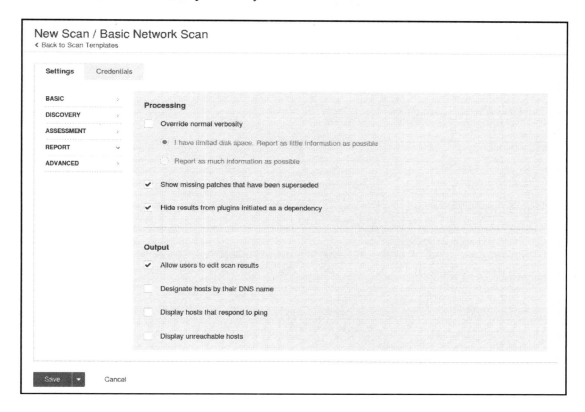

5. The reporting also can be customized as per the requirements using the available options:

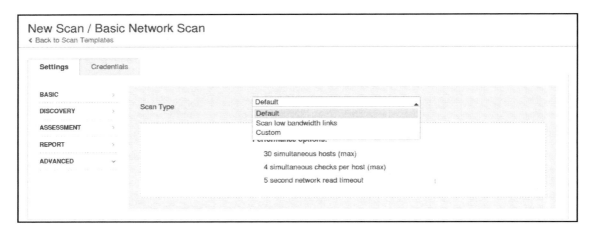

6. The preceding options are very important while scanning critical infrastructure. These options are to ensure we are not producing a lot of traffic and network bandwidth in the target network. Nessus allows us to customize as per the use case and requirements:

7. The preceding screenshot represents whether we already have existing credentials for any service and if it requires scanning, we can mention them here. Nessus will use these credentials to authenticate while scanning and this gives better results. Nessus supports multiple types of authentication services:

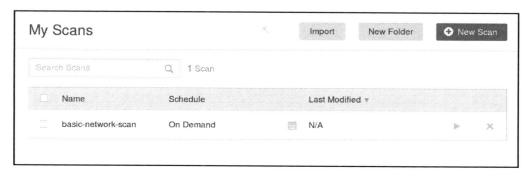

8. Scans can be scheduled if required, or are available on-demand. We can click the **Launch** button (play icon) to start a scan with given configuration parameters:

9. Scan results are available via a dashboard based on host, vulnerabilities, severity level, and so on:

10. The preceding screenshot shows how Nessus will produce detailed results of the existing vulnerabilities with sample **Proof of Concept (POC)** or command output as well. It also provides a detailed summary of the fix, vulnerability, and references.

Running a scan using AutoNessus

With the AutoNessus script, we can do the following:

- List scans
- List scan policies
- Do actions on scans such as start, stop, pause, and resume

The best part of AutoNessus is that since this is a command-line tool, it can easily become part of scheduled tasks and other automation workflows.

Download AutoNessus from https://github.com/redteamsecurity/
AutoNessus.

Setting up AutoNessus

The following code is the Ansible playbook snippet to set up AutoNessus and configure it to use Nessus using credentials. This playbook will allow the setup of the `autoNessus` tool in the path and we can use it as a simple system tool:

```
- name: installing python-pip
  apt:
    name: python-pip
    update_cache: yes
    state: present

- name: install python requests
  pip:
    name: requests

- name: setting up autonessus
  get_url:
    url:
"https://github.com/redteamsecurity/AutoNessus/raw/master/autoNessus.py"
    dest: /usr/bin/autoNessus
    mode: 0755

- name: updating the credentials
  replace:
    path: /usr/bin/autoNessus
    regexp: "{{ item.src }}"
    replace: "{{ item.dst }}"
    backup: yes
  no_log: True

  with_items:
    - { src: "token = ''", dst: "token = '{{ nessus_user_token }}'" }
    - { src: "url = 'https://localhost:8834'", dst: "url = '{{ nessus_url
}}'" }
    - { src: "username = 'xxxxx'", dst: "username = '{{ nessus_user_name
}}'" }
    - { src: "password = 'xxxxx'", dst: "password = '{{
nessus_user_password }}'" }
```

> no_log: True will censor the output in the log console of Ansible output. It will be very useful when we are using secrets and keys inside playbooks.

Running scans using AutoNessus

The following playbook code snippets can be used to perform scans on demand as well as ones that are scheduled. This can also be used in Ansible Tower, Jenkins, or Rundeck.

Before running the automated scans using AutoNessus, we have to create them in the Nessus portal with required customization, and we can use these automated playbooks to perform tasks on top of it.

Listing current available scans and IDs

The following snippet will return the currently available scans and returns the IDs with information:

```
- name: list current scans and IDs using autoNessus
  command: "autoNessus -l"
  register: list_scans_output

- debug:
    msg: "{{ list_scans_output.stdout_lines }}"
```

Ansible output returning list of available scans with IDs information

Starting a specified scan using scan ID

The following snippet will start the specified scan based on scan_id and returns the status information:

```
- name: starting nessus scan "{{ scan_id }}" using autoNessus
  command: "autoNessus -sS {{ scan_id }}"
  register: start_scan_output

- debug:
    msg: "{{ start_scan_output.stdout_lines }}"
```

```
TASK [startscan : starting nessus scan "17" using autoNessus] *************************************
changed: [192.168.33.109]

TASK [startscan : debug] *************************************
ok: [192.168.33.109] => {
    "msg": [
        "Script started: 11-06-17 @ 17:52:34",
        "Logging in...",
        "Logged in!",
        "",
        "",
        "Launching Scan 17",
        "",
        "Scan Name          Status  ",
        "------------------------------------------------",
        "webapp           :  running"
    ]
}
```

Ansible output returning scan status after starting

Similarly, we can perform pause, resume, stop, list policies, and so on. Using the AutoNessus program, these playbooks are available. This can be improved by advancing the Nessus API scripts.

Storing results

We can also get a detailed view of the vulnerability, solutions, and risk information related to vulnerability:

The entire report can be exported into multiple formats, such as HTML, CSV, and Nessus. This helps to give more a detailed structure of vulnerabilities found, solutions with risk rating, and other references:

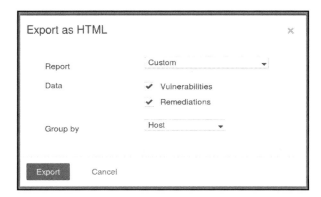

The output report can be customized based on the audience, if it goes to the technical team, we can list all the vulnerabilities and remediation. For example, if management wants to get the report, we can only get the executive summary of the issues.

> Reports can be sent by email as well using notification options in Nessus configuration.

The following screenshots are the detailed reports from the exported HTML format of the recent basic network scan. This can be used to analyze and fix the vulnerabilities based on hosts:

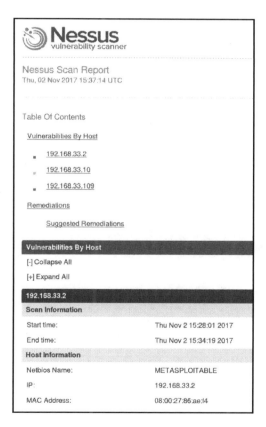

We can see vulnerabilities categorized by hosts previously. We can see each vulnerability in detail in the following screenshot:

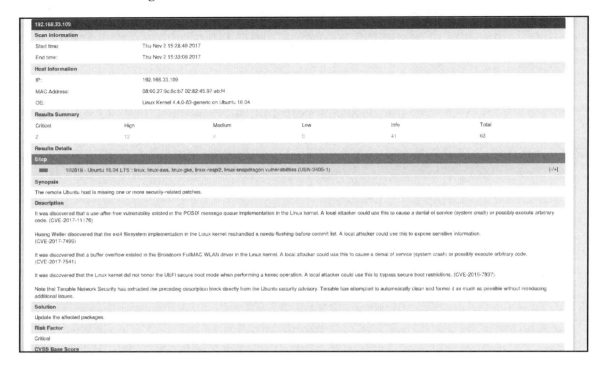

Installing the Nessus REST API Python client

Official API documentation can be obtained by connecting to your Nessus server under `8834/nessus6-api.html`.

To perform any operations using the Nessus REST API, we have to obtain the API keys from the portal. This can be found in user settings. Please make sure to save these keys:

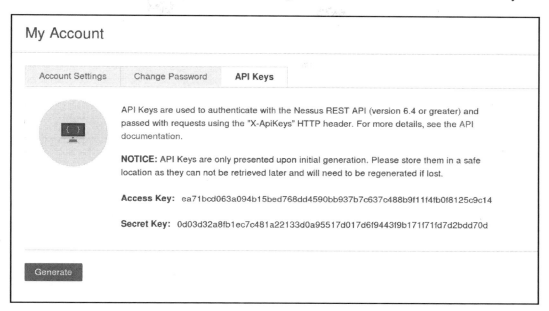

Downloading reports using the Nessus REST API

The following playbook will use the Nessus REST API to perform export requests for the report for the given `scan_id`. It will automate the whole process using a simple playbook. This will return the HTML output of the report:

```
- name: working with nessus rest api
  connection: local
  hosts: localhost
  gather_facts: no
  vars:
    scan_id: 17
    nessus_access_key: 620fe4ffaed47e9fe429ed749207967ecd7a77471105d8
    nessus_secret_key: 295414e22dc9a56abc7a89dab713487bd397cf860751a2
    nessus_url: https://192.168.33.109:8834
    nessus_report_format: html

  tasks:
    - name: export the report for given scan "{{ scan_id }}"
      uri:
```

```
      url: "{{ nessus_url }}/scans/{{ scan_id }}/export"
      method: POST
      validate_certs: no
      headers:
          X-ApiKeys: "accessKey={{ nessus_access_key }}; secretKey={{
nessus_secret_key }}"
      body: "format={{ nessus_report_format
}}&chapters=vuln_by_host;remediations"
      register: export_request

  - debug:
      msg: "File id is {{ export_request.json.file }} and scan id is {{
scan_id }}"

  - name: check the report status for "{{ export_request.json.file }}"
    uri:
      url: "{{ nessus_url }}/scans/{{ scan_id }}/export/{{
export_request.json.file }}/status"
      method: GET
      validate_certs: no
      headers:
          X-ApiKeys: "accessKey={{ nessus_access_key }}; secretKey={{
nessus_secret_key }}"
      register: report_status

  - debug:
      msg: "Report status is {{ report_status.json.status }}"

  - name: downloading the report locally
    uri:
      url: "{{ nessus_url }}/scans/{{ scan_id }}/export/{{
export_request.json.file }}/download"
      method: GET
      validate_certs: no
      headers:
```

```
        X-ApiKeys: "accessKey={{ nessus_access_key }}; secretKey={{
nessus_secret_key }}"
        return_content: yes
        dest: "./{{ scan_id }}_{{ export_request.json.file }}.{{
nessus_report_format }}"
      register: report_output

    - debug:
        msg: "Report can be found at ./{{ scan_id }}_{{
export_request.json.file }}.{{ nessus_report_format }}"
```

 Read more at about the Nessus REST API https://cloud.tenable.com/
api#/overview.

An Ansible playbook for automatic report generation using Nessus REST API:

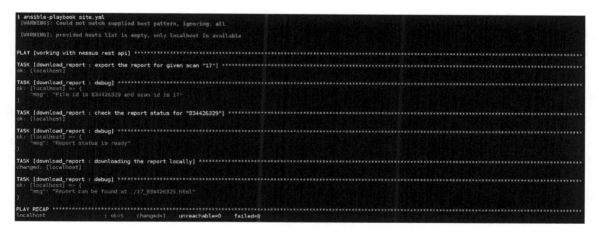

Ansible playbook for automatic report generation and export using Nessus REST API

Nessus configuration

Nessus allows us to create different users with role-based authentication to perform scans and review with different access levels:

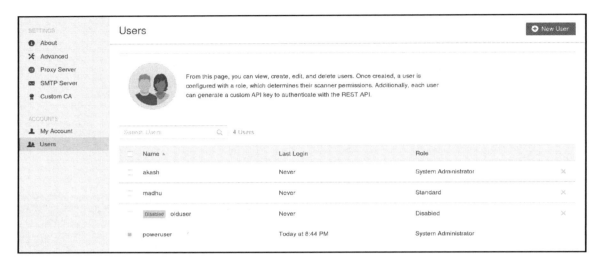

The following screenshot shows how to create a new user with a role to perform the Nessus activities:

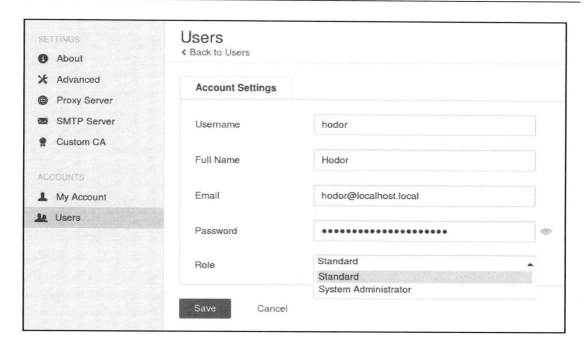

Summary

Security teams and IT teams rely on tools for vulnerability scanning, management, remediation, and continuous security processes. Nessus, by being one of the most popular and useful tools, was an automatic choice for the authors to try and automate.

In this chapter, we looked at the main activities of vulnerability scanning, such as being able to install and deploy the tool, initiate a scan, and download a report.

In the next chapter, we will delve deeper into system security and hardening. We will look at various open security initiatives and benchmarking projects such as STIG, OpenSCAP, and **Center for Internet Security (CIS)**. We will learn how to integrate them with our playbooks and automation tools, such as Tower and Jenkins. This chapter on vulnerability scanning, and the next one on the security hardening of networks and applications create a solid base to explore more ideas on security automation and keeping your systems secure and hardened.

7
Security Hardening for Applications and Networks

Security hardening is the most obvious task for any security-conscious endeavor. By doing the effort of securing systems, applications, and networks, one can achieve multiple security goals given as follows:

- Ensuring that applications and networks are not compromised (sometimes)
- Making it difficult for compromises to stay hidden for long
- Securing by default ensures that compromises in one part of the network don't propagate further and more

The Ansible way of thinking about automation around security is a great fit for automating security hardening. In this chapter, we will introduce security benchmarks and frameworks that can be used to build playbooks that will allow us to do the following things:

- Secure our master images so that as soon as the applications and systems are part of the network, they offer decent security
- Execute audit processes so that we can verify and measure periodically if the applications, systems, and networks are in line with the security policies that are required by the organization

This is by no stretch a new idea. Extensive work has taken place in this sphere. We will look at projects such as dev-sec.io (`http://dev-sec.io/`), which make it simple to start with security hardening of our applications and networks.

Topics to be covered in this chapter are as follows:

- Security hardening with benchmarks such as **Center for Internet Security (CIS)**, **Security Technical Implementation Guides (STIG)**, and **National Institute of Standards and Technology (NIST)**
- Automating security audit checks for networking devices using Ansible
- Automating security audit checks for applications using Ansible
- Automated patching approaches using Ansible

Security hardening with benchmarks such as CIS, STIGs, and NIST

Benchmarks provide a great way for anyone to gain assurance of their individual security efforts. Created by security experts globally or led by security mature government departments such as NIST, benchmarks cover a whole range of systems, configurations, software, and more.

Hardening for security mostly boils down to do the following:

1. Agreeing on what is the minimal set of configuration that qualifies as secure configuration. This is usually defined as a hardening benchmark or framework.
2. Making changes to all the aspects of the system that are touched by such configuration.
3. Measuring periodically if the application and system are still in line with the configuration or if there is any deviation.
4. If any deviation is found, take corrective action to fix that.
5. If no deviation is found, log that.
6. Since software is always getting upgraded, staying on top of the latest configuration guidelines and benchmarks is most important.

The three important benchmarks/frameworks for our discussion are:

- CIS Benchmarks
- STIG guides
- NIST's **National Checklist Program (NCP)**

These CIS Benchmarks are usually expressed as PDF documents available to anyone who would like to get an idea of how secure their system is compared with what CIS experts think about it.

 CIS is a not-for-profit organization with not-for-profit standards for internet security, and are a recognized global standard and best practices for securing IT systems and data against attacks. CIS Benchmarks are the only consensus-based, best-practice security configuration guides both developed and accepted by the government, business, industry, and academia. For more information, visit https://www.cisecurity.org/cis-benchmarks.

STIG is related to the configuration of information systems by US Government's department named **DISA**.

 The STIGs contain technical guidance to **lock down** information systems/software that might otherwise be vulnerable to a malicious computer attack. For more information, visit https://iase.disa.mil/stigs/Pages/index.aspx.

NIST maintains a checklist program that are expressed in files that follows the **Security Content Automation Protocol (SCAP)**. Software tools can read these files to automate the configuration changes and audit running configurations.

 SCAP enables validated security tools to automatically perform configuration checking using SCAP-expressed NCP checklists. For more information, visit https://www.nist.gov/programs-projects/national-checklist-program.

Operating system hardening for baseline using an Ansible playbook

Till now, we have created multiple playbooks to perform certain operations. Now, we will see how we can use existing playbooks from the community (**Ansible Galaxy**).

Hardening Framework is a project by Deutsche Telekom to manage thousands of servers for security, compliance, and maintenance. The goal of this project is to create a common layer for hardening operating systems and services easily.

 If your organization is using chef or puppet tools as configuration management tools, the concepts are completely the same. You can find related cookbooks and details at `http://dev-sec.io`.

The following playbook provides multiple security configurations, standards, and ways to protect operating system against different attacks and security vulnerabilities.

Some of the tasks it will perform include the following:

- Configures package management, for example, allows only signed packages
- Remove packages with known issues
- Configures `pam` and `pam_limits` modules
- Shadow password suite configuration
- Configures system path permissions
- Disable core dumps via soft limits
- Restrict root logins to system console
- Set SUIDs
- Configures kernel parameters via `sysctl`

Downloading and executing Ansible playbooks from galaxy is as simple as follows:

```
$ ansible-galaxy install dev-sec.os-hardening

- hosts: localhost
  become: yes
  roles:
    - dev-sec.os-hardening
```

The dev-sec.os-hardening playbook in execution

The preceding playbook will detect the operating system and perform hardening steps based on the different guidelines. This can be configured as required by updating the default variables values. Refer to https://github.com/dev-sec/ansible-os-hardening for more details about the playbook.

STIGs Ansible role for automated security hardening for Linux hosts

OpenStack has an awesome project named **ansible-hardening** (https://github.com/openstack/ansible-hardening), which applies the security configuration changes as per the STIGs standards. More details about the STIGs benchmarks for Unix/Linux operating systems can be found at https://iase.disa.mil/stigs/os/unix-linux/Pages/index.aspx.

It performs security hardening for the following domains:

- accounts: User account security controls
- aide: Advanced Intrusion Detection Environment
- auditd: Audit daemon
- auth: Authentication

- `file_perms`: Filesystem permissions
- `graphical`: Graphical login security controls
- `kernel`: Kernel parameters
- `lsm`: Linux Security Modules
- `misc`: Miscellaneous security controls
- `packages`: Package managers
- `sshd`: SSH daemon

The `ansible-hardening` playbook supports multiple Linux operating systems

- CentOS 7
- Debian jessie
- Fedora 26
- openSUSE Leap 42.2 and 42.3
- Red Hat Enterprise Linux 7
- SUSE Linux Enterprise 12 (experimental)
- Ubuntu 16.04

For more details about the project and documentation, see `https://docs.openstack.org/ansible-hardening/latest`.

Download the role from the GitHub repository itself using `ansible-galaxy` as follows:

```
$ ansible-galaxy install git+https://github.com/openstack/ansible-hardening
```

The playbook looks like the following. As similar to the previous playbook, this can be configured as required by changing the default variables values:

```
- name: STIGs ansible-hardening for automated security hardening
  hosts: servers
  become: yes
  remote_user: "{{ remote_user_name }}"
  vars:
    remote_user_name: vagrant
    security_ntp_servers:
      - time.nist.gov
      - time.google.com

  roles:
    - ansible-hardening
```

An Ansible-hardening playbook in execution CentOS-7 for STIGs checklist

The preceding playbook is executing on a CentOS-7 server against the STIG checklist.

Continuous security scans and reports for OpenSCAP using Ansible Tower

OpenSCAP is a set of security tools, policies, and standards to perform security compliance checks against the systems by following SCAP. SCAP is the U.S. standard maintained by NIST.

The SCAP scanner application reads a SCAP security policy and checks whether the system is compliant with it. It goes through all of the rules defined in the policy one by one and reports whether each rule is fulfilled. If all checks pass, the system is compliant with the security policy.

OpenSCAP follows these steps to perform scanning on your system:

- Install SCAP Workbench or OpenSCAP Base (for more information, visit https://www.open-scap.org)
- Choose a policy

- Adjust your settings
- Evaluate the system

The following playbook will install `openscap-scanner` and `scap-security-guide` software to perform checks. Then, it will perform the scan as per the given profile and policy using the `oscap` tool.

As you can see, the variable `oscap_profile` is to use the profile from the list of available profiles and `oscap_policy` is to choose the specific policy to scan the system:

```
- hosts: all
  become: yes
  vars:
    oscap_profile: xccdf_org.ssgproject.content_profile_pci-dss
    oscap_policy: ssg-rhel7-ds

  tasks:
  - name: install openscap scanner
    package:
      name: "{{ item }}"
      state: latest
    with_items:
    - openscap-scanner
    - scap-security-guide

  - block:
    - name: run openscap
      command: >
        oscap xccdf eval
        --profile {{ oscap_profile }}
        --results-arf /tmp/oscap-arf.xml
        --report /tmp/oscap-report.html
        --fetch-remote-resources
        /usr/share/xml/scap/ssg/content/{{ oscap_policy }}.xml

    always:
    - name: download report
      fetch:
        src: /tmp/oscap-report.html
        dest: ./{{ inventory_hostname }}.html
        flat: yes
```

Check playbook reference at `https://medium.com/@jackprice/ansible-openscap-for-compliance-automation-14200fe70663`.

Now, we can use this playbook to perform continuously automated checks using Ansible Tower:

1. First, we need to create a directory in Ansible Tower server in order to store this playbook with the `awx` user permission to add the custom playbook.
2. Create a new project in Ansible Tower to perform the **OpenSCAP** setup and scan against the checks:

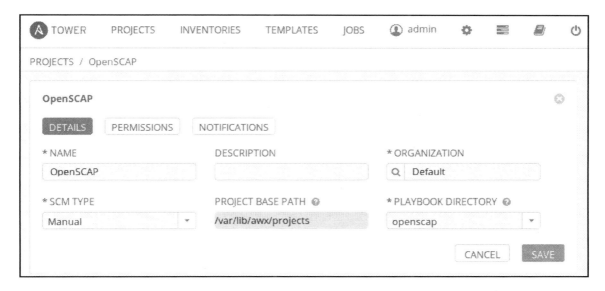

3. Then, we have to create a new job to execute the playbook. Here, we can include the list of hosts, credentials for login, and other details required to perform the execution:

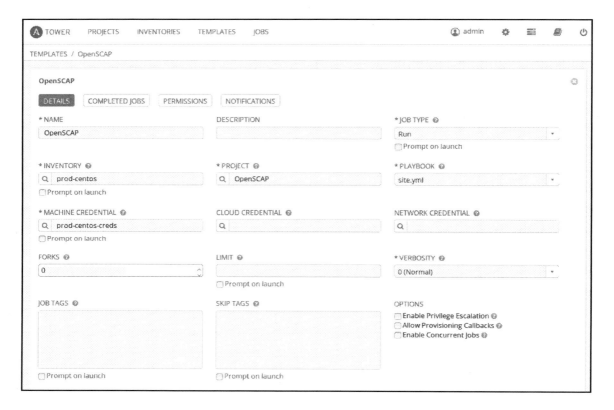

4. This audit can be scheduled to perform frequently. Here you can see that we scheduled every day, this can be modified as per compliance frequency (security compliance requires to perform these kinds of audits frequently):

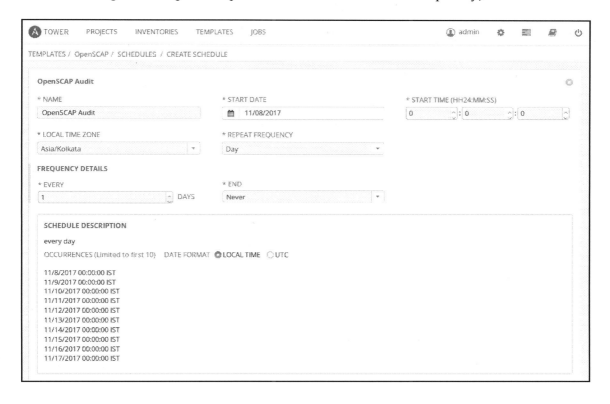

5. We can also launch this job on demand when required. The playbook execution looks as follows:

6. The output of the playbook will generate the OpenSCAP report, and it will be fetched to Ansible Tower. We can access this playbook at the /tmp/ location. Also, we can send this report to the other centralized reporting server if required.

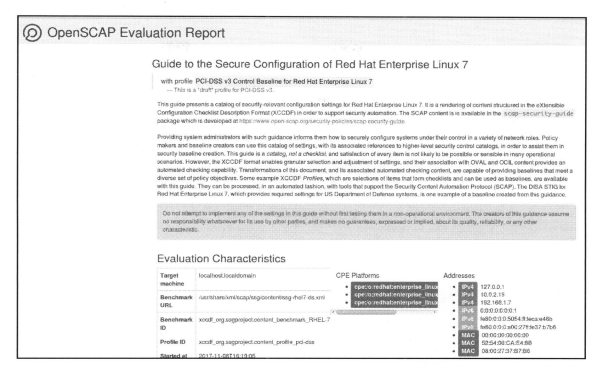

7. We can also set up notifications based on playbook execution results. By doing this, we can send this notifications to respective channels, such as email, slack, and message.

CIS Benchmarks

CIS has benchmarks for different type OS, software, and services. The following are some high-level categories:

- Desktops and web browsers
- Mobile devices
- Network devices
- Security metrics
- Servers – operating systems
- Servers – other
- Virtualization platforms, cloud, and other

Read more about CIS benchmarks at https://www.cisecurity.org.

Ubuntu CIS Benchmarks (server level)

CIS Benchmarks Ubuntu provides prescriptive guidance to establish a secure configuration posture for Ubuntu Linux systems running on x86 and x64 platforms. This benchmark is intended for system and application administrators, security specialists, auditors, help desk, and platform deployment personnel who plan to develop, deploy, assess, or secure solutions that incorporate Linux platform.

Here are the high-level six domains that are part of CIS Ubuntu 16.04 LTS benchmarks:

- Initial setup:
    - Filesystem configuration
    - Configure software updates
    - Filesystem integrity checking
    - Secure boot settings
    - Additional process hardening
    - Mandatory access control
    - Warning banners

- Services:
  - Inted Services
  - Special purpose services
  - Service clients
- Network configuration:
  - Network parameters (host only)
  - Network parameters (host and router)
  - IPv6
  - TCP wrappers
  - Uncommon network protocols
- Logging and auditing:
  - Configure system accounting (`auditd`)
  - Configure logging
- Access, authentication, and authorization:
  - Configure cron
  - SSH server configuration
  - Configure PAM
  - User accounts and environment
- System maintenance:
  - System file permissions
  - User and group settings

Here are the Ansible Playbooks for 14.04 LTS and 16.04 LTS, respectively:

- https://github.com/oguya/cis-ubuntu-14-ansible
- https://github.com/grupoversia/cis-ubuntu-ansible

```
$ git clone https://github.com/oguya/cis-ubuntu-14-ansible.git
$ cd cis-ubuntu-14-ansible
```

Then, update the variables and inventory and execute the playbook using the following command. The variables are not required mostly, as this performs against different CIS checks unless, if we wanted to customize the benchmarks as per the organization:

```
$ ansible-playbook -i inventory cis.yml
```

CIS Ubuntu Benchmarks Ansible playbook execution

The preceding playbook will execute the CIS security benchmark against an Ubuntu server and performs all the checks listed in the CIS guidelines.

AWS benchmarks (cloud provider level)

AWS CIS Benchmarks provides prescriptive guidance to configure security options for a subset of AWS with an emphasis on foundational, testable, and architecture agnostic settings. It is intended for system and application administrators, security specialists, auditors, help desk, platform deployment, and/or DevOps personnel who plan to develop, deploy, assess, or secure solutions in AWS.

Here are the high-level domains, which are part of AWS CIS Benchmarks:

- Identity and access management
- Logging
- Monitoring
- Networking
- Extra

Currently, there is a tool named **prowler** (`https://github.com/Alfresco/prowler`) based on AWS-CLI commands for AWS account security assessment and hardening.

This tools follows the guidelines of the CIS Amazon Web Services Foundations Benchmark 1.1

Before running the playbook, we have to provide AWS API keys to perform security audit. This can be created using IAM role in AWS service. If you have an already existing account with required privileges, these steps can be skipped:

1. Create a new user in your AWS account with programmatic access:

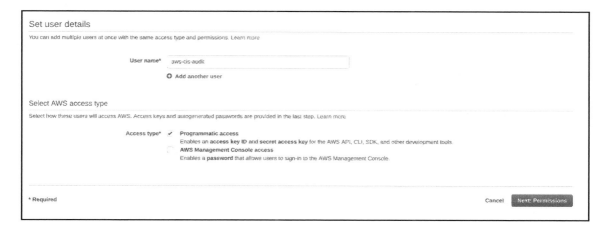

2. Apply the **SecurityAudit** policy for the user from existing policies in IAM console:

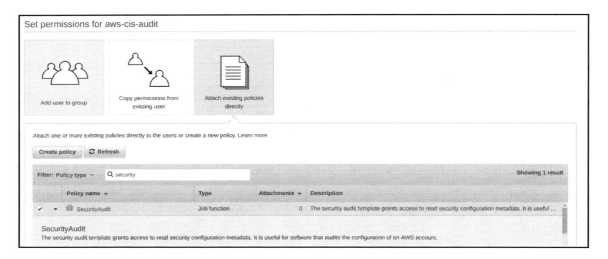

3. Then, create the new user by following the steps. Make sure that you safely save the **Access key ID** and **Secret access key** for later use:

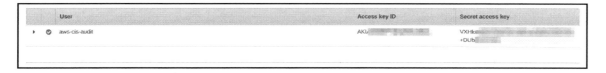

4. Here is the simple playbook to set up and execute checks using the prowler tool. Provide the access and secret keys from the previous steps.

5. The following playbook assume that you already have installed `python` and `pip` in your local system:

```
- name: AWS CIS Benchmarks playbook
  hosts: localhost
  become: yes
  vars:
    aws_access_key: XXXXXXXX
    aws_secret_key: XXXXXXXX

  tasks:
    - name: installing aws cli and ansi2html
      pip:
        name: "{{ item }}"

      with_items:
        - awscli
        - ansi2html

    - name: downloading and setting up prowler
      get_url:
        url:
https://raw.githubusercontent.com/Alfresco/prowler/master
/prowler
        dest: /usr/bin/prowler
        mode: 0755

    - name: running prowler full scan
      shell: "prowler | ansi2html -la > ./aws-cis-report-{{
ansible_date_time.epoch }}.html"
      environment:
        AWS_ACCESS_KEY_ID: "{{ aws_access_key }}"
        AWS_SECRET_ACCESS_KEY: "{{ aws_secret_key }}"

    - name: AWS CIS Benchmarks report downloaded
      debug:
        msg: "Report can be found at ./aws-cis-report-{{
ansible_date_time.epoch }}.html"
```

6. The playbook will trigger the setup and security audit scan for AWS CIS Benchmarks using the prowler tool:

```
$ ansible-playbook main.yml
 [WARNING]: Could not match supplied host pattern, ignoring: all

 [WARNING]: provided hosts list is empty, only localhost is available


PLAY [AWS CIS Benchmarks playbook] ***********************************************

TASK [Gathering Facts] ***********************************************
ok: [localhost]

TASK [installing python2] ***********************************************
changed: [localhost]

TASK [installing pip] ***********************************************
ok: [localhost]

TASK [installing aws cli and ansi2html] ***********************************************
ok: [localhost] => (item=awscli)
ok: [localhost] => (item=ansi2html)

TASK [downloading and setting up prowler] ***********************************************
ok: [localhost]

TASK [running prowler full scan] ***********************************************
changed: [localhost]

TASK [AWS CIS Benchmarks report downloaded] ***********************************************
ok: [localhost] => {
    "msg": "Report can be found at ./aws-cis-report-1510253857.html"
}

PLAY RECAP ***********************************************
localhost                  : ok=7    changed=2    unreachable=0    failed=0
```

7. Prowler-generated HTML report looks as follows, and the report can be downloaded in different formats as required and also scanning checks can be configured as required:

```
 prowler
 | CIS based AWS Account Hardening Tool

 Date: Thu Nov  9 18:57:46 UTC 2017

 Colors Code for results:  INFORMATIVE, OK (RECOMMENDED VALUE),  WARNING (FIX REQUIRED)

 This report is being generated using credentials below:

 AWS-CLI Profile: [ENV] AWS API Region: [us-east-1] AWS Filter Region: [all]

 Caller Identity:
 -----------------------------------------------------------------
 |                      GetCallerIdentity                        |
 +---------+-----------------------------------------------------+
 | Account |                                                     |
 | Arn     | arn:aws:iam::              :user/aws-cis-audit       |
 | UserId  |                                                     |
 +---------+-----------------------------------------------------+


 0.1  Generating AWS IAM Credential Report...

 1 Identity and Access Management *****************************************

 1.1  Avoid the use of the root account (Scored).
      INFO! Root account last accessed (password key_1 key_2): 2017-11-09T18:28:52+00:00 N/A N/A

 1.2  Ensure multi-factor authentication (MFA) is enabled for all IAM users that have a console password (Scored)
      OK!  No users found with Password enabled and MFA disabled

 1.3  Ensure credentials unused for 90 days or greater are disabled (Scored)
      OK!  No users found with password enabled

 1.4  Ensure access keys are rotated every 90 days or less (Scored)
      WARNING!  stack has not rotated access key1 in over 90 days
      OK!  No users with access key 2.

 1.5  Ensure IAM password policy requires at least one uppercase letter (Scored)
      WARNING! Password Policy missing upper-case requirement

 1.6  Ensure IAM password policy require at least one lowercase letter (Scored)
      WARNING! Password Policy missing lower-case requirement
```

More reference about the tool can be found at `https://github.com/Alfresco/prowler`.

Lynis – open source security auditing tool for Unix/Linux systems

Lynis is an open source security auditing tool. Used by system administrators, security professionals, and auditors, to evaluate the security defenses of their Linux and Unix-based systems. It runs on the host itself, so it performs more extensive security scans than vulnerability scanners.

Supported Operating Systems: Lynis runs on almost all Unix-based systems and versions, including the following:

- AIX
- FreeBSD
- HP-UX
- Linux
- macOS
- NetBSD
- OpenBSD
- Solaris and others

As stated in `https://cisofy.com/lynis`:

> *"It even runs on systems like the Raspberry Pi, or QNAP storage devices."*

The playbook looks as follows:

```
- name: Lynis security audit playbook
  hosts: lynis
  remote_user: ubuntu
  become: yes
  vars:
    # refer to https://packages.cisofy.com/community
    code_name: xenial
  tasks:
    - name: adding lynis repo key
      apt_key:
        keyserver: keyserver.ubuntu.com
        id: C80E383C3DE9F082E01391A0366C67DE91CA5D5F
        state: present
```

```yaml
    - name: installing apt-transport-https
      apt:
        name: apt-transport-https
        state: present

    - name: adding repo
      apt_repository:
        repo: "deb https://packages.cisofy.com/community/lynis/deb/ {{
code_name }} main"
        state: present
        filename: "cisofy-lynis"
    - name: installing lynis
      apt:
        name: lynis
        update_cache: yes
        state: present
    - name: audit scan the system
      shell: lynis audit system > /tmp/lynis-output.log
    - name: downloading report locally
      fetch:
        src: /tmp/lynis-output.log
        dest: ./{{ inventory_hostname }}-lynis-report-{{
ansible_date_time.date }}.log
        flat: yes

    - name: report location
      debug:
        msg: "Report can be found at ./{{ inventory_hostname }}-lynis-
report-{{ ansible_date_time.date }}.log"
```

The preceding playbook will set up the Lynis, run the system audit scan against it, and finally fetches the report locally:

```
$ ansible-playbook -i inventory main.yml --ask-pass
SSH password:

PLAY [Lynis security audit playbook] ********************************************

TASK [Gathering Facts] *********************************************************
ok: [192.168.1.5]

TASK [adding lynis repo key] ***************************************************
ok: [192.168.1.5]

TASK [installing apt-transport-https] ******************************************
ok: [192.168.1.5]

TASK [adding repo] *************************************************************
ok: [192.168.1.5]

TASK [installing lynis] ********************************************************
ok: [192.168.1.5]

TASK [audit scan the system] **************************************************
changed: [192.168.1.5]

TASK [downloading report locally] *********************************************
changed: [192.168.1.5]

TASK [report location] ********************************************************
ok: [192.168.1.5] => {
    "msg": "Report can be found at ./192.168.1.5-lynis-report-2017-11-13.log"
}

PLAY RECAP ********************************************************************
192.168.1.5                : ok=8    changed=2    unreachable=0    failed=0
```

Lynis system audit scan playbook in execution

The following screenshot is the report from the recent audit scan:

```
$ cat ./192.168.1.5-lynis-report-2017-11-13.log

[ Lynis 2.5.7 ]

################################################################################
  Lynis comes with ABSOLUTELY NO WARRANTY. This is free software, and you are
  welcome to redistribute it under the terms of the GNU General Public License.
  See the LICENSE file for details about using this software.

  2007-2017, CISOfy - https://cisofy.com/lynis/
  Enterprise support available (compliance, plugins, interface and tools)
################################################################################


[+] Initializing program
------------------------------------
  - Detecting OS...                                        [ DONE ]
  - Checking profiles...                                   [ DONE ]


  ---------------------------------------------------
  Program version:          2.5.7
  Operating system:         Linux
  Operating system name:    Ubuntu Linux
  Operating system version: 16.04
  Kernel version:           4.4.0
  Hardware platform:        x86_64
  Hostname:                 ubuntu-xenial
  ---------------------------------------------------
  Profiles:                 /etc/lynis/default.prf
  Log file:                 /var/log/lynis.log
  Report file:              /var/log/lynis-report.dat
  Report version:           1.0
  Plugin directory:         /usr/share/lynis/plugins
  ---------------------------------------------------
  Auditor:                  [Not Specified]
  Language:                 en
  Test category:            all
  Test group:               all
  ---------------------------------------------------
  - Program update status...                               [ NO UPDATE ]

[+] System Tools
------------------------------------
  - Scanning available tools...
  - Checking system binaries...
```

Lynis system audit scan report

This can be run via Ansible Tower and other automation tools to perform periodical checks against systems using Lynis for audit scans.

Lynis commands and advanced options

The Lynis has multiple options and commands that can be used to perform different options. For example, we can use `audit dockerfile <filename>` to perform analysis of Dockerfiles and the `--pentest` option to perform scan-related for pentesting.

```
[+] Initializing program
------------------------------------

Usage: lynis command [options]

Command:

   audit
       audit system                    : Perform local security scan
       audit system remote <host>      : Remote security scan
       audit dockerfile <file>         : Analyze Dockerfile

   show
       show                            : Show all commands
       show version                    : Show Lynis version
       show help                       : Show help

   update
       update info                     : Show update details

Options:

   --no-log                            : Don't create a log file
   --pentest                           : Non-privileged scan (useful for pentest)
   --profile <profile>                 : Scan the system with the given profile file
   --quick (-Q)                        : Quick mode, don't wait for user input

   Layout options
   --no-colors                         : Don't use colors in output
   --quiet (-q)                        : No output
   --reverse-colors                    : Optimize color display for light backgrounds

   Misc options
   --debug                             : Debug logging to screen
   --view-manpage (--man)              : View man page
   --verbose                           : Show more details on screen
   --version (-V)                      : Display version number and quit

   Enterprise options
   --plugin-dir "<path>"               : Define path of available plugins
   --upload                            : Upload data to central node

More options available. Run '/usr/sbin/lynis show options', or use the man page.
>
```

Windows server audit using Ansible playbooks

Most of the enterprises use Windows to centrally manage their policies and updates through the organization using Active Directory type of features. Also, it is a very critical asset to protect and check for security issues in the organizations. We know that Ansible supports Windows operating system using WinRM to perform configuration changes. Let's see some examples to add security to your Windows servers using Ansible playbooks.

Windows security updates playbook

The following playbook is a simple reference from the Ansible documentation at `https://docs.ansible.com/ansible/devel/windows_usage.html#installing-updates`:

```
- name: Windows Security Updates
  hosts: winblows

  tasks:
    - name: install all critical and security updates
      win_updates:
        category_names:
        - CriticalUpdates
        - SecurityUpdates
        state: installed
      register: update_result

    - name: reboot host if required
      win_reboot:
      when: update_result.reboot_required
```

Windows updates playbook in action

The preceding playbook will perform an automated Windows security updates of critical severity and restart the computer if required to apply the updated changes.

Windows workstation and server audit

The following Ansible playbook is created based on `https://github.com/alanrenouf/` `Windows-Workstation-and-Server-Audit`, and it will perform an audit of the system and generates a detailed HTML report. This is an example of how we can perform an audit using the PowerShell script. This can be extended by adding more checks and also adding other security audits scripts.

The playbook looks as follows:

```
- name: Windows Audit Playbook
  hosts: winblows

  tasks:
    - name: download audit script
      win_get_url:
        url:
https://raw.githubusercontent.com/alanrenouf/Windows-Workstation-and-Server
-Audit/master/Audit.ps1
        dest: C:\Audit.ps1

    - name: running windows audit script
      win_shell: C:\Audit.ps1
      args:
        chdir: C:\
```

Windows Audit Playbook in Action

Once the playbook execution completed, we can see the output report in HTML format with detailed information about running services, security patches, events, logging and other configuration details.

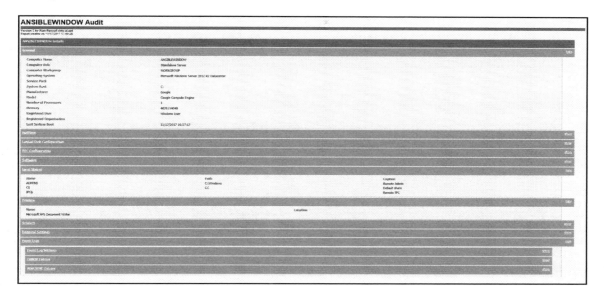

Automating security audit checks for networking devices using Ansible

We have seen that Ansible lends itself really well to work with a variety of tools, and we can use this to do security audit checks for networking devices.

Nmap scanning and NSE

Network Mapper (Nmap) is a free open source software to perform network discovery, scanning, audit, and many others. It has a various amount of features such as OS detection, system fingerprinting, firewall detection, and many other features. **Nmap Scripting Engine (Nmap NSE)** provides advanced capabilities like scanning for particular vulnerabilities and attacks. We can also write and extend Nmap using our own custom script. Nmap is a swiss army knife for pen testers (security testers) and network security teams.

Read more about Nmap at `https://nmap.org`. Ansible also has a module to perform the inventory using Nmap `https://github.com/ansible/ansible/pull/32857/files`.

The following playbook will install Nmap if not available and perform the basic network port scan using the specified flags:

```
- name: Basic NMAP Scan Playbook
  hosts: localhost
  gather_facts: false
  vars:
    top_ports: 1000
    network_hosts:
      - 192.168.1.1
      - scanme.nmap.org
      - 127.0.0.1
      - 192.168.11.0/24

  tasks:
    - name: check if nmap installed and install
      apt:
        name: nmap
        update_cache: yes
        state: present
      become: yes

    - name: top ports scan
      shell: "nmap --top-ports {{ top_ports }} -Pn -oA nmap-scan-%Y-%m-%d
{{ network_hosts|join(' ') }}"
```

- `{{ network_hosts|join(' ') }}` is a Jinja2 feature named **filter arguments** to parse the given `network_hosts` by space delimited
- `network_hosts` variable holds the list of IPs, network range (CIDR), hosts, and so on to perform scan using Nmap
- `top_ports` is the number that is ranging from 0 to 65535. Nmap by default picks commonly opened top ports
- `-Pn` specifies that scans the host if ping (ICMP) doesn't work also
- `-oA` gets the output in all formats, which includes gnmap (greppable format), Nmap, and XML

- More details about the options and documentation for nmap can be found at `https://nmap.org/book/man.html`

```
$ ansible-playbook main.yml --ask-sudo-pass
[DEPRECATION WARNING]: The sudo command line option has been deprecated in favor
Deprecation warnings can be disabled by setting deprecation_warnings=False in ans
SUDO password:
 [WARNING]: Could not match supplied host pattern, ignoring: all

 [WARNING]: provided hosts list is empty, only localhost is available


PLAY [Basic NMAP Scan Playbook] ************************************************

TASK [check if nmap installed and install] ************************************
ok: [localhost]

TASK [top ports scan] *********************************************************
changed: [localhost]

PLAY RECAP ********************************************************************
localhost                  : ok=2    changed=1    unreachable=0    failed=0
```

Nmap basic port scan playbook execution

The output of playbook for running a basic Nmap scan is:

```
$ ls -l
total 52
-rw-rw-r-- 1 madhuakula madhuakula  556 Nov 14 21:10 main.yml
-rw-rw-r-- 1 madhuakula madhuakula  472 Nov 14 21:10 nmap-scan-2017-11-14.gnmap
-rw-rw-r-- 1 madhuakula madhuakula  591 Nov 14 21:10 nmap-scan-2017-11-14.nmap
-rw-rw-r-- 1 madhuakula madhuakula 5992 Nov 14 21:10 nmap-scan-2017-11-14.xml
```

Figure: Playbook scan output in 3 different formats

The playbook after executing has created three reports of the format Nmap supports:

```
$ cat nmap-scan-2017-11-14.nmap
# Nmap 7.01 scan initiated Tue Nov 14 21:19:32 2017 as: nmap --top-ports 1000 -Pn -oA nmap-scan-%Y-%m-%d 192.168.1.1 scanme.nmap.org 127.0.0.1
Nmap scan report for 192.168.1.1
Host is up (0.013s latency).
Not shown: 994 closed ports
PORT     STATE SERVICE
21/tcp   open  ftp
22/tcp   open  ssh
23/tcp   open  telnet
53/tcp   open  domain
80/tcp   open  http

Nmap scan report for scanme.nmap.org (45.33.32.156)
Host is up (0.23s latency).
Other addresses for scanme.nmap.org (not scanned): 2600:3c01::f03c:91ff:fe18:bb2f
Not shown: 986 closed ports
PORT      STATE    SERVICE
22/tcp    open     ssh
80/tcp    open     http
135/tcp   filtered msrpc
139/tcp   filtered netbios-ssn
445/tcp   filtered microsoft-ds
554/tcp   filtered rtsp
1022/tcp  filtered exp2
1023/tcp  filtered netvenuechat
1026/tcp  filtered LSA-or-nterm
1720/tcp  filtered h323q931
1863/tcp  filtered msnp
5190/tcp  filtered aol
9898/tcp  filtered monkeycom
31337/tcp open     Elite

Nmap scan report for localhost (127.0.0.1)
Host is up (0.00011s latency).
Not shown: 998 closed ports
PORT     STATE SERVICE
53/tcp   open  domain

# Nmap done at Tue Nov 14 21:20:05 2017 -- 3 IP addresses (3 hosts up) scanned in 32.50 seconds
```

Figure: Playbook scan output in nmap format

By seeing the output of the `.nmap` file, we can easily see exactly what was found by the Nmap scan.

Nmap NSE scanning playbook

The following playbook will perform enumeration of directories used by popular web applications and servers using `http-enum` and finds options that are supported by an HTTP server using `http-methods` using Nmap scripts.

 More about Nmap NSE can be found at `https://nmap.org/book/nse.html`.

The following playbook will perform `http-enum` and `http-methods` scans against `scanme.nmap.org` of ports `80` and `443`:

```
- name: Advanced NMAP Scan using NSE
  hosts: localhost
  vars:
    ports:
      - 80
      - 443
    scan_host: scanme.nmap.org

  tasks:
    - name: Running Nmap NSE scan
      shell: "nmap -Pn -p {{ ports|join(',') }} --script {{ item }} -oA
nmap-{{ item }}-results-%Y-%m-%d {{ scan_host }}"

      with_items:
        - http-methods
        - http-enum
```

The following playbook will execute the Nmap NSE script using Ansible playbook for the HTTP enumeration and methods check:

Nmap NSE Playbook execution

The output of the playbook when we run a simple NSE script is as follows:

```
$ cat nmap-http-*.nmap
# Nmap 7.01 scan initiated Tue Nov 14 22:49:33 2017 as: nmap -Pn -p 80,443 --script http-enum -oA nmap-http-enum-results-%Y-%m-%d scanme.nmap.org
Nmap scan report for scanme.nmap.org (45.33.32.156)
Host is up (0.23s latency).
Other addresses for scanme.nmap.org (not scanned): 2600:3c01::f03c:91ff:fe18:bb2f
PORT    STATE SERVICE
80/tcp  open  http
| http-enum:
|   /images/: Potentially interesting directory w/ listing on 'apache/2.4.7 (ubuntu)'
|_  /shared/: Potentially interesting directory w/ listing on 'apache/2.4.7 (ubuntu)'
443/tcp closed https

# Nmap done at Tue Nov 14 22:50:01 2017 -- 1 IP address (1 host up) scanned in 28.03 seconds
# Nmap 7.01 scan initiated Tue Nov 14 22:49:30 2017 as: nmap -Pn -p 80,443 --script http-methods -oA nmap-http-methods-results-%Y-%m-%d scanme.nmap.org
Nmap scan report for scanme.nmap.org (45.33.32.156)
Host is up (0.24s latency).
Other addresses for scanme.nmap.org (not scanned): 2600:3c01::f03c:91ff:fe18:bb2f
PORT    STATE SERVICE
80/tcp  open  http
| http-methods:
|_  Supported Methods: GET HEAD POST OPTIONS
443/tcp closed https

# Nmap done at Tue Nov 14 22:49:33 2017 -- 1 IP address (1 host up) scanned in 2.28 seconds
```

Nmap NSE scans output in .nmap format

The `http-enum` script runs additional tests against network ports where web servers are detected. In the preceding screenshot, we can see that two folders were discovered by the script and additionally all HTTP methods that are supported got enumerated as well.

AWS security audit using Scout2

Scout2 is an open source AWS security auditing tool and it is used to assess AWS environments security posture using AWS Python API. The scan output will be stored in JSON format, and the final results of the Scout2 will be produced as a simple HTML website with detailed information of AWS cloud security posture. It performs the scans and audits based on its existing rule set and test cases, and this can be extended based on our custom scripts and scenarios.

 More details about the tool can be found at `https://github.com/nccgroup/Scout2`. This tool requires AWS IAM credentials to perform the scan; refer to `https://github.com/nccgroup/AWS-recipes/blob/master/IAM-Policies/Scout2-Default.json` for user policy creation.

Installing AWS Scout2 is very simple using the following playbook:

```
- name: AWS Security Audit using Scout2
  hosts: localhost
  become: yes
  tasks:
    - name: installing python and pip
      apt:
        name: "{{ item }}"
        state: present
        update_cache: yes
      with_items:
        - python
        - python-pip
    - name: install aws scout2
      pip:
        name: awsscout2
```

There are multiple rules configured to perform the audit, and the following snippet is the example of IAM password policy rule:

```
#
https://raw.githubusercontent.com/nccgroup/Scout2/master/tests/data/rule-co
nfigs/iam-password-policy.json
{
    "aws_account_id": "123456789012",
    "services": {
        "iam": {
            "password_policy": {
                "ExpirePasswords": false,
                "MinimumPasswordLength": "1",
                "PasswordReusePrevention": false,
                "RequireLowercaseCharacters": false,
                "RequireNumbers": false,
                "RequireSymbols": false,
                "RequireUppercaseCharacters": false
            }
        }
    }
}
```

The following playbook will perform the AWS Scout2 scan and returns the report in HTML format:

```
- name: AWS Security Audit using Scout2
  hosts: localhost
  vars:
    aws_access_key: XXXXXXXX
    aws_secret_key: XXXXXXXX
  tasks:
    - name: running scout2 scan
      # If you are performing from less memory system add --thread-config 1
to below command
      command: "Scout2"
      environment:
        AWS_ACCESS_KEY_ID: "{{ aws_access_key }}"
        AWS_SECRET_ACCESS_KEY: "{{ aws_secret_key }}"
    - name: AWS Scout2 report downloaded
      debug:
        msg: "Report can be found at ./report.html"
```

Account ID:

Dashboard

Summary:

Service	# of Resources	# of Rules	# of Findings	# of Checks
Cloudformation	1	1	0	1
CloudTrail	0	5	15	16
CloudWatch	1	1	0	1
Directconnect	0	0	0	0
EC2	38	22	93	1258
EFS	0	0	0	0
Elasticache	0	0	0	0
Elb	0	1	0	0

AWS Scout2 report high-level overview

The preceding screenshot is of a high-level report, and the detailed report is as follows:

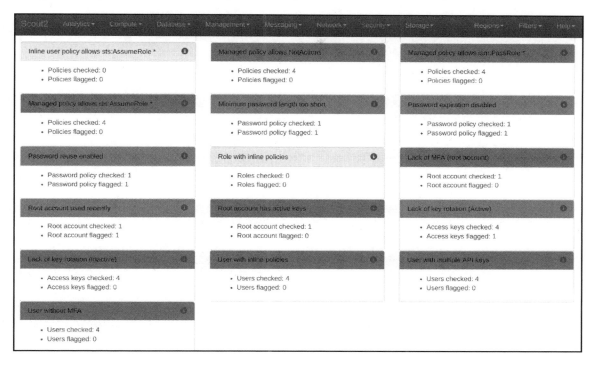

AWS Scout2 report detailed results for IAM section

Automation security audit checks for applications using Ansible

Modern applications can get pretty complex fairly quickly. Having the ability to run automation to do security tasks is almost a mandatory requirement.

The different types of application security scanning we can do can range from the following:

1. Run CI/CD scanning against the source code (for example, RIPS and brakeman).
2. Dependency checking scanners (for example, OWASP dependency checker and snyk.io (https://snyk.io/)).

3. Once deployed then run the web application scanner (for example, Nikto, Arachni, and w3af).
4. Framework-specific security scanners (for example, WPScan and Droopscan) and many other.

Source code analysis scanners

This is one of the first and common way to minimize the security risk while applications going to production. Source code analysis scanner also known as **Static Application Security Testing (SAST)** will help to find security issues by analyzing the source code of the application. This kind of tools and testing methodology allows developers to scan their code for security vulnerabilities repeatedly and automatically in the process of **continuous integration/continuous delivery (CI/CD)**.

There are multiple stages we can introduce these tools to effectively identify security vulnerabilities like integrated with IDE (code editors such as Eclipse, Visual Studio Code, and so on) and integrating in CI/CD process tools (Jenkins, Travis CI, and so on).

Source code analysis is kind of white box testing and looking through code. This kind of testing methodology may not find 100% coverage of security vulnerabilities, and it requires manual testing as well. For example, finding logical vulnerabilities requires some kind of user interactions such as dynamic functionalities.

There are many open source and commercial tools available in the market to perform static code analysis. Also, some of the tools are specific to the technology and frameworks you are using. For example, if you are scanning PHP code, then RIPS (http://rips-scanner. sourceforge.net/); if it's Ruby on Rails code, then it's Brakeman (https:// brakemanscanner.org/); and if it's python, then Bandit (https://wiki.openstack.org/ wiki/Security/Projects/Bandit); and so on.

 For more reference, visit https://www.owasp.org/index.php/Source_ Code_Analysis_Tools.

Brakeman scanner – Rails security scanner

Brakeman is an open source tool to do a static security analysis of Ruby on Rails applications. This can be applied at any stage of development and deployment process that includes staging, QA, production, and so on.

A simple playbook to execute Brakeman against our application looks like the following:

```
- name: Brakeman Scanning Playbook
  hosts: scanner
  remote_user: ubuntu
  become: yes
  gather_facts: false
  vars:
    repo_url: https://github.com/OWASP/railsgoat.git
    output_dir: /tmp/railsgoat/
    report_name: report.html

  tasks:
    - name: installing ruby and git
      apt:
        name: "{{ item }}"
        update_cache: yes
        state: present

      with_items:
        - ruby-full
        - git

    - name: installing brakeman gem
      gem:
        name: brakeman
        state: present
    - name: cloning the {{ repo_url }}
      git:
        repo: "{{ repo_url }}"
        dest: "{{ output_dir }}"
    - name: Brakeman scanning in action
      # Output available in text, html, tabs, json, markdown and csv
formats
      command: "brakeman -p {{ output_dir }} -o {{ output_dir
}}report.html"
      # Error handling for brakeman output
      failed_when: result.rc != 3
```

```
      register: result
    - name: Downloading the report
      fetch:
        src: "{{ output_dir }}/report.html"
        dest: "{{ report_name }}"
        flat: yes

    - debug:
        msg: "Report can be found at {{ report_name }}"
```

```
$ ansible-playbook -i inventory main.yml --ask-pass
SSH password:

PLAY [Brakeman Scanning Playbook] **********************************************

TASK [installing ruby and git] ************************************************
ok: [192.168.1.5] => (item=[u'ruby-full', u'git'])

TASK [installing brakeman gem] ************************************************
ok: [192.168.1.5]

TASK [cloning the https://github.com/OWASP/railsgoat.git] *********************
changed: [192.168.1.5]

TASK [Brakeman scanning in action] ********************************************
changed: [192.168.1.5]

TASK [Downloading the report] *************************************************
changed: [192.168.1.5]

TASK [debug] ******************************************************************
ok: [192.168.1.5] => {
    "msg": "Report can be found at ./report.html"
}

PLAY RECAP ********************************************************************
192.168.1.5               : ok=6    changed=3    unreachable=0    failed=0
```

Brakeman Playbook in Action against Rails goat project

Brakeman report overview is:

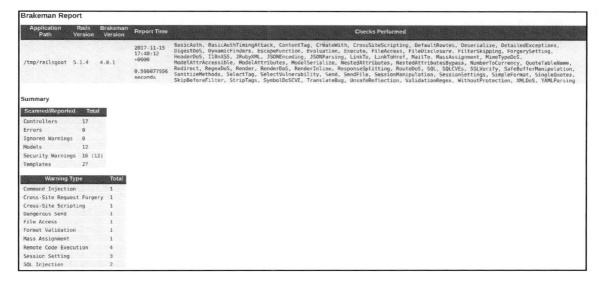

Brakeman report overview at high level

Here is Brakeman report in detail:

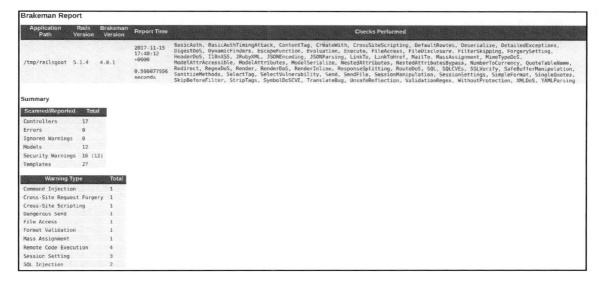

This is the detailed report with code and issue-level.

Reference about the Brakeman tool and options can be found at `https://` `brakemanscanner.org`.

Dependency-checking scanners

Most of the developers use third-party libraries while developing applications, and it's very common to see using open source plugins and modules inside their code. Many of the open source projects might be vulnerable to known attacks such as Cross-Site Scripting and SQL injection. If developers don't know the vulnerability that exists in the library they use, that means their entire application becomes vulnerable the attacker because of a bad library.

So dependency checks will allow us to find using components with known vulnerabilities (OWASP A9) issues in application code by scanning the libraries against the CVE and NIST vulnerability database.

There are multiple projects out there in the market for performing these checks, and some of them includes the following:

- OWASP Dependency-Check
- Snyk.io (`https://snyk.io/`)
- Retire.js
- [:] SourceClear and many other

OWASP Dependency-Check

OWASP Dependency-Check is an open source tool to perform checks for known vulnerabilities in Java and .NET applications primarily. It also supports other platforms such as Node.js and Python as an experiment analyzer. This can also produce false positives and can be configured to fine tune the scanning as required.

This tool can also be run in multiple ways such as CLI, build tools (Ant, Gradle, Maven, and so on) and CI/CD (Jenkins) process.

 More details about the project can be found at `https://www.owasp.org/` `index.php/OWASP_Dependency_Check`.

The following code snippet is to set up and perform a scan using OWASP Dependency-Check tool on vulnerable Java project:

```
- name: OWASP Dependency Check Playbook
  hosts: scanner
  remote_user: ubuntu
  become: yes
  vars:
    repo_url: https://github.com/psiinon/bodgeit.git
    output_dir: /tmp/bodgeit/
    project_name: bodgeit
    report_name: report.html
  tasks:
    - name: installing pre requisuites
      apt:
        name: "{{ item }}"
        state: present
        update_cache: yes

      with_items:
        - git
        - unzip
        - mono-runtime
        - mono-devel
        - default-jre

    - name: downloading owasp dependency-check
      unarchive:
        src:
http://dl.bintray.com/jeremy-long/owasp/dependency-check-3.0.2-release.zip
        dest: /usr/share/
        remote_src: yes
    - name: adding symlink to the system
      file:
        src: /usr/share/dependency-check/bin/dependency-check.sh
        dest: /usr/bin/dependency-check
        mode: 0755
        state: link
    - name: cloning the {{ repo_url }}
      git:
        repo: "{{ repo_url }}"
        dest: "{{ output_dir }}"
    - name: updating CVE database
      command: "dependency-check --updateonly"

    - name: OWASP dependency-check scanning in action
      # Output available in XML, HTML, CSV, JSON, VULN, ALL formats
```

```
      command: "dependency-check --project {{ project_name }} --scan {{
output_dir }} -o {{ output_dir }}{{ project_name }}-report.html"
    - name: Downloading the report
      fetch:
        src: "{{ output_dir }}{{ project_name }}-report.html"
        dest: "{{ report_name }}"
        flat: yes

    - debug:
        msg: "Report can be found at {{ report_name }}"
```

```
$ ansible-playbook -i inventory main.yml

PLAY [OWASP Dependency Check Playbook] ****************************************************

TASK [Gathering Facts] *******************************************************************
ok: [192.168.1.10]

TASK [installing pre requisuites] ********************************************************
ok: [192.168.1.10] => (item=[u'git', u'unzip', u'mono-runtime', u'mono-devel', u'default-jre'])

TASK [downloading owasp dependency-check] ************************************************
changed: [192.168.1.10]

TASK [adding symlink to the system] *****************************************************
changed: [192.168.1.10]

TASK [cloning the https://github.com/psiinon/bodgeit.git] *******************************
changed: [192.168.1.10]

TASK [updating CVE database] ************************************************************
changed: [192.168.1.10]

TASK [OWASP dependency-check scanning in action] ***************************************
changed: [192.168.1.10]

TASK [Downloading the report] **********************************************************
changed: [192.168.1.10]

TASK [debug] **************************************************************************
ok: [192.168.1.10] => {
    "msg": "Report can be found at ./report.html"
}

PLAY RECAP **************************************************************************
192.168.1.10               : ok=9    changed=6    unreachable=0    failed=0
```

OWASP Dependency-Check scan against Bodgeit project using Ansible playbook

OWASP Dependency-Check report in high level:

DEPENDENCY-CHECK

Dependency-Check is an open source tool performing a best effort analysis of 3rd party dependencies; false positives and false negatives may exist in the analysis performed by the tool. Use of the tool and the reporting provided constitutes acceptance for use in an AS IS condition, and there are NO warranties, implied or otherwise, with regard to the analysis or its use. Any use of the tool and the reporting provided is at the user's risk. In no event shall the copyright holder or OWASP be held liable for any damages whatsoever arising out of or in connection with the use of this tool, the analysis performed, or the resulting report.

How to read the report | Suppressing false positives | Getting Help: google group | github issues

Project: bodgeit

Scan Information (show all):
- *dependency-check version*: 3.0.2
- *Report Generated On*: Nov 16, 2017 at 19:46:09 +00:00
- *Dependencies Scanned*: 52 (49 unique)
- *Vulnerable Dependencies*: 19
- *Vulnerabilities Found*: 108
- *Vulnerabilities Suppressed*: 0
- *. . .*

Display: Showing Vulnerable Dependencies (click to show all)

Dependency	CPE	GAV	Highest Severity	CVE Count	CPE Confidence	Evidence Count
servlet-api.jar	cpe:/a:apache_tomcat:apache_tomcat:6.0.13 cpe:/a:apache:tomcat:6.0.13 cpe:/a:apache_software_foundation:tomcat:6.0.13	org.apache.tomcat:servlet-api:6.0.13 ✓	High	75	Highest	15
selenium-server-standalone-2.43.0.jar/META-INF/maven/org.apache.httpcomponents/httpclient/pom.xml	cpe:/a:apache:httpclient:4.3.4	org.apache.httpcomponents:httpclient:4.3.4	Medium	2	Highest	15
selenium-server-standalone-2.43.0.jar/META-INF/maven/org.apache.httpcomponents/httpmime/pom.xml	cpe:/a:apache:httpclient:4.3.4	org.apache.httpcomponents:httpmime:4.3.4	Medium	2	Highest	15
selenium-server-standalone-2.43.0.jar/META-INF/maven/commons-collections/commons-collections/pom.xml	cpe:/a:apache:commons_collections:3.2.1	commons-collections:commons-collections:3.2.1	High	1	Highest	16
selenium-server-standalone-2.43.0.jar/META-INF/maven/com.google.protobuf/protobuf-java/pom.xml	cpe:/a:google:protobuf:2.4.1	com.google.protobuf:protobuf-java:2.4.1	Medium	1	Low	16

High-level report of OWASP Dependency-Check tool

Here is a detailed report with vulnerability, fixes, and the references:

A detailed report with vulnerability, fixes, and reference

The report format looks like the following at high level:

- **Dependency**: The file name of the dependency scanned
- **CPE**: Any Common Platform Enumeration identifiers found
- **GAV**: The Maven Group, Artifact, and Version (GAV)
- **Highest severity**: The highest severity of any associated CVEs
- **CVE count**: The number of associated CVEs
- **CPE confidence**: A ranking of how confident Dependency-check is that the CPE was identified correctly
- **Evidence count**: The quantity of data extracted from the dependency that was used to identify CPE

 More detailed documentation can be found at https://jeremylong.
github.io/DependencyCheck.

Running web application security scanners

This is the phase where the application went live to QA, stage, (or) Production. Then, we wanted to perform security scans like an attacker (black box view). At this stage, an application will have all the dynamic functionalities and server configurations applied.

These scanner results tell us how good the server configured and any other application security issues before releasing the replica copy into the production.

At this stage, most of the scanners just work at a certain level only. And we need to put some manual testing using human brain to find logical vulnerabilities and other security vulnerabilities that can't be detected by security scanners and tools.

As we have seen in other sections, there are many tools in the market to do these jobs for you in both open source and commercial world. Some of them includes the following:

- Nikto
- Arachni
- w3af
- Acunetix and many other

Nikto – web server scanner

Nikto is an open source web server assessment tool written in Perl to perform security configuration checks and web server and application scanning using its checklist of items to scan.

Some of the checks Nikto does includes the following:

- Server and software misconfigurations
- Default files and programs
- Insecure files and programs
- Outdated servers and programs

Nikto setup and execution Ansible playbook looks like the following:

```
- name: Nikto Playbook
  hosts: scanner
  remote_user: ubuntu
  become: yes
  vars:
    domain_name: idontexistdomainnamewebsite.com # Add the domain to scan
    report_name: report.html
  tasks:
    - name: installing pre requisuites
      apt:
        name: "{{ item }}"
        state: present
        update_cache: yes

      with_items:
        - git
        - perl
        - libnet-ssleay-perl
        - openssl
        - libauthen-pam-perl
        - libio-pty-perl
        - libmd-dev

    - name: downloading nikto
      git:
        repo: https://github.com/sullo/nikto.git
        dest: /usr/share/nikto/

    - name: Nikto scanning in action
      # Output available in csv, html, msf+, nbe, txt, xml formats
      command: "/usr/share/nikto/program/nikto.pl -h {{ domain_name }} -o
/tmp/{{ domain_name }}-report.html"
    - name: downloading the report
      fetch:
        src: "/tmp/{{ domain_name }}-report.html"
        dest: "{{ report_name }}"
        flat: yes

    - debug:
        msg: "Report can be found at {{ report_name }}"
```

```
$ ansible-playbook -i inventory main.yml

PLAY [Nikto Playbook] ***********************************************************

TASK [Gathering Facts] **********************************************************
ok: [192.168.1.10]

TASK [installing pre requisuites] ***********************************************
ok: [192.168.1.10] => (item=[u'git', u'perl', u'libnet-ssleay-perl', u'openssl', u'libauthen-pam-perl', u'libio-pty-perl', u'libmd-dev'])

TASK [downloading nikto] ********************************************************
ok: [192.168.1.10]

TASK [Nikto scanning in action] *************************************************
changed: [192.168.1.10]

TASK [downloading the report] ***************************************************
changed: [192.168.1.10]

TASK [debug] ********************************************************************
ok: [192.168.1.10] => {
    "msg": "Report can be found at ./report.html"
}

PLAY RECAP **********************************************************************
192.168.1.10               : ok=6    changed=2    unreachable=0    failed=0
```

Nikto Playbook in action

Playbook to download, install, and run Nikto with report output is:

idontexistdomainnamewebsite.com / idontexistdomainnamewebsite.com port 80	
Target IP	idontexistdomainnamewebsite.com
Target hostname	idontexistdomainnamewebsite.com
Target Port	80
HTTP Server	Apache/2.4.7 (Ubuntu)
Site Link (Name)	http://idontexistdomainnamewebsite.com:80/
Site Link (IP)	http://idontexistdomainnamewebsite.com:80/
URI	/
HTTP Method	GET
Description	Retrieved x-powered-by header: PHP/5.5.9-1ubuntu4.20
Test Links	http://idontexistdomainnamewebsite.com:80/ http://idontexistdomainnamewebsite.com:80/
OSVDB Entries	OSVDB-0
URI	/
HTTP Method	GET
Description	The anti-clickjacking X-Frame-Options header is not present.
Test Links	http://idontexistdomainnamewebsite.com:80/ http://idontexistdomainnamewebsite.com:80/
OSVDB Entries	OSVDB-0
URI	/
HTTP Method	GET
Description	The X-XSS-Protection header is not defined. This header can hint to the user agent to protect against some forms of XSS
Test Links	http://idontexistdomainnamewebsite.com:80/ http://idontexistdomainnamewebsite.com:80/
OSVDB Entries	OSVDB-0
URI	/
HTTP Method	GET
Description	The X-Content-Type-Options header is not set. This could allow the user agent to render the content of the site in a different fashion to the MIME type
Test Links	http://idontexistdomainnamewebsite.com:80/ http://idontexistdomainnamewebsite.com:80/
OSVDB Entries	OSVDB-0

Nikto HTML scan report

Read more about Nikto options and documentation at `https://cirt.net/Nikto2`.

Framework-specific security scanners

This kind of check and scanning is to perform against specific to framework, CMS, and platforms. It allows to get more detailed results by validating against multiple security test cases and checks. Again, there are multiple tools and scanners available in both open source and commercial world.

Some of the examples includes the following:

- Scanning against WordPress CMS using WPScan: `https://github.com/wpscanteam/wpscan`
- Scanning against JavaScript libraries using Retire.js: `https://retirejs.github.io/retire.js`
- Scanning against Drupal CMS using Droopescan - `https://github.com/droope/droopescan` and many others

WordPress vulnerability scanner – WPScan

WPScan is black box WordPress vulnerability scanner written in Ruby to perform security scanning and vulnerability checks against WordPress CMS using WPScan vulnerability database (`https://wpvulndb.com`).

Some of the checks it does includes but not limited to are as follows:

- WordPress core
- WordPress plugins and themes
- Old software known vulnerabilities
- Username, attachment enumeration
- Brute force attacks
- Security misconfiguration and many other

The following playbook will perform WPScan as per the given domain and produces the scan report with list of issues and references.

Update the `domain_name` and `output_dir` values as required in the playbook. Also, the following playbook assumes that you already have Docker installed in the system:

```
- name: WPScan Playbook
  hosts: localhost
  vars:
    domain_name: www.idontexistdomainnamewebsite.com # Specify the domain
to scan
    wpscan_container: wpscanteam/wpscan
    scan_name: wpscan
    output_dir: /tmp # Specify the output directory to store results
  tasks:
    # This playbook assumes docker already installed
    - name: Downloading {{ wpscan_container }} docker container
      docker_image:
        name: "{{ wpscan_container }}"

    - name: creating output report file
      file:
        path: "{{output_dir }}/{{ domain_name }}.txt"
        state: touch

    - name: Scanning {{ domain_name }} website using WPScan
      docker_container:
        name: "{{ scan_name }}"
        image: "{{ wpscan_container }}"
        interactive: yes
        auto_remove: yes
```

```
        state: started
        volumes: "/tmp/{{ domain_name }}.txt:/wpscan/data/output.txt"
        command: ["--update", "--follow-redirection", "--url", "{{
domain_name }}", "--log", "/wpscan/data/output.txt"]
    - name: WPScan report downloaded
      debug:
        msg: "The report can be found at /tmp/{{ domain_name }}.txt"
```

```
$ ansible-playbook main.yml
 [WARNING]: Could not match supplied host pattern, ignoring: all

 [WARNING]: provided hosts list is empty, only localhost is available

PLAY [WPScan Playbook] ***********************************************************************

TASK [Gathering Facts] ***********************************************************************
ok: [localhost]

TASK [Downloading wpscanteam/wpscan docker container] ***************************************
ok: [localhost]

TASK [creating output report file] *********************************************************
changed: [localhost]

TASK [Scanning www.idontexistdomainnamewebsite.com website using WPScan] ********************
changed: [localhost]

TASK [WPScan report downloaded] ************************************************************
ok: [localhost] => {
    "msg": "The report can be found at /tmp/www.idontexistdomainnamewebsite.com.txt"
}

PLAY RECAP ******************************************************************************
localhost                  : ok=5    changed=2    unreachable=0    failed=0
```

WPScan Ansible playbook execution

Playbook output of downloading, executing, and storing the scan results for WPScan:

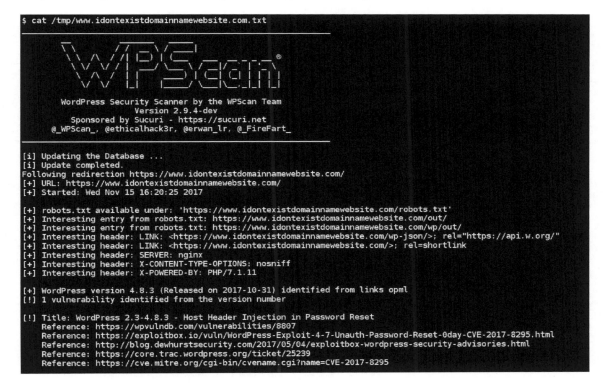

WPScan output report with issue details and references

These scans can be integrated into our CI/CD pipeline and execute once the deployment completed to validate against the security checks and configuration checks. Also, this scan can be customized as required based on the WPScan; refer to the WPScan documentation for more reference https://github.com/wpscanteam/wpscan.

Automated patching approaches using Ansible

Patching and updating is a task that everyone who has to manage production systems has to deal with. There are two approaches that we will look are as follows:

- Rolling updates
- BlueGreen deployments

Rolling updates

Imagine that we have five web servers behind a load balancer. What we would like to do is a zero downtime upgrade of our web application. Using certain keywords available in Ansible, we can make this happen.

In our example, we want to achieve the following:

- Tell the load balancer that web server node is down
- Bring down the web server on that node
- Copy the updated application files to that node
- Bring up the web server on that node

The first keyword for us to look at is `serial`. Let's see this example from Ansible documentation:

```
- name: test play
  hosts: webservers
  serial: 1
```

The example is from http://docs.ansible.com/ansible/latest/playbooks_delegation. html#rolling-update-batch-size.

This ensures that the execution of the playbook is done serially rather than in parallel. So the steps we listed previously can be done for one node at a time. The load balancer distributes traffic to the website on running nodes, and we achieve rolling updates.

Apart from giving a number to serial, we can also use percentage. Therefore, the example becomes as follows:

```
- name: test play
  hosts: webservers
  serial: "20%"
```

The example is from `http://docs.ansible.com/ansible/latest/playbooks_delegation.html#rolling-update-batch-size`.

We can choose to provide a percentage value or numeric value to serial. In this case the the play will run against 1, then 20% of the remaining nodes and finally all the remaining ones.

```
# The batch sizes can be a list as well
- name: test play
  hosts: webservers
  serial:
    - "1"
    - "20%"
    - "100%"
```

Example is from `http://docs.ansible.com/ansible/latest/playbooks_delegation.html#rolling-update-batch-size`.

A great example for this way of doing updates is given in the following link

Episode #47 - Zero-downtime Deployments with Ansible: `https://sysadmincasts.com/episodes/47-zero-downtime-deployments-with-ansible-part-4-4`

BlueGreen deployments

The concept of BlueGreen is attributed to Martin Fowler. A good reference is this article `http://martinfowler.com/bliki/BlueGreenDeployment.html` on it. The idea is to consider our current live production workload as blue. Now what we want to do is upgrade the application. So a replica of blue is brought up behind the same load balancer. The replica of the infrastructure has the updated application.

Once it is up and running, the load balancer configuration is switched from current blue to point to green. Blue keeps running in case there are any operational issues. Once we are happy with the progress, we can tear down the older host. The following playbook demonstrate this in a very simplistic manner:

- The first playbook brings up three hosts. Two web servers running nginx behind a load balancer
- The second playbook switches what is live (blue) to green

BlueGreen deployment setup playbook

The following playbook will set up three nodes, which includes load balancer and two web server nodes. Follow https://www.upcloud.com/support/haproxy-load-balancer-ubuntu to create a playbook.

The following snippet is the `inventory` file:

```
[proxyserver]
proxy ansible_host=192.168.100.100 ansible_user=ubuntu
ansible_password=passwordgoeshere

[blue]
blueserver ansible_host=192.168.100.10 ansible_user=ubuntu
ansible_password=passwordgoeshere

[green]
greenserver ansible_host=192.168.100.20 ansible_user=ubuntu
ansible_password=passwordgoeshere

[webservers:children]
blue
green

[prod:children]
webservers
proxyserver
```

Then, the `main.yml` playbook file looks like the following, which describes what roles to execute on which nodes and flow:

```
- name: running common role
  hosts: prod
  gather_facts: false
  become: yes
  serial: 100%
  roles:
    - common

- name: running haproxy role
  hosts: proxyserver
  become: yes
  roles:
    - haproxy

- name: running webserver role
  hosts: webservers
  become: yes
  serial: 100%
  roles:
    - nginx

- name: updating blue code
  hosts: blue
  become: yes
  roles:
    - bluecode

- name: updating green code
  hosts: green
  become: yes
  roles:
    - greencode
```

Each role has it's own functionality to perform; the following is the common role to perform across all the nodes:

```
- name: installing python if not installed
  raw: test -e /usr/bin/python || (apt -y update && apt install -y python-
minimal)

- name: updating and installing git, curl
  apt:
    name: "{{ item }}"
    state: present
    update_cache: yes
  with_items:
    - git
    - curl

# Also we can include common any monitoring and security hardening tasks
```

Then, the proxy server role looks like the following to set up and configure the haproxy server:

```
- name: adding haproxy repo
  apt_repository:
    repo: ppa:vbernat/haproxy-1.7

- name: updating and installing haproxy
  apt:
    name: haproxy
    state: present
    update_cache: yes

- name: updating the haproxy configuration
  template:
    src: haproxy.cfg.j2
    dest: /etc/haproxy/haproxy.cfg

- name: starting the haproxy service
  service:
    name: haproxy
    state: started
    enabled: yes
```

The `haproxy.cfg.j2` looks as follows, it has all the configuration required to perform the setup. This can be improved based on what configuration we want to add (or) remove like SSL/TLS certificates and exposing `haproxy` stats and so on:

```
global
  log /dev/log local0
  log /dev/log local1 notice
  chroot /var/lib/haproxy
  stats socket /run/haproxy/admin.sock mode 660 level admin
  stats timeout 30s
  user haproxy
  group haproxy
  daemon

  # Default SSL material locations
  ca-base /etc/ssl/certs
  crt-base /etc/ssl/private

  # Default ciphers to use on SSL-enabled listening sockets.
  # For more information, see ciphers(1SSL). This list is from:
  # https://hynek.me/articles/hardening-your-web-servers-ssl-ciphers/
  # An alternative list with additional directives can be obtained from
  #
https://mozilla.github.io/server-side-tls/ssl-config-generator/?server=haproxy
  ssl-default-bind-ciphers
ECDH+AESGCM:DH+AESGCM:ECDH+AES256:DH+AES256:ECDH+AES128:DH+AES:RSA+AESGCM:RSA+AES:!aNULL:!MD5:!DSS
  ssl-default-bind-options no-sslv3

defaults
  log global
  mode http
  option httplog
  option dontlognull
        timeout connect 5000
        timeout client 50000
        timeout server 50000
  errorfile 400 /etc/haproxy/errors/400.http
  errorfile 403 /etc/haproxy/errors/403.http
  errorfile 408 /etc/haproxy/errors/408.http
  errorfile 500 /etc/haproxy/errors/500.http
  errorfile 502 /etc/haproxy/errors/502.http
  errorfile 503 /etc/haproxy/errors/503.http
  errorfile 504 /etc/haproxy/errors/504.http
```

```
frontend http_front
    bind *:80
    stats uri /haproxy?stats
    default_backend http_back

backend http_back
    balance roundrobin
    server {{ hostvars.blueserver.ansible_host }} {{
hostvars.blueserver.ansible_host }}:80 check
    #server {{ hostvars.greenserver.ansible_host }} {{
hostvars.greenserver.ansible_host }}:80 check
```

The following snippet will add the servers as part of load balancer and serves when user requested. We can add multiple servers as well. `haproxy` also supports both L7 and L4 load balancing as well:

```
server {{ hostvars.blueserver.ansible_host }} {{
hostvars.blueserver.ansible_host }}:80 check
```

The web server is very simple nginx server setup to install and add the service to startup process:

```
- name: installing nginx
  apt:
    name: nginx
    state: present
    update_cache: yes

- name: starting the nginx service
  service:
    name: nginx
    state: started
    enabled: yes
```

Finally, the following code snippets are the code for `blue` and `green` servers, respectively:

```
<html>
    <body bgcolor="blue">
        <h1 align="center">Welcome to Blue Deployment</h1>
    </body>
</html>


<html>
```

```
    <body bgcolor="green">
        <h1 align="center">Welcome to Green Deployment</h1>
    </body>
</html>
```

The following screenshot is the reference to playbook execution of this entire setup:

```
$ ansible-playbook -i inventory main.yml

PLAY [running common role] ****************************************************

TASK [common : installing python if not installed] ***************************
changed: [blueserver]
changed: [greenserver]
changed: [proxy]

TASK [common : updating and installing git, curl] ****************************
ok: [greenserver] => (item=[u'git', u'curl'])
ok: [blueserver] => (item=[u'git', u'curl'])
ok: [proxy] => (item=[u'git', u'curl'])

PLAY [running haproxy role] **************************************************

TASK [Gathering Facts] ******************************************************
ok: [proxy]

TASK [haproxy : adding haproxy repo] ****************************************
ok: [proxy]

TASK [haproxy : updating and installing haproxy] ***************************
ok: [proxy]

TASK [haproxy : updating the haproxy configuration] ***********************
ok: [proxy]

TASK [haproxy : starting the haproxy service] ****************************
ok: [proxy]

PLAY [running webserver role] ***********************************************

TASK [Gathering Facts] ******************************************************
ok: [blueserver]
ok: [greenserver]

TASK [nginx : installing nginx] ********************************************
ok: [greenserver]
ok: [blueserver]

TASK [nginx : starting the nginx service] *********************************
ok: [blueserver]
ok: [greenserver]
```

Once the playbook is completed, we can check the production site at our load balancer IP address to see the blue deployment:

BlueGreen deployment update playbook

Now, the developer has updated the code (or) server is patched for some security vulnerabilities. We want to deploy the new version of production site with green deployment.

The playbook looks very simple as follows, it will update the configuration and reloads the `haproxy` service to serve the new production deployment:

```
- name: Updating to GREEN deployment
  hosts: proxyserver
  become: yes
  tasks:
    - name: updating proxy configuration
      template:
        src: haproxy.cfg.j2
        dest: /etc/haproxy/haproxy.cfg
    - name: updating the service
      service:
        name: haproxy
        state: reloaded

    - debug:
        msg: "GREEN deployment successful. Please check your server :)"
```

```
$ ansible-playbook -i inventory main.yml

PLAY [Updating to GREEN deployment] ************************************

TASK [Gathering Facts] ************************************************
ok: [proxy]

TASK [updating proxy configuration] **********************************
changed: [proxy]

TASK [updating the service] *******************************************
changed: [proxy]

TASK [debug] **********************************************************
ok: [proxy] => {
    "msg": "GREEN deployment successful. Please check your server :)"
}

PLAY RECAP ************************************************************
proxy                      : ok=4    changed=2    unreachable=0    failed=0
```

Then, we can check our production site again to see the update deployment by navigating to the load balancer IP:

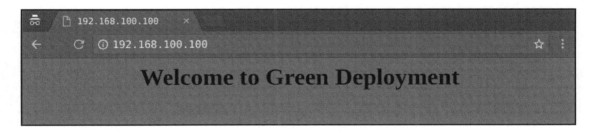

Now, we can see that our production site is running the new updated deployment. There are multiple advanced options available in HAProxy to perform different kind of updates and can be configurable as required.

Summary

This chapter touched upon various use cases for application and network security. By combining various tools with the power of Ansible playbooks, we created powerful workflows for security automation in this space. Based on requirements, you may use benchmarks in order to enable secure defaults or periodic checks for compliance and fulfill audit requirements. We looked at tools that allow us to do the same for AWS Cloud as well. From application security scanners to approaches to doing software updates and patches in a secure configuration-driven manner, we tried to cover a wide variety of tasks that are made powerful by Ansible automation.

In the next chapter, we will focus on one of the most exciting emerging areas of IT and operations, that is, containers. Docker being synonymous with containers has become a widely deployed technology for developers, system administrators, and a core part of the modern software development and deployment pipelines. Let's explore what does Ansible have in store to work with Docker containers.

8
Continuous Security Scanning for Docker Containers

Docker containers are the new way developers package applications. The best feature of containers is the fact that they contain the code, runtime, system libraries, and all the settings that are required for the application to work. Due to the ease of use and deployment, more and more applications are getting deployed in containers for production use.

With so many moving parts, it becomes imperative that we have the capability to continuously scan Docker containers for security issues. In this chapter, we will look at various ways of doing just that. Starting with the familiar CIS benchmark scripts invoked using Ansible, we will move on to clair-scanner, which is a great tool to scan for existing vulnerabilities and integrates well with your existing CI/CD workflow, if you need.

In detail, we will explore the following topics in this chapter:

- Understanding continuous security concepts
- Automating vulnerability assessments of Docker containers using Ansible
- Scheduled scans using Ansible Tower for Docker security
- Scheduled scans using Ansible Tower for operating systems and kernel security
- Scheduled scans for file integrity checks, host level monitoring using Ansible for various compliance initiatives

Understanding continuous security concepts

One of the key approaches to emerge out of DevOps is the idea of immutable infrastructure. It means that every time there needs to be a runtime change, either in application code or configuration, the containers are built and deployed again and the existing running ones are torn down.

Since that allows for predictability, resilience, and simplifies deployment choices at runtime, it is no surprise that many operations teams are moving toward it. With that comes the question of when these containers should be tested for security and compliance. By embracing the process of continuous security scanning and monitoring, as discussed in this chapter, you can automate for a variety of workloads and workflows.

Automating vulnerability assessments of Docker containers using Ansible

Containers are everywhere. Let's look at some of the techniques and tools to perform scans and assess the Docker containers and environments using Ansible.

There are many different ways of evaluating the security of containers. In this chapter, we will look at some of them and how they can be used with Ansible:

Tool	Description
Docker Bench	A security shell script to perform checks based on CIS
Clair	A tool to perform vulnerability analysis based on the CVE database
Anchore	A tool to perform security evaluation and make runtime policy decisions
`vuls`	An agent-less vulnerability scanner with CVE, OVAL database
`osquery`	OS instrumentation framework for OS analytics to do HIDS-type activities

Docker Bench for Security

Docker Bench for Security is a shell script to perform multiple checks against the Docker container environment. It will give a more detailed view of the security configuration based on CIS benchmarks. This script supports most of the Unix operating systems as it was built based on the POSIX 2004 compliant.

More details about the tool information can be found at `https://github.com/docker/docker-bench-security`.

The following are the high-level areas of checks this script will perform:

- Host configuration
- Docker daemon configuration and files
- Docker container images
- Docker runtime
- Docker security operations
- Docker swarm configuration

The following playbook will perform a Docker bench security scan against the Docker environment and return a detailed report:

```
- name: Docker bench security playbook
  hosts: docker
  remote_user: ubuntu
  become: yes
  tasks:
    - name: make sure git installed
      apt:
        name: git
        state: present

    - name: download the docker bench security
      git:
        repo: https://github.com/docker/docker-bench-security.git
        dest: /opt/docker-bench-security
    - name: running docker-bench-security scan
      command: docker-bench-security.sh -l /tmp/output.log
      args:
        chdir: /opt/docker-bench-security/
    - name: downloading report locally
      fetch:
        src: /tmp/output.log
        dest: "{{ playbook_dir }}/{{ inventory_hostname }}-docker-report-{{
```

```
ansible_date_time.date }}.log"
      flat: yes

  - name: report location
    debug:
      msg: "Report can be found at {{ playbook_dir }}/{{
inventory_hostname }}-docker-report-{{ ansible_date_time.date
}}.log"</mark>
```

Docker bench security Ansible playbook in action:

```
$ ansible-playbook -i inventory main.yml --ask-pass
SSH password:

PLAY [Docker bench security playbook] *******************************************

TASK [Gathering Facts] *******************************************
ok: [192.168.1.9]

TASK [make sure git installed] *******************************************
ok: [192.168.1.9]

TASK [download the docker bench security] *******************************************
ok: [192.168.1.9]

TASK [running docker-bench-security scan] *******************************************
changed: [192.168.1.9]

TASK [downloading report locally] *******************************************
changed: [192.168.1.9]

TASK [report location] *******************************************
ok: [192.168.1.9] => {
    "msg": "Report can be found at ./192.168.1.9-docker-report-2017-11-09.log"
}

PLAY RECAP *******************************************
192.168.1.9                : ok=6    changed=2    unreachable=0    failed=0
```

Docker bench security Ansible playbook in action

The output of the playbook will download and scan the containers based on the CIS benchmark and store the results in a log file, the output of which can be seen here:

```
$ cat ./192.168.1.9-docker-report-2017-11-09.log
Initializing Thu Nov  9 20:31:12 UTC 2017


[INFO] 1 - Host Configuration
[WARN] 1.1  - Ensure a separate partition for containers has been created
[NOTE] 1.2  - Ensure the container host has been Hardened
[INFO] 1.3  - Ensure Docker is up to date
[INFO]      * Using 17.09.0, verify is it up to date as deemed necessary
[INFO]      * Your operating system vendor may provide support and security maintenance for Docker
[INFO] 1.4  - Ensure only trusted users are allowed to control Docker daemon
[INFO]      * docker:x:999:
[WARN] 1.5  - Ensure auditing is configured for the Docker daemon
[WARN] 1.6  - Ensure auditing is configured for Docker files and directories - /var/lib/docker
[WARN] 1.7  - Ensure auditing is configured for Docker files and directories - /etc/docker
[INFO] 1.8  - Ensure auditing is configured for Docker files and directories - docker.service
[INFO]      * File not found
[INFO] 1.9  - Ensure auditing is configured for Docker files and directories - docker.socket
[INFO]      * File not found
[WARN] 1.10 - Ensure auditing is configured for Docker files and directories - /etc/default/docker
[INFO] 1.11 - Ensure auditing is configured for Docker files and directories - /etc/docker/daemon.json
[INFO]      * File not found
[WARN] 1.12 - Ensure auditing is configured for Docker files and directories - /usr/bin/docker-containerd
[WARN] 1.13 - Ensure auditing is configured for Docker files and directories - /usr/bin/docker-runc


[INFO] 2 - Docker daemon configuration
[WARN] 2.1  - Ensure network traffic is restricted between containers on the default bridge
[PASS] 2.2  - Ensure the logging level is set to 'info'
[PASS] 2.3  - Ensure Docker is allowed to make changes to iptables
[PASS] 2.4  - Ensure insecure registries are not used
[WARN] 2.5  - Ensure aufs storage driver is not used
[INFO] 2.6  - Ensure TLS authentication for Docker daemon is configured
[INFO]      * Docker daemon not listening on TCP
[INFO] 2.7  - Ensure the default ulimit is configured appropriately
[INFO]      * Default ulimit doesn't appear to be set
[WARN] 2.8  - Enable user namespace support
[PASS] 2.9  - Ensure the default cgroup usage has been confirmed
[PASS] 2.10 - Ensure base device size is not changed until needed
[WARN] 2.11 - Ensure that authorization for Docker client commands is enabled
[WARN] 2.12 - Ensure centralized and remote logging is configured
[WARN] 2.13 - Ensure operations on legacy registry (v1) are Disabled
[WARN] 2.14 - Ensure live restore is Enabled
[WARN] 2.15 - Ensure Userland Proxy is Disabled
[INFO] 2.16 - Ensure daemon-wide custom seccomp profile is applied, if needed
[PASS] 2.17 - Ensure experimental features are avoided in production
[PASS] 2.18 - Ensure containers are restricted from acquiring new privileges
```

Detailed Docker bench security analysis report

Clair

Clair allows us to perform static vulnerability analysis against containers by checking with the existing vulnerability database. It allows us to perform vulnerability analysis checks against our Docker container images using the Clair database. More details about Clair can be found at https://github.com/coreos/clair.

Setting up Clair itself is really difficult and scanning using the API with Docker images makes more difficult. Here comes clair-scanner, it makes really simple to set up and perform scans using the REST API.

 Read more about clair-scanner at `https://github.com/arminc/clair-scanner`.

Clair-scanner can trigger a simple scan against a container based on certain events, to check for existing vulnerabilities. Furthermore, this report can be forwarded to perform the team responsible for fixes and so on.

The following playbook will set up the required Docker containers and configuration to perform clair-scanning. It assumes that the target system has Docker and the required libraries installed:

```
- name: Clair Scanner Server Setup
  hosts: docker
  remote_user: ubuntu
  become: yes
  tasks:
    - name: setting up clair-db
      docker_container:
        name: clair_db
        image: arminc/clair-db
        exposed_ports:
          - 5432

    - name: setting up clair-local-scan
      docker_container:
        name: clair
        image: arminc/clair-local-scan:v2.0.1
        ports:
          - "6060:6060"
        links:
          - "clair_db:postgres"
```

The following screenshot is the execution of clair-scanner setup with Docker Containers using Ansible

```
$ ansible-playbook -i inventory main.yaml

PLAY [Clair Scanner Server Setup] ***********************************************

TASK [Gathering Facts] **********************************************************
ok: [192.168.1.10]

TASK [setting up clair-db] ******************************************************
changed: [192.168.1.10]

TASK [setting up clair-local-scan] **********************************************
changed: [192.168.1.10]

PLAY RECAP **********************************************************************
192.168.1.10               : ok=3    changed=2    unreachable=0    failed=0

$
```

Setting up clair-scanner with Docker containers using Ansible

 It will take a while to download and setup the CVE database after playbook execution.

The following playbook will be used to run clair-scanner to perform an analysis on the containers by making an API request to the server:

```
- name: Scanning containers using clair-scanner
  hosts: docker
  remote_user: ubuntu
  become: yes
  vars:
    image_to_scan: "debian:sid"    #container to scan for vulnerabilities
    clair_server: "http://192.168.1.10:6060"    #clair server api endpoint
  tasks:
    - name: downloading and setting up clair-scanner binary
      get_url:
        url:
https://github.com/arminc/clair-scanner/releases/download/v6/clair-scanner_
linux_amd64
        dest: /usr/local/bin/clair-scanner
        mode: 0755
    - name: scanning {{ image_to_scan }} container for vulnerabilities
      command: clair-scanner -r /tmp/{{ image_to_scan }}-scan-report.json -
c {{ clair_server }} --ip 0.0.0.0 {{ image_to_scan }}
```

```
    register: scan_output
    ignore_errors: yes
  - name: downloading the report locally
    fetch:
      src: /tmp/{{ image_to_scan }}-scan-report.json
      dest: {{ playbook_dir }}/{{ image_to_scan }}-scan-report.json
      flat: yes
```

The following screenshot is the clair-scanner in action for the requested docker images. As you can see fatal error, so when it found any issues with docker image it returns error and we can handle it using `ignore_errors`.

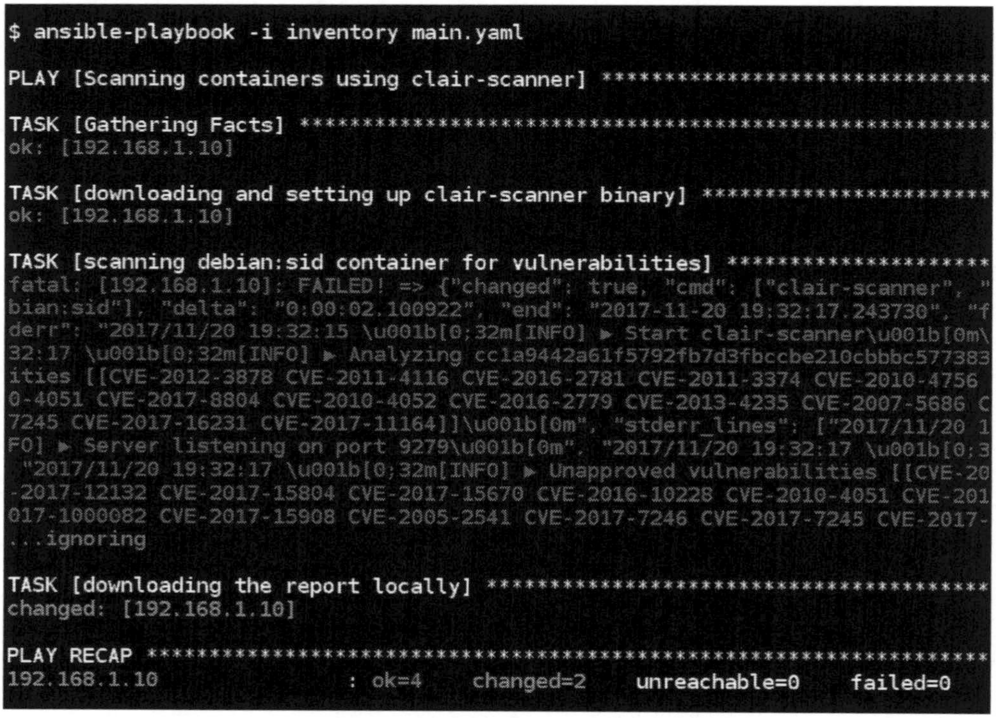

Clair-scanner execution in action

Here is the output of the playbook running clair-scanner and the output of the report in JSON format:

```
$ cat debian\:sid-scan-report.json
{
    "image": "debian:sid",
    "unaproved": [
        "CVE-2011-3374",
        "CVE-2007-5686",
        "CVE-2017-12424",
        "CVE-2013-4235",
        "CVE-2013-4392",
        "CVE-2017-1000082",
        "CVE-2017-7245",
        "CVE-2017-7246",
        "CVE-2017-11164",
        "CVE-2010-4052",
        "CVE-2010-4051",
        "CVE-2015-8985",
        "CVE-2017-12132",
        "CVE-2010-4756",
        "CVE-2016-10228",
        "CVE-2017-8804",
        "CVE-2016-2779",
        "CVE-2012-3878",
        "CVE-2011-4116",
        "CVE-2016-2781",
        "CVE-2011-3389",
        "CVE-2005-2541"
    ],
    "vulnerabilities": [
        {
            "vulnerability": "CVE-2011-3374",
            "namespace": "debian:unstable",
            "severity": "Negligible"
        },
        {
            "vulnerability": "CVE-2007-5686",
            "namespace": "debian:unstable",
            "severity": "Negligible"
        },
        {
            "vulnerability": "CVE-2017-12424",
            "namespace": "debian:unstable",
            "severity": "High"
        },
        {
            "vulnerability": "CVE-2013-4235",
            "namespace": "debian:unstable",
            "severity": "Negligible"
        },
```

The output of the report includes vulnerability CVE and severity

Scheduled scans using Ansible Tower for Docker security

Continuous security processes are all about the loop of planning, doing, measuring, and acting:

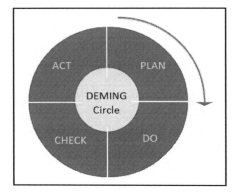

The Deming Cycle from Wikimedia Commons

By following standard checklists and benchmarks and using Ansible to execute them on containers, we can check for security issues and act on them. Anchore is an analysis and inspection platform for containers.

Anchore – open container compliance platform

Anchore is one of the most popular tools and services to perform analysis, inspection, and certification of container images. It provides multiple services and platforms to set up, the most stable and powerful way is to set up the local service using Anchore Engine, which can be accessed via the REST API. In the following documentation, we will see how to set up the service using Anchore Engine and how we can use this REST API to perform continuous security scanning and analysis of Docker containers.

The following items are high level operations Anchore can perform:

- Policy evaluation operations
- Image operations
- Policy operations
- Registry operations
- Subscription operations
- System operations

Read more about the Anchore Engine service at `https://github.com/anchore/anchore-engine`.

Anchore Engine service setup

The following playbook will set up the Anchore Engine service, which contains the engine container as well as the `postgres` to store database information. The `admin_password` variable is the admin user password to access the REST API of Anchore:

```
- name: anchore server setup
  hosts: anchore
  become: yes
  vars:
    db_password: changeme
    admin_password: secretpassword

  tasks:
    - name: creating volumes
      file:
        path: "{{ item }}"
        recurse: yes
        state: directory
      with_items:
        - /root/aevolume/db
        - /root/aevolume/config
    - name: copying anchore-engine configuration
      template:
        src: config.yaml.j2
        dest: /root/aevolume/config/config.yaml

    - name: starting anchore-db container
      docker_container:
        name: anchore-db
        image: postgres:9
        volumes:
```

```
            - "/root/aevolume/db/:/var/lib/postgresql/data/pgdata/"
        env:
          POSTGRES_PASSWORD: "{{ db_password }}"
          PGDATA: "/var/lib/postgresql/data/pgdata/"

  - name: starting anchore-engine container
    docker_container:
      name: anchore-engine
      image: anchore/anchore-engine
      ports:
        - 8228:8228
        - 8338:8338
      volumes:
        - "/root/aevolume/config/config.yaml:/config/config.yaml:ro"
        - "/var/run/docker.sock:/var/run/docker.sock:ro"
      links:
        - anchore-db:anchore-db
```

The following screenshot is the Ansible playbook execution of Anchore engine service setup:

Anchore Engine service setup using Ansible playbook

Anchore CLI scanner

Now that we have the Anchore Engine service REST API with access details, we can use this to perform the scanning of container images in any host. The following steps are the Ansible Tower setup to perform continuous scanning of container images for vulnerabilities.

The playbook for scanning a container image is shown as follows:

```
- name: anchore-cli scan
  hosts: anchore
  become: yes
  vars:
    scan_image_name: "docker.io/library/ubuntu:latest"
    anchore_vars:
      ANCHORE_CLI_URL: http://localhost:8228/v1
      ANCHORE_CLI_USER: admin
      ANCHORE_CLI_PASS: secretpassword

  tasks:
    - name: installing anchore-cli
      pip:
        name: "{{ item }}"

      with_items:
        - anchorecli
        - pyyaml
    - name: downloading image
      docker_image:
        name: "{{ scan_image_name }}"

    - name: adding image for analysis
      command: "anchore-cli image add {{ scan_image_name }}"
      environment: "{{anchore_vars}}"
    - name: wait for analysis to compelte
      command: "anchore-cli image content {{ scan_image_name }} os"
      register: analysis
      until: analysis.rc != 1
      retries: 10
      delay: 30
      ignore_errors: yes
      environment: "{{anchore_vars}}"

    - name: vulnerabilities results
      command: "anchore-cli image vuln {{ scan_image_name }} os"
      register: vuln_output
      environment: "{{anchore_vars}}"
```

```
- name: "vulnerabilities in {{ scan_image_name }}"
  debug:
    msg: "{{ vuln_output.stdout_lines }}"
```

 The options to perform `anchore-cli` can be customized as required, please refer to the documentation at `https://github.com/anchore/anchore-cli`.

Now, we have to create the new project in Ansible Tower to add the playbook. Then we can select the playbook source from version control, or required source with details:

Then we have to create a new job template to provide the options for executing the playbook using Ansible Tower:

We can also pass variables via Ansible Tower UI. As you can see, we are passing some secrets and we will see how we can leverage Ansible Vault to store and use them securely:

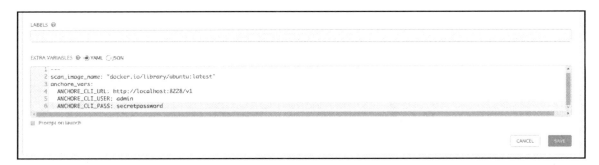

We can also schedule this playbook to run weekly or monthly, as required. Also note this can be customized based on use cases:

Then we can also perform on-demand scans by launching the job. The following screenshot is the reference for the `ubuntu:latest` Docker image vulnerabilities with CVE details and list of packages vulnerable:

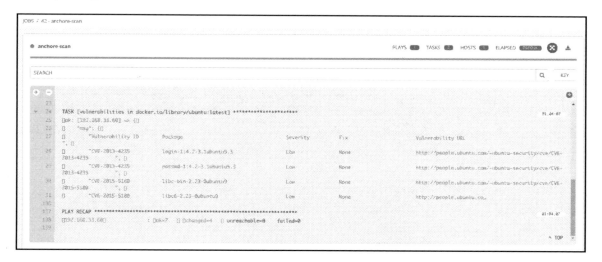

Scheduled scans using Ansible Tower for operating systems and kernel security

Continuous security scanning requires us to manage it in a software like Ansible Tower. While most of the discussed tools can be used for scanning and maintaining a benchmark for security, we should think about the entire process of the incident response and threat detection workflow:

1. Preparation
2. Detection and analysis
3. Containment, eradication, and recovery
4. Post-incident activity

Setting up all such scanners is our preparation. Using the output of these scanners gives us the ability to detect and analyze. Both containment and recovery are beyond the scope of such tools. For the process of recovery and post-incident activity, you may want to consider playbooks that can trash the current infrastructure and recreate it as it is.

As part of our preparation, it may be useful to get familiar with the following terms as you will see them being used repeatedly in the world of vulnerability scanners and vulnerability management tools:

Term	Full form (if any)	Description of the term
CVE	Common Vulnerabilities and Exposures	It is a list of cybersecurity vulnerability identifiers. Usage typically includes CVE IDs.
OVAL	Open Vulnerability and Assessment Language	A language for finding out and naming vulnerabilities and configuration issues in computer systems.
CWE	Common Weakness Enumeration	A common list of software security weaknesses.
NVD	National Vulnerability Database	A US government vulnerability management database available for public use in XML format.

Vuls – vulnerability scanner

Vuls is an agent-less scanner written in golang. It supports a different variety of Linux operating systems. It performs the complete end-to-end security system administrative tasks such as scanning for security vulnerabilities and security software updates. It analyzes the system for required security vulnerabilities, performs security risk analysis based on the CVE score, sends notifications via Slack and email, and also provides a simple web report with historical data.

 Read more about vuls at `https://github.com/future-architect/vuls`.

Vuls setup playbook

The following playbook is used to set up `vuls` in an Ubuntu 16.04 system using Docker containers. The following playbook assumes that you already have docker installed and the required packages.

The playbook has mainly two roles for setting up `vuls` using Docker containers.

- `vuls_containers_download`
- `vuls_database_download`

```
- name: setting up vuls using docker containers
  hosts: vuls
  become: yes

  roles:
    - vuls_containers_download
    - vuls_database_download
```

Pulling the Docker containers locally using the `docker_image` module:

```
- name: pulling containers locally
  docker_image:
    name: "{{ item }}"
    pull: yes
  with_items:
    - vuls/go-cve-dictionary
    - vuls/goval-dictionary
    - vuls/vuls
```

Then downloading the CVE and OVAL databases for the required operating systems and distributions versions:

```
- name: fetching NVD database locally
  docker_container:
    name: "cve-{{ item }}"
    image: vuls/go-cve-dictionary
    auto_remove: yes
    interactive: yes
    state: started
    command: fetchnvd -years "{{ item }}"
    volumes:
      - "{{ vuls_data_directory }}:/vuls"
      - "{{ vuls_data_directory }}/go-cve-dictionary-log:/var/log/vuls"
  with_sequence: start=2002 end="{{ nvd_database_years }}"

- name: fetching redhat oval data
  docker_container:
    name: "redhat-oval-{{ item }}"
    image: vuls/goval-dictionary
    auto_remove: yes
    interactive: yes
    state: started
    command: fetch-redhat "{{ item }}"
    volumes:
      - "{{ vuls_data_directory }}:/vuls"
      - "{{ vuls_data_directory }}/goval-dictionary-log:/var/log/vuls"
  with_items: "{{ redhat_oval_versions }}"

- name: fetching ubuntu oval data
  docker_container:
    name: "ubuntu-oval-{{ item }}"
    image: vuls/goval-dictionary
    auto_remove: yes
    interactive: yes
    state: started
    command: "fetch-ubuntu {{ item }}"
    volumes:
      - "{{ vuls_data_directory }}:/vuls"
      - "{{ vuls_data_directory }}/goval-dictionary-log:/var/log/vuls"
  with_items: "{{ ubuntu_oval_versions }}"
```

The global variables file looks as follows. We can add more `redhat_oval_versions`, such as 5. The `nvd_database_years` will download the CVE database up until the end of 2017:

```
vuls_data_directory: "/vuls_data"
nvd_database_years: 2017
```

```
redhat_oval_versions:
  - 6
  - 7
ubuntu_oval_versions:
  - 12
  - 14
  - 16
```

The following screenshot is the Ansible playbook execution for vuls setup:

```
$ ansible-playbook -i inventory main.yml

PLAY [setting up vuls using docker containers] *****************************

TASK [Gathering Facts] ****************************************************
ok: [192.168.33.60]

TASK [vuls_containers_download : pulling containers locally] ***************
ok: [192.168.33.60] => (item=vuls/go-cve-dictionary)
ok: [192.168.33.60] => (item=vuls/goval-dictionary)
ok: [192.168.33.60] => (item=vuls/vuls)

TASK [vuls_database_download : fetching NVD database locally] **************
changed: [192.168.33.60] => (item=2002)
changed: [192.168.33.60] => (item=2003)
changed: [192.168.33.60] => (item=2004)
changed: [192.168.33.60] => (item=2005)
changed: [192.168.33.60] => (item=2006)
changed: [192.168.33.60] => (item=2007)
changed: [192.168.33.60] => (item=2008)
changed: [192.168.33.60] => (item=2009)
changed: [192.168.33.60] => (item=2010)
changed: [192.168.33.60] => (item=2011)
changed: [192.168.33.60] => (item=2012)
changed: [192.168.33.60] => (item=2013)
changed: [192.168.33.60] => (item=2014)
changed: [192.168.33.60] => (item=2015)
changed: [192.168.33.60] => (item=2016)
changed: [192.168.33.60] => (item=2017)

TASK [vuls_database_download : fetching redhat oval data] ******************
changed: [192.168.33.60] => (item=6)
changed: [192.168.33.60] => (item=7)

TASK [vuls_database_download : fetching ubuntu oval data] ******************
changed: [192.168.33.60] => (item=12)
changed: [192.168.33.60] => (item=14)
changed: [192.168.33.60] => (item=16)

PLAY RECAP ****************************************************************
192.168.33.60              : ok=5    changed=3    unreachable=0    failed=0
```

Vuls setup playbook in action

Vuls scanning playbook

Now, it's time to perform the scanning and reporting using the `vuls` Docker containers. The following playbook contains simple steps to perform the `vuls` scan against virtual machines and containers, and send the report to slack and web:

```
- name: scanning and reporting using vuls
  hosts: vuls
  become: yes
  vars:
    vuls_data_directory: "/vuls_data"
    slack_web_hook_url:
https://hooks.slack.com/services/XXXXXXX/XXXXXXXXXXXXXXXXXXXXX
    slack_channel: "#vuls"
    slack_emoji: ":ghost:"
    server_to_scan: 192.168.33.80
    server_username: vagrant
    server_key_file_name: 192-168-33-80

  tasks:
  - name: copying configuraiton file and ssh keys
    template:
      src: "{{ item.src }}"
      dest: "{{ item.dst }}"
      mode: 0400
    with_items:
      - { src: 'config.toml', dst: '/root/config.toml' }
      - { src: '192-168-33-80', dst: '/root/.ssh/192-168-33-80' }

  - name: running config test
    docker_container:
      name: configtest
      image: vuls/vuls
      auto_remove: yes
      interactive: yes
      state: started
      command: configtest -config=/root/config.toml
      volumes:
        - "/root/.ssh:/root/.ssh:ro"
        - "{{ vuls_data_directory }}:/vuls"
        - "{{ vuls_data_directory }}/vuls-log:/var/log/vuls"
        - "/root/config.toml:/root/config.toml:ro"
  - name: running vuls scanner
    docker_container:
      name: vulsscan
      image: vuls/vuls
      auto_remove: yes
```

```
        interactive: yes
        state: started
        command: scan -config=/root/config.toml
        volumes:
          - "/root/.ssh:/root/.ssh:ro"
          - "{{ vuls_data_directory }}:/vuls"
          - "{{ vuls_data_directory }}/vuls-log:/var/log/vuls"
          - "/root/config.toml:/root/config.toml:ro"
          - "/etc/localtime:/etc/localtime:ro"
        env:
          TZ: "Asia/Kolkata"

    - name: sending slack report
      docker_container:
        name: vulsreport
        image: vuls/vuls
        auto_remove: yes
        interactive: yes
        state: started
        command: report -cvedb-path=/vuls/cve.sqlite3 -ovaldb-
path=/vuls/oval.sqlite3 --to-slack -config=/root/config.toml
        volumes:
          - "/root/.ssh:/root/.ssh:ro"
          - "{{ vuls_data_directory }}:/vuls"
          - "{{ vuls_data_directory }}/vuls-log:/var/log/vuls"
          - "/root/config.toml:/root/config.toml:ro"
          - "/etc/localtime:/etc/localtime:ro"

    - name: vuls webui report
      docker_container:
        name: vulswebui
        image: vuls/vulsrepo
        interactive: yes
        volumes:
          - "{{ vuls_data_directory }}:/vuls"
        ports:
          - "80:5111"
```

The following file is the configuration file for `vuls` to perform the scanning. This holds the configuration for slack alerting and also the server to perform scanning. This can be configured very effectively as required using `vuls` documentation:

```
[slack]
hookURL = "{{ slack_web_hook_url}}"
channel = "{{ slack_channel }}"
iconEmoji = "{{ slack_emoji }}"

[servers]

[servers.{{ server_key_file_name }}]
host = "{{ server_to_scan }}"
user = "{{ server_username }}"
keyPath = "/root/.ssh/{{ server_key_file_name }}"
```

The following screenshot is Ansible playbook execution for vuls scanning in action:

```
$ ansible-playbook -i inventory main.yml

PLAY [scanning and reporting using vuls] ************************************************

TASK [Gathering Facts] ****************************************************************
ok: [192.168.33.60]

TASK [copying configuraiton file and ssh keys] ************************************
ok: [192.168.33.60] => (item={u'src': u'config.toml', u'dst': u'/root/config.toml'})
ok: [192.168.33.60] => (item={u'src': u'192-168-33-80', u'dst': u'/root/.ssh/192-168-33-80'})

TASK [running config test] **********************************************************
changed: [192.168.33.60]

TASK [running vuls scanner] *********************************************************
changed: [192.168.33.60]

TASK [sending slack report] *********************************************************
changed: [192.168.33.60]

TASK [vuls webui report] ************************************************************
changed: [192.168.33.60]

PLAY RECAP *************************************************************************
192.168.33.60              : ok=6     changed=4    unreachable=0    failed=0
```

Vuls scanning playbook in action

Once the reporting container has executed, based on the configuration options, `vuls` will notify the issues to the respective slack channel:

192-168-33-80 (ubuntu14.04)

Total: 10 (High:10 Medium:0 Low:0 ?:0)

CVE-2017-1000111
8.9 (HIGH)

> *Linux kernel: heap out-of-bounds in AF_PACKET sockets. This new issue is analogous to previously disclosed CVE-2016-8655. In both cases, a socket option that changes socket state may race with safety checks in packet_set_ring. Previously with PACKET_VERSION. This time with PACKET_RESERVE. The solution is similar: lock the socket for the update. This issue may be exploitable, we did not investigate further. As this issue affects PF_PACKET sockets, it requires CAP_NET_RAW in the*

Show more...

Installed   **Candidate**
linux-image-3.13.0-125-generic-   Not Fixed Yet
3.13.0-125.174

CVE-2017-1000112
8.9 (HIGH)

> *Linux kernel: Exploitable memory corruption due to UFO to non-UFO path switch. When building a UFO packet with MSG_MORE __ip_append_data() calls ip_ufo_append_data() to append. However in between two send() calls, the append path can be switched from UFO to non-UFO one, which leads to a memory corruption. In case UFO packet lengths exceeds MTU, copy = maxfraglen - skb->len becomes negative on the non-UFO path and the branch to allocate new skb is taken. This triggers fragmentation*

Show more...

Installed   **Candidate**
linux-image-3.13.0-125-generic-   Not Fixed Yet
3.13.0-125.174

We can also visit the web UI interface of the `vuls` server IP address to see the detailed results in tabular and portable format. This is very useful to manage large amount of servers and patches at scale:

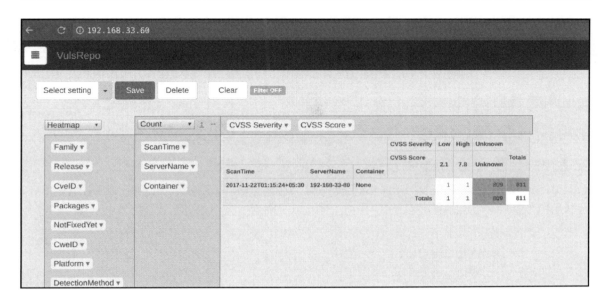

We can also get deeper by digging into the issues, severity, operating system, and so on in the report:

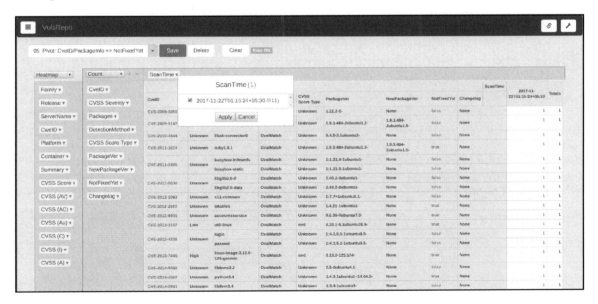

This can be part of the CI/CD life cycle as an infrastructure code and then we can run this as a scheduled scan using Ansible Tower or Jenkins.

Scheduled scans for file integrity checks, host-level monitoring using Ansible for various compliance initiatives

One of the many advantages of being able to execute commands on the host using Ansible is the ability to get internal system information, such as:

- File hashes
- Network connections
- List of running processes

It can act as a lightweight **Host-Based Intrusion Detection System (HIDS)**. While this may not eliminate the case for a purpose-built HIDS in many cases, we can execute the same kind of security tasks using a tool such as Facebook's osquery along with Ansible.

osquery

osquery is an operating system instrumentation framework by Facebook and written in C++, that supports Windows, Linux, OS X (macOS), and other operating systems. It provides an interface to query an operating system using an SQL like syntax. By using this, we can perform low-level activities such as running processes, kernel configurations, network connections, and file integrity checks. Overall it's like a **host-based intrusion detection system (HIDS)** endpoint security. It provides osquery as a service, system interactive shell, and so on. Hence we can use this to perform centralized monitoring and security management solutions. Read more about osquery at https://osquery.io.

Here is a high-level overview of what osquery looks like:

```
osquery> SELECT * FROM users;
+-------+-------+------------+------------+-----------+-----------------------------------------+-----------------------+-------------------+------+
| uid   | gid   | uid_signed | gid_signed | username  | description                             | directory             | shell             | uuid |
+-------+-------+------------+------------+-----------+-----------------------------------------+-----------------------+-------------------+------+
| 0     | 0     | 0          | 0          | root      | root                                    | /root                 | /bin/bash         |      |
| 1     | 1     | 1          | 1          | daemon    | daemon                                  | /usr/sbin             | /usr/sbin/nologin |      |
| 2     | 2     | 2          | 2          | bin       | bin                                     | /bin                  | /usr/sbin/nologin |      |
| 3     | 3     | 3          | 3          | sys       | sys                                     | /dev                  | /usr/sbin/nologin |      |
| 4     | 65534 | 4          | 65534      | sync      | sync                                    | /bin                  | /bin/sync         |      |
| 5     | 60    | 5          | 60         | games     | games                                   | /usr/games            | /usr/sbin/nologin |      |
| 6     | 12    | 6          | 12         | man       | man                                     | /var/cache/man        | /usr/sbin/nologin |      |
| 7     | 7     | 7          | 7          | lp        | lp                                      | /var/spool/lpd        | /usr/sbin/nologin |      |
| 8     | 8     | 8          | 8          | mail      | mail                                    | /var/mail             | /usr/sbin/nologin |      |
| 9     | 9     | 9          | 9          | news      | news                                    | /var/spool/news       | /usr/sbin/nologin |      |
| 10    | 10    | 10         | 10         | uucp      | uucp                                    | /var/spool/uucp       | /usr/sbin/nologin |      |
| 13    | 13    | 13         | 13         | proxy     | proxy                                   | /bin                  | /usr/sbin/nologin |      |
| 33    | 33    | 33         | 33         | www-data  | www-data                                | /var/www              | /usr/sbin/nologin |      |
| 34    | 34    | 34         | 34         | backup    | backup                                  | /var/backups          | /usr/sbin/nologin |      |
| 38    | 38    | 38         | 38         | list      | Mailing List Manager                    | /var/list             | /usr/sbin/nologin |      |
| 39    | 39    | 39         | 39         | irc       | ircd                                    | /var/run/ircd         | /usr/sbin/nologin |      |
| 41    | 41    | 41         | 41         | gnats     | Gnats Bug-Reporting System (admin)      | /var/lib/gnats        | /usr/sbin/nologin |      |
| 65534 | 65534 | 65534      | 65534      | nobody    | nobody                                  | /nonexistent          | /usr/sbin/nologin |      |
| 100   | 101   | 100        | 101        | libuuid   |                                         | /var/lib/libuuid      |                   |      |
| 101   | 104   | 101        | 104        | syslog    |                                         | /home/syslog          | /bin/false        |      |
| 102   | 106   | 102        | 106        | messagebus|                                         | /var/run/dbus         | /bin/false        |      |
| 103   | 109   | 103        | 109        | landscape |                                         | /var/lib/landscape    | /bin/false        |      |
| 104   | 65534 | 104        | 65534      | sshd      |                                         | /var/run/sshd         | /usr/sbin/nologin |      |
| 105   | 1     | 105        | 1          | pollinate |                                         | /var/cache/pollinate  | /bin/false        |      |
| 1000  | 1000  | 1000       | 1000       | vagrant   |                                         | /home/vagrant         | /bin/bash         |      |
| 106   | 112   | 106        | 112        | colord    | colord colour management daemon,..      | /var/lib/colord       | /bin/false        |      |
| 107   | 65534 | 107        | 65534      | statd     |                                         | /var/lib/nfs          | /bin/false        |      |
| 108   | 114   | 108        | 114        | puppet    | Puppet configuration management daemon,,,| /var/lib/puppet      | /bin/false        |      |
| 1001  | 1001  | 1001       | 1001       | ubuntu    | Ubuntu                                  | /home/ubuntu          | /bin/bash         |      |
| 109   | 116   | 109        | 116        | mysql     | MySQL Server,,,                         | /nonexistent          | /bin/false        |      |
+-------+-------+------------+------------+-----------+-----------------------------------------+-----------------------+-------------------+------+
```

osquery getting a list of users with groups and other information using a SQL query

The following playbook is to set up and configure the osquery agent in your Linux servers to monitor and look for vulnerabilities, file integrity monitoring, and many other compliance activities, and then log them for sending to a centralized logging monitoring system:

```
- name: setting up osquery
  hosts: linuxservers
  become: yes

  tasks:
    - name: installing osquery
      apt:
        deb: https://pkg.osquery.io/deb/osquery_2.10.2_1.linux.amd64.deb
        update_cache: yes
    - name: adding osquery configuration
      template:
        src: "{{ item.src }}"
        dest: "{{ item.dst }}"
      with_items:
        - { src: fim.conf, dst: /usr/share/osquery/packs/fim.conf }
        - { src: osquery.conf, dst: /etc/osquery/osquery.conf }
    - name: starting and enabling osquery service
```

```
service:
  name: osqueryd
  state: started
  enabled: yes
```

The following `fim.conf` code snippet is the pack for file integrity monitoring and it monitors for file events in the `/home`, `/etc`, and `/tmp` directories every 300 seconds. It uses **Secure Hash Algorithm (SHA)** checksum to validate the changes. This can be used to find out whether attackers add their own SSH keys or audit log changes against system configuration changes for compliance and other activities:

```
{
  "queries": {
    "file_events": {
      "query": "select * from file_events;",
      "removed": false,
      "interval": 300
    }
  },
  "file_paths": {
    "homes": [
      "/root/.ssh/%%",
      "/home/%/.ssh/%%"
    ],
      "etc": [
      "/etc/%%"
    ],
      "home": [
      "/home/%%"
    ],
      "tmp": [
      "/tmp/%%"
    ]
  }
}
```

The following configuration is used by the `osquery` daemon to perform checks and monitoring based on specified options, packs, and custom queries. We are also using different packs (that contain multiple queries) to look for different monitoring and configuration checks.

 `osquery`, by default, has multiple packs for incident response, vulnerability management, compliance, rootkit, hardware monitoring, and so on. Read more at `https://osquery.io/schema/packs`.

The following code snippet is the `osquery` service configuration. This can be modified as required to monitor and log by `osquery` service:

```json
{
  "options": {
    "config_plugin": "filesystem",
    "logger_plugin": "filesystem",
    "logger_path": "/var/log/osquery",
    "disable_logging": "false",
    "log_result_events": "true",
    "schedule_splay_percent": "10",
    "pidfile": "/var/osquery/osquery.pidfile",
    "events_expiry": "3600",
    "database_path": "/var/osquery/osquery.db",
    "verbose": "false",
    "worker_threads": "2",
    "enable_monitor": "true",
    "disable_events": "false",
    "disable_audit": "false",
    "audit_allow_config": "true",
    "host_identifier": "hostname",
    "enable_syslog": "true",
    "audit_allow_sockets": "true",
    "schedule_default_interval": "3600"
  },
  "schedule": {
    "crontab": {
      "query": "SELECT * FROM crontab;",
      "interval": 300
    },
    "system_profile": {
      "query": "SELECT * FROM osquery_schedule;"
    },
    "system_info": {
      "query": "SELECT hostname, cpu_brand, physical_memory FROM
system_info;",
      "interval": 3600
    }
  },
  "decorators": {
    "load": [
      "SELECT uuid AS host_uuid FROM system_info;",
      "SELECT user AS username FROM logged_in_users ORDER BY time DESC
LIMIT 1;"
    ]
  },
  "packs": {
```

```
        "fim": "/usr/share/osquery/packs/fim.conf",
        "osquery-monitoring": "/usr/share/osquery/packs/osquery-
monitoring.conf",
        "incident-response": "/usr/share/osquery/packs/incident-
response.conf",
        "it-compliance": "/usr/share/osquery/packs/it-compliance.conf",
        "vuln-management": "/usr/share/osquery/packs/vuln-management.conf"
    }
}
```

 The reference tutorial can be followed at `https://www.digitalocean.com/community/tutorials/how-to-monitor-your-system-security-with-osquery-on-ubuntu-16-04`.

The playbook can be executed to set up the `osquery` configuration in Linux servers to set up and log the events generated by the `osquery` agent:

```
$ ansible-playbook -i inventory main.yml

PLAY [setting up osquery] ***********************************************************

TASK [Gathering Facts] *************************************************************
ok: [192.168.33.60]

TASK [installing osquery] **********************************************************
changed: [192.168.33.60]

TASK [adding osquery configuration] ************************************************
changed: [192.168.33.60] => (item={u'src': u'fim.conf', u'dst': u'/usr/share/osquery/packs/fim.conf'})
changed: [192.168.33.60] => (item={u'src': u'osquery.conf', u'dst': u'/etc/osquery/osquery.conf'})

TASK [starting and enabling osquery service] ***************************************
changed: [192.168.33.60]

PLAY RECAP *************************************************************************
192.168.33.60              : ok=4    changed=3    unreachable=0    failed=0

$
```

osquery setup playbook in action

The goal is not just setting up `osquery`, we can use the logs to build a centralized real-time monitoring system using our Elastic stack. We can use the Filebeat agent to forward these logs to our Elastic stack and we can view them and build a centralized dashboard for alerting and monitoring.

The following is an example of the logs generated by `osquery`, we can see that the `authorized_keys` file is getting modified by the Ubuntu user at **November 22nd 2017,23:59:21.000**:

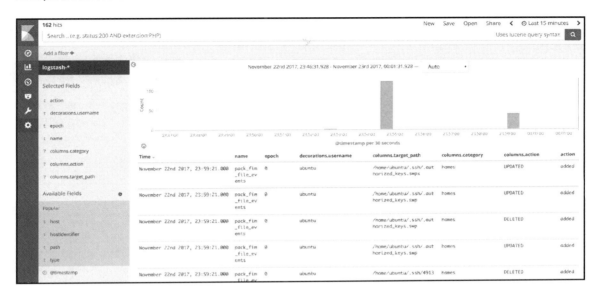

This idea can be extended for building some automated defences by taking actions against attacks by using automated Ansible playbooks for known actions.

The world is moving toward containers and this kind of monitoring gives us a look at low-level things such as kernel security checks, and file integrity checks on host level. When attackers try to bypass containers and get access to hosts to escalate privileges, we can detect and defend them using this kind of setup.

Summary

Containers are rapidly changing the world of developers and operations teams. The rate of change is accelerating, and in this new world, security automation gets to play a front and center role. By leveraging our knowledge of using Ansible for scripting play-by-play commands along with excellent tools such as Archore and `osquery`, we can measure, analyze, and benchmark our containers for security. This allows us to build end-to-end automatic processes of securing, scanning and remediating containers.

In the next chapter, we will look at a specialized use case for security automation. We will look at how can we improve the tasks around malware analysis by automating certain parts of it. We will especially focus on lightweight dynamic analysis workflow integrating Cuckoo sandbox, one of the most popular malware analysis tools out there.

9
Automating Lab Setups for Forensics Collection and Malware Analysis

Malware is one of the biggest challenges faced by the security community. It impacts everyone who gets to interact with information systems. While there is a massive effort required in keeping computers safe from malware for operational systems, a big chunk of work in malware defenses is about understanding where they come from and what they are capable of.

This is the part where Ansible can be used for automation and enabling experts who do malware analysis. In this chapter, we will look at various workflows which are all for classification, analysis of malware using tools like Cuckoo Sandbox, and more. Also, we will be looking into creating Ansible playbooks for labs for isolated environments and for collection and storage with secure backup of forensic artifacts.

Creating Ansible playbooks for labs for isolated environments

We will start by using VirusTotal and move on to Cuckoo with a Windows virtual machine in an isolated network. Another important aspect of malware analysis is the ability to collaborate and share threats using the **Malware Information Sharing Platform (MISP)**. We also setup Viper (binary management and analysis framework) to perform the analysis.

Collecting file and domain malware identification and classification

One of the initial phases of malware analysis is identification and classification. The most popular source is using VirusTotal to scan and get the results of the malware samples, domain information, and so on. It has a very rich API and a lot of people have written custom apps that leverage the API to perform the automated scans using the API key for identifying the malware type. The following example is to set up the VirusTotal tool in the system, scan the malware samples against the VirusTotal API, and identify whether or not it's really malware. It generally checks using more than 60 antivirus scanners and tools and provides detailed information.

VirusTotal API tool set up

The following playbook will set up the VirusTotal API tool (`https://github.com/doomedraven/VirusTotalApi`), which is officially supported in the VirusTotal page itself:

```
- name: setting up VirusTotal
  hosts: malware
  remote_user: ubuntu
  become: yes
  tasks:
    - name: installing pip
      apt:
        name: "{{ item }}"
      with_items:
        - python-pip
        - unzip
    - name: checking if vt already exists
      stat:
        path: /usr/local/bin/vt
      register: vt_status

    - name: downloading VirusTotal api tool repo
      unarchive:
        src:
"https://github.com/doomedraven/VirusTotalApi/archive/master.zip"
        dest: /tmp/
        remote_src: yes
      when: vt_status.stat.exists == False

    - name: installing the dependencies
      pip:
        requirements: /tmp/VirusTotalApi-master/requirements.txt
```

```
        when: vt_status.stat.exists == False
    -  name: installing vt
        command: python /tmp/VirusTotalApi-master/setup.py install
        when: vt_status.stat.exists == False
```

The playbook execution will download the repository and set up the VirusTotal API tool and this will get us ready for scanning the malware samples:

```
$ ansible-playbook -i inventory main.yml

PLAY [setting up VirusTotal] ***************************************************>

TASK [Gathering Facts] ********************************************************>
ok: [192.168.33.21]

TASK [installing pip] *********************************************************>
ok: [192.168.33.21] => (item=[u'python-pip', u'unzip'])

TASK [checking if vt already exists] ******************************************>
ok: [192.168.33.21]

TASK [downloading VirusTotal api tool repo] ***********************************>
changed: [192.168.33.21]

TASK [installing the dependencies] ********************************************>
changed: [192.168.33.21]

TASK [installing vt] **********************************************************>
changed: [192.168.33.21]

PLAY RECAP ********************************************************************>
192.168.33.21              : ok=6    changed=3    unreachable=0    failed=0
```

VirusTotal API scan for malware samples

Once we have the setup ready, it is as simple as using the Ansible playbook to run a scan for the list of malware samples. The following playbook will find and copy the local malware samples to a remote system and scan them recursively and return the results. Once the scan has been completed, it will remove the samples from the remote system:

```
-  name: scanning file in VirusTotal
   hosts: malware
   remote_user: ubuntu
   vars:
     vt_api_key: XXXXXXXXXXXXXXXXXXXXXXXXXXXXXXXXX #use Ansible-vault
     vt_api_type: public # public/private
     vt_intelligence_access: False # True/False
```

```
      files_in_local_system: /tmp/samples/
      files_in_remote_system: /tmp/sample-file/

  tasks:
    - name: creating samples directory
      file:
        path: "{{ files_in_remote_system }}"
        state: directory

    - name: copying file to remote system
      copy:
        src: "{{ files_in_local_system }}"
        dest: "{{ files_in_remote_system }}"
        directory_mode: yes
    - name: copying configuration
      template:
        src: config.j2
        dest: "{{ files_in_remote_system }}/.vtapi"

    - name: running VirusTotal scan
      command: "vt -fr {{ files_in_remote_system }}"
      args:
        chdir: "{{ files_in_remote_system }}"
      register: vt_scan
    - name: removing the samples
      file:
        path: "{{ files_in_remote_system }}"
        state: absent

    - name: VirusTotal scan results
      debug:
        msg: "{{ vt_scan.stdout_lines }}"
```

The results of the malware sample scan using the VirusTotal API looks like this. It returns the hashes and pointers to the VirusTotal API scan report for detailed results:

```
TASK [virus total scan results] *********************************************************************************************
ok: [192.168.33.21] => {
    "msg": [
        "",
        "Calculating hash for: /tmp/sample-file/random",
        "",
        "Scanned on : ",
        "\t2017-11-29 17:57:33",
        "",
        "Detections:",
        "\t 0/59 Positives/Total",
        "",
        "\tResults for MD5    : 04a9a0cadce634da6e3e83dd324c264c",
        "\tResults for SHA1   : aa3b2783e55cfd9d2eb687d607d7b8afd3fa83d3",
        "\tResults for SHA256 : cc1d5297f2904dec59294cc1bb34915a44fc7d17c00267e24040cc71bca6e67a",
        "",
        "\tPermanent Link : https://www.virustotal.com/file/cc1d5297f2904dec59294cc1bb34915a44fc7d17c00267e24040cc71bca6e67a/analysis/1511978253/",
        "",
        "Calculating hash for: /tmp/sample-file/rootkit.ex1",
        "",
        "Scanned on : ",
        "\t2017-11-29 16:48:46",
        "",
        "Detections:",
        "\t 60/68 Positives/Total",
        "",
        "\tResults for MD5    : 9219e2cfcc64ccde2d8de507538b9991",
        "\tResults for SHA1   : 181a59680d657dc6b31a3b19d7f4f75381a3425e",
        "\tResults for SHA256 : 5af3fd53aea5e008d8725c720ea0290e2e0cd485d8a953053ccf02e5e81a94a0",
        "",
        "\tPermanent Link : https://www.virustotal.com/file/5af3fd53aea5e008d8725c720ea0290e2e0cd485d8a953053ccf02e5e81a94a0/analysis/1511974126/"
    ]
}
```

Setting up the Cuckoo Sandbox environment

Cuckoo Sandbox is one of the most popular open source automated malware analysis systems. It has a lot of integrations to perform the malware analysis of suspicious files. Its setup requirements include dependencies, and other software such as VirtualBox, yara, ssdeep, and volatility. Also, the VM analysis is Windows and it requires some prerequisites to perform the analysis.

Read more about Cuckoo Sandbox at `https://cuckoosandbox.org`.

Setting up the Cuckoo host

The following Ansible Playbook will set up the host operating system and dependencies required for Cuckoo Sandbox to work. This has different roles to install all the required packages in the Ubuntu operating system.

The following roles are included to set up the host system:

```
- name: setting up cuckoo
  hosts: cuckoo
  remote_user: ubuntu
  become: yes

  roles:
    - dependencies
```

```
            - virtualbox
            - yara
            - cuckoo
            - start-cukcoo
```

The dependencies role has lot of `apt` packages that have to be installed to perform other installations. Then we will set up capabilities for the `tcpdump` package, so Cuckoo can access them for analysis:

```
  - name: installing pre requirements
    apt:
      name: "{{ item }}"
      state: present
      update_cache: yes
    with_items:
      - python
      - python-pip
      - python-dev
      - libffi-dev
      - libssl-dev
      - python-virtualenv
      - python-setuptools
      - libjpeg-dev
      - zlib1g-dev
      - swig
      - tcpdump
      - apparmor-utils
      - mongodb
      - unzip
      - git
      - volatility
      - autoconf
      - libtool
      - libjansson-dev
      - libmagic-dev
      - postgresql
      - volatility
      - volatility-tools
      - automake
      - make
      - gcc
      - flex
      - bison

  - name: setting capabilitites to tcpdump
    capabilities:
      path: /usr/sbin/tcpdump
```

```
      capability: "{{ item }}+eip"
      state: present
    with_items:
      - cap_net_raw
      - cap_net_admin
```

Then we will install the VirtualBox, so the VM analysis can be installed in VirtualBox. Cuckoo uses the VirtualBox API to interact with VM analysis to perform operations:

```
- name: adding virtualbox apt source
  apt_repository:
    repo: "deb http://download.virtualbox.org/virtualbox/debian xenial
contrib"
    filename: 'virtualbox'
    state: present

- name: adding virtualbox apt key
  apt_key:
    url: "https://www.virtualbox.org/download/oracle_vbox_2016.asc"
    state: present

- name: install virtualbox
  apt:
    name: virtualbox-5.1
    state: present
    update_cache: yes
```

After that, we will install some additional packages and tools for Cuckoo to use in the analysis:

```
- name: copying the setup scripts
  template:
    src: "{{ item.src }}"
    dest: "{{ item.dest }}"
    mode: 0755
  with_items:
    - { src: "yara.sh", dest: "/tmp/yara.sh" }
    - { src: "ssdeep.sh", dest: "/tmp/ssdeep.sh" }

- name: downloading ssdeep and yara releases
  unarchive:
    src: "{{ item }}"
    dest: /tmp/
    remote_src: yes

  with_items:
    - https://github.com/plusvic/yara/archive/v3.4.0.tar.gz
    -
```

```
https://github.com/ssdeep-project/ssdeep/releases/download/release-2.14.1/s
sdeep-2.14.1.tar.gz

- name: installing yara and ssdeep
  shell: "{{ item }}"
  ignore_errors: yes

  with_items:
    - /tmp/yara.sh
    - /tmp/ssdeep.sh

- name: installing M2Crypto
  pip:
    name: m2crypto
    version: 0.24.0
```

The custom scripts have the build scripts to install the yara and ssdeep packages:

```
# yara script
#!/bin/bash

cd /tmp/yara-3.4.0
./bootstrap
./configure --with-crypto --enable-cuckoo --enable-magic
make
make install
cd yara-python
python setup.py build
python setup.py install


# ssdeep script
#!/bin/bash

cd /tmp/ssdeep-2.14.1
./configure
./bootstrap
make
make install
```

Finally, we will install the Cuckoo and other required settings, such as creating users, to the vboxusers group. The configuration files are taken from templates, so these will be modified based on the VM analysis environment:

```
  - name: adding cuckoo to vboxusers
    group:
      name: cuckoo
```

```
        state: present

- name: creating new user and add to groups
  user:
    name: cuckoo
    shell: /bin/bash
    groups: vboxusers, cuckoo
    state: present
    append: yes

- name: upgrading pip, setuptools and cuckoo
  pip:
    name: "{{ item }}"
    state: latest
  with_items:
    - pip
    - setuptools
    - pydeep
    - cuckoo
    - openpyxl
    - ujson
    - pycrypto
    - distorm3
    - pytz
    - weasyprint

- name: creating cuckoo home direcotry
  command: "cuckoo"
  ignore_errors: yes

- name: adding cuckoo as owner
  file:
    path: "/root/.cuckoo"
    owner: cuckoo
    group: cuckoo
    recurse: yes
```

The following playbook will copy the configurations and start the Cuckoo and web server to perform the Cuckoo analysis:

```
- name: copying the configurationss
  template:
    src: "{{ item.src }}"
    dest: /root/.cuckoo/conf/{{ item.dest }}
  with_items:
    - { src: "cuckoo.conf", dest: "cuckoo.conf"}
    - { src: "auxiliary.conf", dest: "auxiliary.conf"}
    - { src: "virtualbox.conf", dest: "virtualbox.conf"}
```

```
        - { src: "reporting.conf", dest: "reporting.conf"}

    - name: starting cuckoo server
      command: cuckoo -d
      ignore_errors: yes

    - name: starting cuckoo webserver
      command: "cuckoo web runserver 0.0.0.0:8000"
        args:
          chdir: "/root/.cuckoo/web"
      ignore_errors: yes
```

Setting up Cuckoo guest

Most of the settings will need to be performed in the Windows operating system. The following guide will help you set up the Windows Guest VM for Cuckoo analysis. Refer to https://cuckoo.sh/docs/installation/guest/index.html.

The following screenshots are the reference that the first adapter is the **Host-only Adapter**:

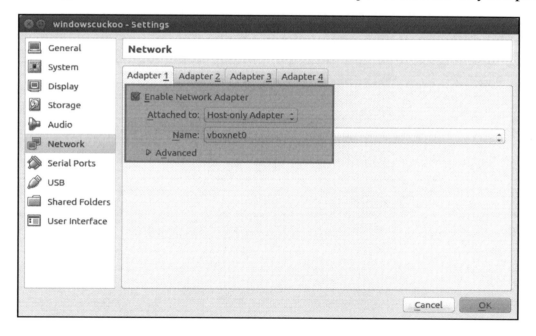

And the second adapter is the **NAT**:

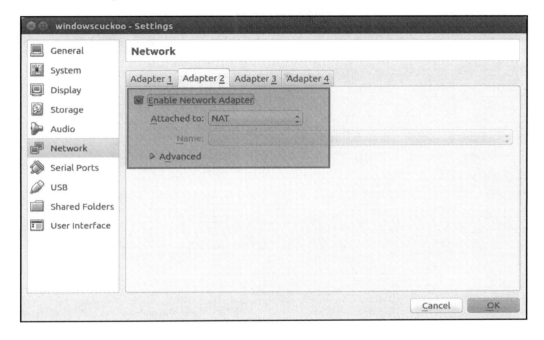

Once the Windows VM starts, we need to install the VirtualBox guest addition tools. This allows Cuckoo to perform analysis using a command-line utility called VBoxManage:

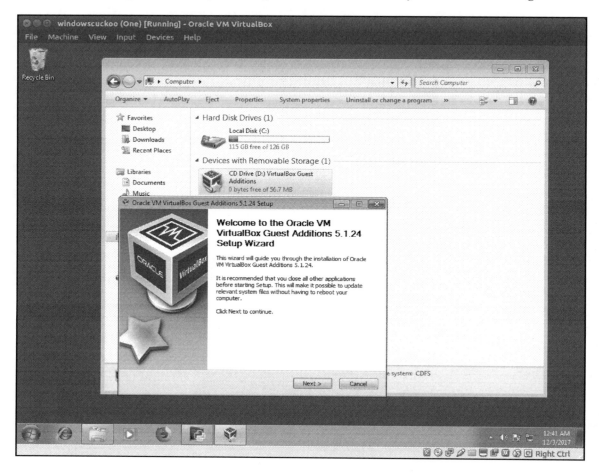

Next, we have to install Python locally to start the Cuckoo agent locally, we can install Python from the official Python website: https://www.python.org/downloads/release/python-2714.

Now download the agent from the Cuckoo host, it will be available in the Cuckoo working directory in the `agent` folder. We need to keep this in the Windows VM for the Cuckoo server to interact with:

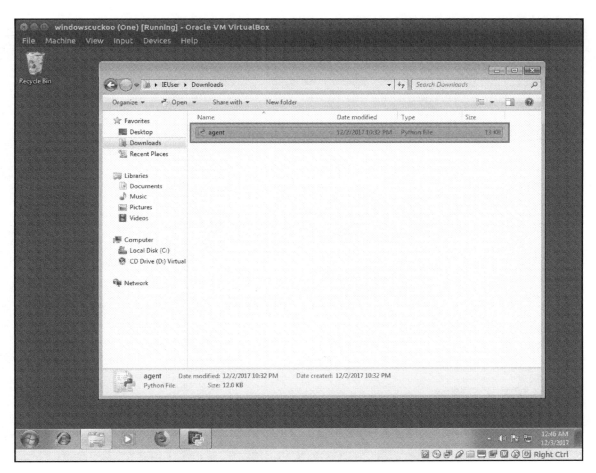

Then, we have to add the Python file path to the system startups using the `regedit` command. This can be done by navigating to
`HKEY_LOCAL_MACHINE\SOFTWARE\Microsoft\Windows\Current\Version\Run`. Then, add the new string in the registry editor right side, with name Cuckoo and give the full path for the `agent.py` file in the value section:

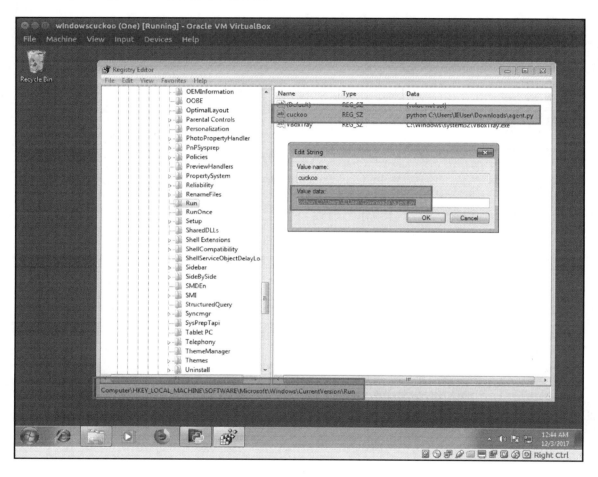

Now, we can take a snapshot and update the configurations in the Cuckoo host. Once this is done, we are ready to start the Cuckoo server and web server.

The following screenshot is the home page of the Cuckoo web server. Once we submit the malware sample, then we can click on analyze to start:

Then, it will take some time to perform the analysis with the VirtualBox Windows VM. This will perform the analysis based on the option you selected:

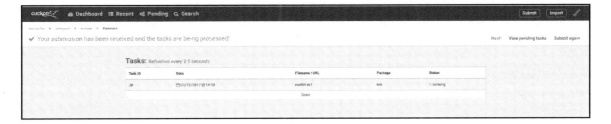

Then, it will give complete detailed information about the sample. It includes submitted file checksum, runtime execution screenshot while Cuckoo performing analysis and other information:

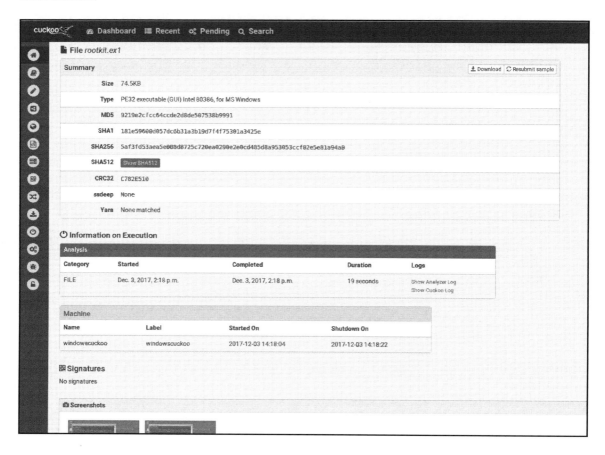

The following screenshot is the behavioral analysis of the malware sample, which includes a detailed analysis of the process tree. The left-side menu contains different options such as dropped files, memory dump analysis, and packet analysis:

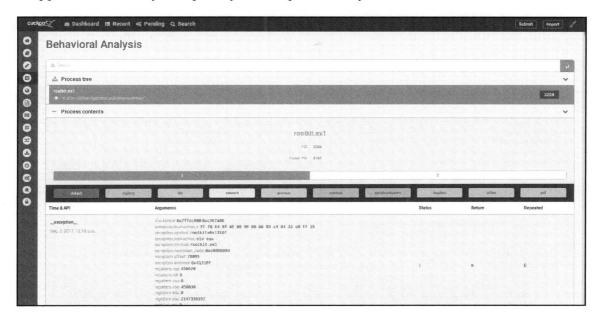

Learn more about Cuckoo usage in the Cuckoo documentation at `http://docs.cuckoosandbox.org/en/latest/usage`.

Submitting samples and reporting using Ansible playbook

The following playbook will perform the analysis of the given malware sample files in a local system path and return the reports to using Ansible playbook:

```
- name: Cuckoo malware sample analysis
  hosts: cuckoo
  vars:
    local_binaries_path: /tmp/binaries

  tasks:
    - name: copying malware sample to cuckoo for analysis
      copy:
        src: "{{ local_binaries_path }}"
        dest: "/tmp/binaries/{{ Ansible_hostname }}"
    - name: submitting the files to cuckoo for analysis
      command: "cuckoo submit /tmp/binaries/{{ Ansible_hostname }}"
      ignore_errors: yes
```

The following screenshot copies the malware samples to a Cuckoo analysis system and submits these files for automated analysis using Ansible playbook:

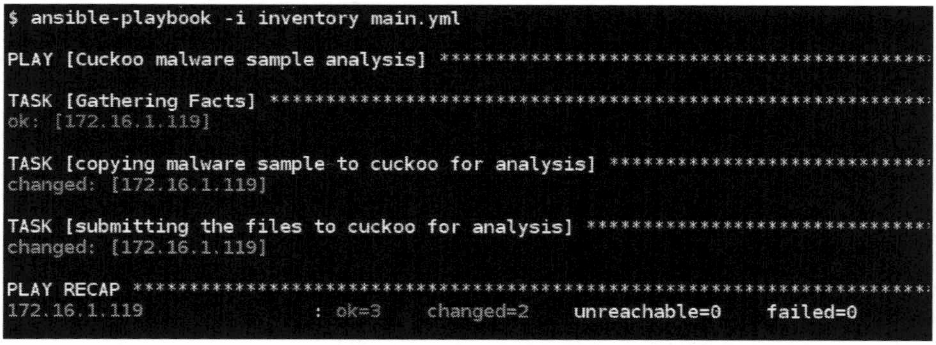

The preceding screenshot copies the local binaries into the remote Cuckoo host and submits them for analysis using the Cuckoo submit feature:

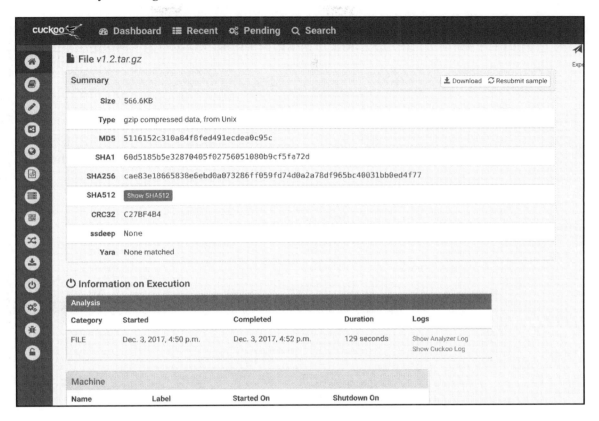

The preceding screenshot is the report of analysis submitted by our Cuckoo scan submission using Ansible Playbook.

Setting up Cuckoo using Docker containers

This will allows us to simplify the Cuckoo setup using Docker containers. The following commands will allow us to set up the Cuckoo Sandbox using Docker containers:

```
$ git clone https://github.com/blacktop/docker-cuckoo
$ cd docker-cuckoo
$ docker-compose up -d
```

It takes a while to download the Docker containers and configure them to work together. Once the installation is complete, we can access Cuckoo using `http://localhost:`

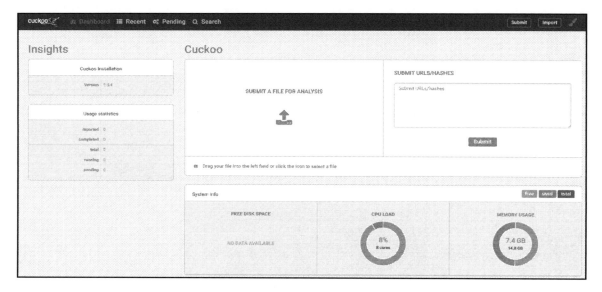

Now, we can submit the malware samples or suspicious files to Cuckoo to perform an analysis using the tool set and it will return with a detailed analysis. We can also choose what analysis to perform by selecting the configuration options before submitting the sample.

Setting up MISP and Threat Sharing

Malware Information Sharing Platform (MISP) is an open source threat-sharing platform (http://www.misp-project.org). It allows us to exchange **Indicators of Compromise (IOCs)** about **Advanced Persistent Threat (APT)** and targeted attacks within the known community and organizations. By doing this, we can gain more knowledge about different attacks and threats and it's easy for organizations to defend against such attacks.

The simplest way to get started with this platform is to use their customized VM by the **Computer Incident Response Center Luxembourg (CIRCL)**, which includes the latest release of the complete setup. This VM is customized to work in different environments.

 The VM and training materials can be found at https://www.circl.lu/services/misp-training-materials.

Setting up MISP using Ansible playbook

We can also set up using the Ansible playbooks. Based on our customized use, there are multiple playbooks available in the community:

- https://github.com/juju4/Ansible-MISP
- https://github.com/StamusNetworks/Ansible-misp

Setting up MISP using existing Ansible playbooks is as simple as cloning the repository and updating the variables for required changes and configurations. Make sure to update the variables before executing the playbook:

```
$ git clone https://github.com/StamusNetworks/Ansible-misp.git
$ cd Ansible-misp
$ Ansible-playbook -i hosts misp.yaml
```

MISP web user interface

The following is the MISP virtual machine web interface. Here are the default credentials for the MISP VM:

```
For the MISP web interface -> admin@admin.test:admin
For the system -> misp:Password1234
```

The following screenshot is the home page of **Malware Information Sharing Platform (MISP)** with login panel:

The following screenshot is the home screen for the MISP platform web interface, it contains options to share the IOCs, add organisations, and perform access control, among other features:

Read more about MISP using their documentation to learn different features available in MISP at `https://www.circl.lu/doc/misp/`.

Setting up Viper - binary management and analysis framework

Viper (`http://viper.li`) is a framework dedicated to malware and exploit researchers. It provides a simple solution to easily organize collections of malware and exploit samples. It provides both a CLI and web interface for researchers to perform analysis on binary files and malware samples.

The following playbook will set up the entire Viper framework. It has two roles, one is to set up the dependencies required to run the Viper framework, and the other is the main setup:

```
- name: Setting up Viper - binary management and analysis framework
  hosts: viper
  remote_user: ubuntu
  become: yes

  roles:
    - dependencies
    - setup
```

The following snippet is to set up the dependencies and other required packages:

```
- name: installing required packages
  apt:
    name: "{{ item }}"
    state: present
    update_cache: yes
  with_items:
    - gcc
    - python-dev
    - python-pip
    - libssl-dev
    - swig

- name: downloading ssdeep release
  unarchive:
    src:
https://github.com/ssdeep-project/ssdeep/releases/download/release-2.14.1/s
sdeep-2.14.1.tar.gz
```

```
      dest: /tmp/
      remote_src: yes

  - name: copy ssdeep setup script
    template:
      src: ssdeep.sh
      dest: /tmp/ssdeep.sh
      mode: 0755

  - name: installing ssdeep
    shell: /tmp/ssdeep.sh
    ignore_errors: yes

  - name: installing core dependencies
    pip:
      name: "{{ item }}"
      state: present
    with_items:
      - SQLAlchemy
      - PrettyTable
      - python-magic
      - pydeep
```

Here, we are using a custom shell script for setting up `ssdeep`, which has to perform compilation and build:

```
#!/bin/bash

cd /tmp/ssdeep-2.14.1
./configure
./bootstrap
make
make install
```

The set up role will install the Viper packages, required dependencies, and it will start the web server to access the Viper web user interface:

```
  - name: downloading the release
    unarchive:
      src: https://github.com/viper-framework/viper/archive/v1.2.tar.gz
      dest: /opt/
      remote_src: yes

  - name: installing pip dependencies
    pip:
      requirements: /opt/viper-1.2/requirements.txt
```

```
- name: starting viper webinterface
  shell: nohup /usr/bin/python /opt/viper-1.2/web.py -H 0.0.0.0 &
  ignore_errors: yes

- debug:
    msg: "Viper web interface is running at http://{{ inventory_hostname
}}:9090"
```

The following screenshot refers to the playbook execution of the Viper framework setup. and it returns the web interface URL to access:

```
$ ansible-playbook -i inventory main.yml

PLAY [Setting up Viper - binary management and analysis framework] *********************************

TASK [Gathering Facts] ****************************************************************************
ok: [192.168.33.22]

TASK [dependencies : installing required packages] **********************************************
changed: [192.168.33.22] => (item=[u'gcc', u'python-dev', u'python-pip', u'libssl-dev', u'swig'])

TASK [dependencies : downloading ssdeep release] **********************************************
changed: [192.168.33.22]

TASK [dependencies : copy ssdeep setup script] **********************************************
changed: [192.168.33.22]

TASK [dependencies : installing ssdeep] *****************************************************
changed: [192.168.33.22]

TASK [dependencies : installing core dependencies] ********************************************
changed: [192.168.33.22] => (item=SQLAlchemy)
changed: [192.168.33.22] => (item=PrettyTable)
changed: [192.168.33.22] => (item=python-magic)
changed: [192.168.33.22] => (item=pydeep)

TASK [setup : downloading the release] *****************************************************
changed: [192.168.33.22]

TASK [setup : installing pip dependencies] *************************************************
changed: [192.168.33.22]

TASK [setup : starting viper webinterface] ************************************************
changed: [192.168.33.22]

TASK [setup : debug] ****************************************************************************
ok: [192.168.33.22] => {
    "msg": "Viper web interface is running at http://192.168.33.22:9090"
}

PLAY RECAP ***********************************************************************************
192.168.33.22              : ok=10    changed=8    unreachable=0    failed=0
```

If we navigate to `http://192.18.33.22:9090`, we can see the web interface with a lot of options to use this framework:

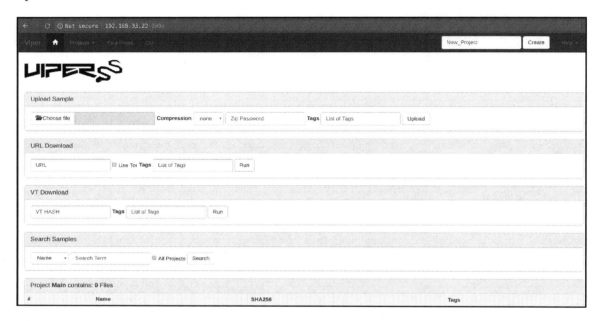

The following screenshot is the output of the sample malware we analyzed. This Viper framework also has module support with YARA ruleset, VirusTotal API, and other modules to perform a deep analysis based on the use case:

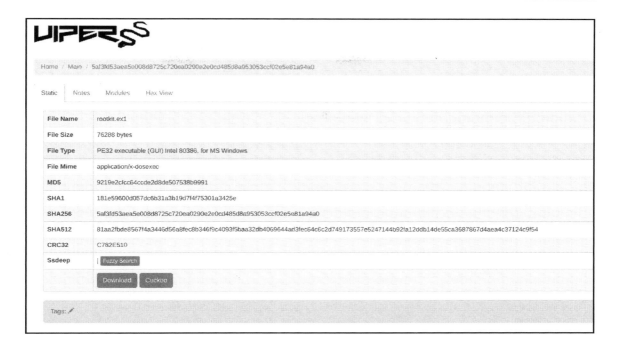

Creating Ansible playbooks for collection and storage with secure backup of forensic artifacts

Ansible is an apt replacement for all kinds of bash scripts. Typically, for most activities that require analysis, we follow a set pattern:

1. Collect logs from running processes into files with a path we already know
2. Copy the content from these log files periodically to a secure storage locally or accessible remotely over SSH or a network file share
3. Once copied successfully, rotate the logs

Since there is a bit of network activity involved, our bash scripts are usually written to be fault tolerant with regard to network connections and become complex very soon. Ansible playbooks can be used to do all of that while being simple to read for everyone.

Collecting log artifacts for incident response

The key phase in incident response is **log analysis**. The following playbook will collect the logs from all the hosts and store it locally. This allows responders to perform the further analysis:

```
# Reference https://www.Ansible.com/security-automation-with-Ansible

- name: Gather log files
  hosts: servers
  become: yes

  tasks:
    - name: List files to grab
      find:
        paths:
          - /var/log
        patterns:
          - '*.log*'
        recurse: yes
      register: log_files

    - name: Grab files
      fetch:
        src: "{{ item.path }}"
        dest: "/tmp/LOGS_{{ Ansible_fqdn }}/"
      with_items: "{{ log_files.files }}"
```

The following playbook execution will collect a list of logs in specified locations in remote hosts using Ansible modules and store them in the local system. The output of the logs from the playbook looks like this:

```
$ tree /tmp/LOGS_*
/tmp/LOGS_blue-server
└── 192.168.100.10
    └── var
        └── log
            ├── apt
            │   ├── history.log
            │   └── term.log
            ├── auth.log
            ├── cloud-init.log
            ├── cloud-init-output.log
            ├── dpkg.log
            ├── kern.log
            └── nginx
                ├── access.log
                └── error.log
/tmp/LOGS_green-server
└── 192.168.100.20
    └── var
        └── log
            ├── apt
            │   ├── history.log
            │   └── term.log
            ├── auth.log
            ├── cloud-init.log
            ├── cloud-init-output.log
            ├── dpkg.log
            ├── kern.log
            └── nginx
                ├── access.log
                └── error.log

10 directories, 18 files
```

Secure backups for data collection

When collecting multiple sets of data from servers, it's important to store them securely with encrypted backups. This can be achieved by backing up the data to storage services such as S3.

The following Ansible playbook allows us to install and copy the collected data to the AWS S3 service with encryption enabled:

```
- name: backing up the log data
  hosts: localhost
  gather_facts: false
  become: yes
  vars:
    s3_access_key: XXXXXXX # Use Ansible-vault to encrypt
    s3_access_secret: XXXXXXX # Use Ansible-vault to encrypt
```

```
      localfolder: /tmp/LOGS/ # Trailing slash is important
      remotebucket: secretforensicsdatausingAnsible # This should be unique
in s3

  tasks:
    - name: installing s3cmd if not installed
      apt:
        name: "{{ item }}"
        state: present
        update_cache: yes
      with_items:
        - python-magic
        - python-dateutil
        - s3cmd
    - name: create s3cmd config file
      template:
        src: s3cmd.j2
        dest: /root/.s3cfg
        owner: root
        group: root
        mode: 0640
    - name: make sure "{{ remotebucket }}" is avilable
      command: "s3cmd mb s3://{{ remotebucket }}/ -c /root/.s3cfg"

    - name: running the s3 backup to "{{ remotebucket }}"
      command: "s3cmd sync {{ localfolder }} --preserve s3://{{
remotebucket }}/ -c /root/.s3cfg"
```

The configuration file looks like the following for the s3cmd configuration:

```
[default]
access_key = {{ s3_access_key }}
secret_key = {{ s3_access_secret }}
host_base = s3.amazonaws.com
host_bucket = %(bucket)s.s3.amazonaws.com
website_endpoint = http://%(bucket)s.s3-website-%(location)s.amazonaws.com/
use_https = True
signature_v2 = True
```

The following screenshot is the Ansible playbook execution of uploading the data to S3 bucket:

```
$ ansible-playbook main.yml
 [WARNING]: Could not match supplied host pattern, ignoring: all

 [WARNING]: provided hosts list is empty, only localhost is available


PLAY [backing up the log data] ************************************************

TASK [installing s3cmd if not installed] ************************************
changed: [localhost] => (item=[u'python-magic', u'python-dateutil', u's3cmd'])

TASK [create s3cmd config file] *********************************************
changed: [localhost]

TASK [make sure "secretforensicsdatausingansible" is avilable] ***************
changed: [localhost]

TASK [running the s3 backup to "secretforensicsdatausingansible"] ***********
changed: [localhost]

PLAY RECAP *****************************************************************
localhost                  : ok=4    changed=4    unreachable=0    failed=0
```

The preceding screenshot shows the Ansible playbook installing s3cmd, creating the new bucket called secretforensicsdatausingAnsible, and copying the local log data to the remote S3 bucket.

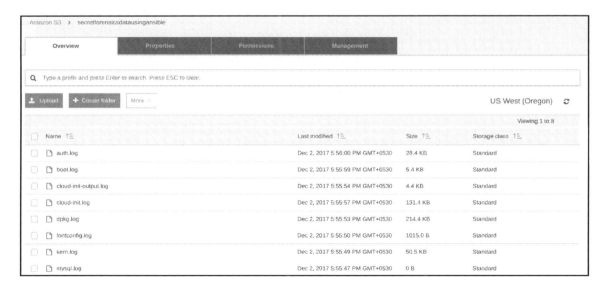

The preceding screenshot is the outcome of the playbook. We can see that the logs are successfully uploaded into the `secretforensicsdatausingAnsible` S3 bucket in AWS S3.

Summary

Being able to automate various workflows required for malware analysis allows us to scale the number of malware being analyzed and the resources required for doing such large-scale analysis. This is one way to address the deluge of malware that gets released every day on the internet and create useful defenses against them.

In the next chapter, we move on to creating an Ansible module for security testing. We will take baby steps at creating the module right from understanding the basics to utilizing and consuming the API of OWASP ZAP for scanning websites. By the end of the chapter, you will have a complete module that can be used with the Ansible CLI or Ansible playbook.

10

Writing an Ansible Module for Security Testing

Ansible primarily works by pushing small bits of code to the nodes it connects to. These codes/programs are what we know as Ansible modules. Typically in the case of a Linux host these are copied over SSH, executed, and then removed from the node.

As stated in the Ansible Developer Guide (the best resource for all things Ansible-related):

> *"Ansible modules can be written in any language that can return JSON."*

Modules can be used by the Ansible command-line, in a playbook, or by the Ansible API. There are already hundreds of modules that ship with Ansible version 2.4.x.

 Have a look at the module index on the Ansible documentation site: `http://docs.ansible.com/ansible/latest/modules_by_category.html`.

Currently, there are over 20 categories of modules with categories such as cloud, storage, Remote Management, and Windows.

Sometimes in spite of all the modules out there, you may need to write your own. This chapter will take you through writing a module that you can use with your Ansible playbooks.

Ansible has an extremely detailed development guide (`http://docs.ansible.com/ansible/latest/dev_guide/index.html`) that is the best place to start if you are planning to contribute your modules to be shipped with Ansible.

This chapter is not at all meant to replace that. Consider that if you plan to write modules for your internal use and you are not fussed about distributing them, this chapter offers you a simple-to-follow path where we will end up with a working module for enabling security automation, which has been our goal throughout.

We will look at the following:

- How to set up the development environment
- Writing an Ansible hello world module to understand the basics
- Where to seek further help
- Defining a security problem statement
- Addressing that problem by writing a module of our own

Along with that, we will try to understand and attempt to answer the following questions:

- What are the good use cases for modules?
- When does it make sense to use roles?
- How do modules differ from plugins?

Let's get started with a simple hello world module.

Getting started with a hello world Ansible module

We will pass one argument to our custom module and show if we have success or failure for the module executing based on that.

Since all of this is new to us, we will look at the following things:

- The source code of the hello world module
- The output of that module for both success and failure
- The command that we will use to invoke it

Before we get started, all of this is based on the Ansible Developer Guide! The following code is in Python.

Code

We use Python for many scripting tasks, but we are not experts in it. But we believe this code is simple enough to understand:

```python
from ansible.module_utils.basic import AnsibleModule

module = AnsibleModule(
    argument_spec=dict(
        answer=dict(choices=['yes', 'no'], default='yes'),
    )
)

answer = module.params['answer']
if answer == 'no':
    module.fail_json(changed=True, msg='Failure! We failed because we answered no.')

module.exit_json(changed=True, msg='Success! We passed because we answered yes.')
```

1. We are importing some modules.
2. The second part is just how we need to declare the arguments we will accept for the module.
3. In our code, we can refer to the arguments the way we have taken the value of the `answer` variable.
4. Based on the answer, if it is `no`, we indicate failure.
5. If the answer is `yes`, we indicate success.

Let's see what the output of this looks like if we provide answer as `yes`:

```
$ ANSIBLE_LIBRARY=. ansible -m ansible_module_hello_world.py -a answer=yes
localhost

 [WARNING]: provided hosts list is empty, only localhost is available

localhost | SUCCESS => {
    "changed": true,
    "msg": "Success! We passed because we answered yes."
}
```

And if the answer is no:

```
$ ANSIBLE_LIBRARY=. ansible -m ansible_module_hello_world -a answer=no
localhost

 [WARNING]: provided hosts list is empty, only localhost is available

localhost | FAILED! => {
    "changed": true,
    "failed": true,
    "msg": "Failure! We failed because we answered no."
}
```

The main difference in the output is the indication of either the SUCCESS or FAILED status and the message that we provided.

Since we haven't set up the development environment so far, we set an environment variable for this command:

- ANSIBLE_LIBRARY=. indicates that search the module to be executed in the current directory
- With -m, we call our module
- With -a, we pass the module argument, which in this case is answered with possible values of yes or no
- We end with the host that we want to run the module on, which is local for this example

> While Ansible is written in Python, please note that the modules can be written in any language capable of returning messages in JSON. A great starting point for Rubyists is the Ansible for Rubyists (https://github.com/ansible/ansible-for-rubyists) repository on Github. Chapter 5 of *Learning Ansible* by Packt has covered this as well.

Setting up the development environment

The primary requirement for Ansible 2.4 is Python 2.6 or higher and Python 3.5 or higher. If you have either of them installed, we can follow the simple steps to get the development environment going.

From the Ansible Developer Guide:

1. **Clone the Ansible repository:** `$ git clone https://github.com/ansible/ansible.git`
2. **Change the directory into the repository root directory:** `$ cd ansible`
3. **Create a virtual environment:** `$ python3 -m venv venv (or for Python 2 $ virtualenv venv`
4. **Note, this requires you to install the** `virtualenv` **package:** `$ pip install virtualenv`
5. **Activate the virtual environment:** `$ . venv/bin/activate`
6. **Install the development requirements:** `$ pip install -r requirements.txt`
7. **Run the environment setup script for each new dev shell process:** `$ . hacking/env-setup`

You should end up with a `venv` prompt at this point. Here is a simple playbook to set up the development environment.

The following playbook will set up the developer environment by installing and setting up the virtual environment:

```
- name: Setting Developer Environment
  hosts: dev
  remote_user: madhu
  become: yes
  vars:
    ansible_code_path: "/home/madhu/ansible-code"

  tasks:
    - name: installing prerequirements if not installed
      apt:
        name: "{{ item }}"
        state: present
        update_cache: yes
      with_items:
        - git
        - virtualenv
        - python-pip
    - name: downloading ansible repo locally
      git:
        repo: https://github.com/ansible/ansible.git
        dest: "{{ ansible_code_path }}/venv"
    - name: creating virtual environment
      pip:
        virtualenv: "{{ ansible_code_path }}"
```

```
virtualenv_command: virtualenv
requirements: "{{ ansible_code_path }}/venv/requirements.txt"
```

The following screenshot shows the playbook execution of the developer environment setup for writing your own Ansible modules using the Python virtual environment:

```
PLAY [Setting Developer Environment] *******************************************

TASK [Gathering Facts] *********************************************************
ok: [172.16.1.119]

TASK [installing prerequirements if not installed] *****************************
ok: [172.16.1.119] => (item=[u'git', u'virtualenv', u'python-pip'])

TASK [downloading ansible repo locally] ****************************************
ok: [172.16.1.119]

TASK [creating virtual environment] ********************************************
changed: [172.16.1.119]

PLAY RECAP *********************************************************************
172.16.1.119              : ok=4    changed=1    unreachable=0    failed=0
```

Planning and what to keep in mind

The Ansible Developer Guide has a section on how should you develop a module (http://docs.ansible.com/ansible/latest/dev_guide/developing_modules.html#should-you-develop-a-module).

In the section, they have multiple points on what to keep in mind before going ahead and developing a module.

Does a similar module already exist? It's always a good idea to check the current modules to see whether what you plan to build has been done before. The good news is, so far nobody has built an **Open Web Application Security Project (OWASP) Zed Attack Proxy (ZAP)** module.

Has someone already worked on a similar *Pull Request?* Again, maybe the module hasn't been published but that doesn't mean that folks are not working on it already. The document provides three convenient links to check if a similar PR is already in place.

Additionally, it asks if rather than a module, we should look at an action plugin or role. The main reason we think it makes sense for us to develop the module is the fact that it will run on the nodes. ZAP provides an API endpoint if it is already running and we intend for our module to make it easy for us to run ZAP scans on hosted ZAP instances.

So, this is the plan for now:

1. Create a module that will connect to a hosted ZAP instance.
2. Provide the module with two main pieces of information:
   - IP address of the hosted ZAP
   - Target URL for scanning
3. By calling the module, we will have a task for scanning the target application.

OWASP ZAP module

OWASP ZAP has an API that we can use. Additionally, there is a Python module for consuming the API. We will try and use that to learn how to write our own Ansible modules.

Create ZAP using Docker

For our development, let's use a Docker container to get ZAP going. Since we plan to use the API, we will run the container in headless mode:

```
$ docker run -u zap -p 8080:8080 -i owasp/zap2docker-stable zap.sh -daemon
-host 0.0.0.0 -port 8080 -config api.disablekey=true -config
api.addrs.addr.name=.* -config api.addrs.addr.regex=true
```

Explanation of the command

- While we are doing dev, we can disable the API key: `-config api.disablekey=true`
- Allow access to the API from any IP: `-config api.addrs.addr.name=.* -config api.addrs.addr.regex=true`
- Listen to port `8080`

If everything worked fine, you will see the following output:

```
2594 [ZAP-daemon] INFO org.parosproxy.paros.extension.ExtensionLoader  - Initializing Easy way to
 replace strings in requests and responses
2689 [ZAP-daemon] INFO org.zaproxy.zap.extension.callback.ExtensionCallback  - Started callback s
erver on 0.0.0.0:40083
2689 [ZAP-daemon] INFO org.zaproxy.zap.extension.dynssl.ExtensionDynSSL  - Creating new root CA c
ertificate
3089 [ZAP-daemon] INFO org.zaproxy.zap.extension.dynssl.ExtensionDynSSL  - New root CA certificat
e created
3091 [ZAP-daemon] INFO org.zaproxy.zap.DaemonBootstrap  - ZAP is now listening on 0.0.0.0:8080
```

Creating a vulnerable application

For a vulnerable application, we can host one of our own but let's use the same online vulnerable application we used for the OWASP ZAP + Jenkins integration in Chapter 5, *Automating Web Application Security Testing Using OWASP ZAP* - `http://testphp.vulnweb.com/`

Ansible module template

We will take the sample code given in the module development guide to get started: `http://docs.ansible.com/ansible/latest/dev_guide/developing_modules_general.html#new-module-development`.

This template has a well-commented code and it is written in a manner that makes it easy for us to get started. The code is divided into the following parts:

- Metadata
- Documenting the module
- Functions we will be using

Metadata

This section contains the information about the modules:

```
ANSIBLE_METADATA = {
    'metadata_version': '1.1',
    'status': ['preview'],
    'supported_by': 'community'
}
```

This module isn't supported officially, hence the use of `community`.

Documenting the module

The module documentation is generated from the module code itself. The `DOCUMENTATION` docstring is compulsory for the modules to be created now.

> The easiest way to get started is to look at this example: `https://github.com/ansible/ansible/blob/devel/examples/DOCUMENTATION.yml`.

The list of fields required here are:

- `module`: Module name
- `short_description`: Short description
- `description`: Description
- `version_added`: Indicated by `X.Y`
- `author`: Your name and twitter/GitHub username
- `options`: Each of the options supported by the module
- `notes`: Anything else that a module user should be aware of
- `requirements`: We list additional package requirements

> For more details about the fields, visit `http://docs.ansible.com/ansible/latest/dev_guide/developing_modules_documenting.html#fields`.

Source code template

Here are some snippets of the source code that we will work with to write our module. We have already discussed the metadata and documentation parts. We also need to write docstrings for examples and what the module will be returning.

Our imports—we can import all the modules we need for our module here:

```
from ansible.module_utils.basic import AnsibleModule
```

The main code block—inside the function `run_module` we work and do the following:

1. Define all the arguments we need for the module to work.
2. Initialize the results dictionary.
3. Create the `AnsibleModule` object and pass it common attributes that we may need:

```
def run_module():
    # define the available arguments/parameters that a user can pass to
    # the module
    module_args = dict(
        name=dict(type='str', required=True),
        new=dict(type='bool', required=False, default=False)
    )

    # seed the result dict in the object
    # we primarily care about changed and state
    # change is if this module effectively modified the target
    # state will include any data that you want your module to pass back
    # for consumption, for example, in a subsequent task
    result = dict(
        changed=False,
        original_message='',
        message=''
    )

    # the AnsibleModule object will be our abstraction working with Ansible
    # this includes instantiation, a couple of common attr would be the
    # args/params passed to the execution, as well as if the module
    # supports check mode
    module = AnsibleModule(
        argument_spec=module_args,
        supports_check_mode=True
    )
```

4. Working with exceptions and results:

```
# during the execution of the module, if there is an exception or a
    # conditional state that effectively causes a failure, run
    # AnsibleModule.fail_json() to pass in the message and the result
    if module.params['name'] == 'fail me':
        module.fail_json(msg='You requested this to fail', **result)

    # in the event of a successful module execution, you will want to
    # simple AnsibleModule.exit_json(), passing the key/value results
    module.exit_json(**result)
```

Just remember the following:

- If we hit any kind of errors or exceptions, we invoke the `fail_json` function of the `AnsibleModule` object
- If everything worked out well, we invoke the `exit_json` function of the same object

Invoking our function completes the code:

```
def main():
    run_module()

if __name__ == '__main__':
    main()
```

At this point, we have the following things in place and we are ready for the next steps:

Template of the module code	Ready
Vulnerable application that we need to scan (target)	Ready
OWASP ZAP Proxy with API enabled and running in headless mode (host and port)	Ready
OWASP ZAP Python API code that we can refer to	Pending

We want to focus on writing the Ansible module rather than spending time learning the complete OWASP ZAP API. While we recommend that you do, it's fine to wait until you have gotten the module working.

OWASP ZAP Python API sample script

OWASP ZAP Python API package comes with a very handy script that is complete in terms of code for spidering and doing an active scan of a web application.

> Download the code to study it from `https://github.com/zaproxy/zaproxy/wiki/ApiPython#an-example-python-script`.

Here are some snippets from sample code that we are interested in at this point. Import the Python API client for OWASP ZAP. This is installed using `pip install python-owasp-zap-v2.4`:

```
from zapv2 import ZAPv2
```

Now, we connect to the ZAP instance API endpoint. We can provide the host and port for the OWASP ZAP instance as an argument to our module:

```
zap = ZAPv2(apikey=apikey, proxies={'http': 'http://127.0.0.1:8090',
'https': 'http://127.0.0.1:8090'})
```

Provide the host/IP address of the website that we want to scan:

```
zap.urlopen(target)
# Give the sites tree a chance to get updated
time.sleep(2)

print 'Spidering target %s' % target
scanid = zap.spider.scan(target)

# Give the Spider a chance to start
time.sleep(2)
while (int(zap.spider.status(scanid)) < 100):
    print 'Spider progress %: ' + zap.spider.status(scanid)
    time.sleep(2)

print 'Spider completed'
# Give the passive scanner a chance to finish
time.sleep(5)

print 'Scanning target %s' % target
scanid = zap.ascan.scan(target)
while (int(zap.ascan.status(scanid)) < 100):
    print 'Scan progress %: ' + zap.ascan.status(scanid)
    time.sleep(5)
```

```
print 'Scan completed'

# Report the results

print 'Hosts: ' + ', '.join(zap.core.hosts)
print 'Alerts: '
pprint (zap.core.alerts())
```

This code is a great starter template for us to use in our module.

Here, we are ready with OWASP ZAP Python API code that we can refer to.

Connect to the ZAP instance. At this point, we copied the important bits of code that:

1. Connect to the target.
2. Initiate spidering and the active security scan.

But we quickly ran into an error. We were returning a string during an exception, which obviously wasn't in the JSON format as required by Ansible.

This resulted in an error which didn't have enough information for us to take action

```
localhost | FAILED! => {
    "changed": false,
    "module_stderr": "",
    "module_stdout": "",
    "msg": "MODULE FAILURE",
    "rc": 0
}
```

Ansible modules should only return JSON, otherwise you may see cryptic errors such as above

A quick reading of conventions, best practices, and pitfalls at http://docs.ansible.com/ansible/latest/dev_guide/developing_modules_best_practices.html#conventions-best-practices-and-pitfalls explained the issue to us.

> We strongly recommend that you go through this guide if you face any issues during your module writing: http://docs.ansible.com/ansible/latest/dev_guide/developing_modules_best_practices.html#conventions-best-practices-and-pitfalls.

Use the OWASP ZAP API documentation to learn more: `https://github.com/zaproxy/zaproxy/wiki/ApiGen_Index`.

Complete code listing

This code is also available on GitHub (`https://github.com/appsecco/ansible-module-owasp-zap`). All comments, metadata, and documentation doctrings have been removed from this listing:

```
try:
    from zapv2 import ZAPv2
    HAS_ZAPv2 = True
except ImportError:
    HAS_ZAPv2 = False

from ansible.module_utils.basic import AnsibleModule
import time
def run_module():
    module_args = dict(
        host=dict(type='str', required=True),
        target=dict(type='str', required=True)
    )

    result = dict(
        changed=False,
        original_message='',
        message=''
    )

    module = AnsibleModule(
        argument_spec=module_args,
        supports_check_mode=True
    )

    if not HAS_ZAPv2:
        module.fail_json(msg = 'OWASP python-owasp-zap-v2.4 required. pip
install python-owasp-zap-v2.4')

    if module.check_mode:
        return result
    host = module.params['host']
    target = module.params['target']
    apikey = None
```

```
zap = ZAPv2(apikey=apikey, proxies={'http':host,'https':host})
zap.urlopen(target)
try:
    scanid = zap.spider.scan(target)
    time.sleep(2)
    while (int(zap.spider.status(scanid)) < 100):
        time.sleep(2)
except:
    module.fail_json(msg='Spidering failed')
time.sleep(5)

try:
    scanid = zap.ascan.scan(target)
    while (int(zap.ascan.status(scanid)) < 100):
        time.sleep(5)
except:
    module.fail_json(msg='Scanning failed')

result['output'] = zap.core.alerts()
result['target'] = module.params['target']
result['host'] = module.params['host']
module.exit_json(**result)

def main():
    run_module()
if __name__ == '__main__':
    main()
```

Depending on the website being spidered and scanned, this can take some time to finish. At the end of its execution, you will have the scanning results in `results['output']`.

Running the module

The choices we have for running the module are as follows:

1. We copy it to the standard path of Ansible library.
2. We provide a path to Ansible library whenever we have our module file.
3. Run this file through a playbook.

The following command will invoke our module for us to test and see the results:

```
ansible -m owasp_zap_test_module localhost -a
"host=http://172.16.1.102:8080 target=http://testphp.vulnweb.com" -vvv
```

Explanation of the command

- `ansible` command line
- `-m` to give the module name, which is `owasp_zap_test_module`
- It will run on `localhost`
- `-a` allows us to pass the `host` and `target` module arguments
- `-vvv` is for the verbosity of output

Playbook for the module

Here is a simple playbook to test whether everything is working:

```
- name: Testing OWASP ZAP Test Module
  connection: local
  hosts: localhost
  tasks:
  - name: Scan a website
    owasp_zap_test_module:
      host: "http://172.16.1.102:8080"
      target: "http://testphp.vulnweb.com"
```

Execute the playbook with this command:

```
ansible-playbook owasp-zap-site-scan-module-playbook.yml
```

```
PLAY [Testing OWASP ZAP Test Module] ************************************************

TASK [Gathering Facts] ************************************************************
ok: [localhost]

TASK [Scan a website] *************************************************************
ok: [localhost]

PLAY RECAP ***********************************************************************
localhost                  : ok=2    changed=0    unreachable=0    failed=0
```

An important thing to remember is that just because we have a working module doesn't mean that the good folks at Ansible will automatically accept our module to ship with their next version of the software. A lot of additional work is required for our module to be ready to be used by everyone.

As usual, the best guide for this is the developer guide mentioned earlier in this chapter.

One of the easy things to add to our module would be the ability to send the API key as an argument. Most ZAP instances that are being used for regular scanning will already have this configured. Additionally, this key can be protected by the Ansible vault when stored in the playbook.

Adding an API key as an argument

Just by making the following changes, we will be able to add `apikey` as an argument:

- First, we add this to the `module_args` dictionary on lines 76-78: `apikey=dict(type='str',required=False,default=None)`

- Then we check whether `module.params['apikey']` is set to a value of `None`
- If it is not, set it to `apikey = module.params['apikey']`
- Now, if the module is used with the Ansible command-line tool, pass it along with the `target` and `host`, and if it is used in the playbook, pass it there

Adding scan type as an argument

If you have followed so far, you may realize that the scan that we ran is an active scan. The scanner sends attack traffic against the target in an active scan.

Due to that fact, sometimes if the website is large, it may take a long time to finish.

 More information about active scans can be found at `https://github.com/zaproxy/zap-core-help/wiki/HelpStartConceptsAscan`.

We would like to add an argument for being able to provide the type of scan to run. So far we have two types:

- **Active**: Sends attack traffic
- **Passive**: Parses all the site files downloaded during the spidering phase

We start by adding this as part of the `module_args`:

```
module_args = dict(
    host=dict(type='str', required=True),
    target=dict(type='str', required=True),
    apikey=dict(type='str',required=False,default=None),
```

```
        scantype=dict(default='passive', choices=['passive','active'])
)
```

The newly added line is in bold to highlight the change. Notice that we have defined the default value now and this argument is only allowed two choices currently. So if nothing is set, we do the faster, less invasive, passive scan.

We need to get the value of module param into a variable called scantype:

```
scantype = module.params['scantype']
```

The logic changes to accommodate two possible values now:

```
if scantype == 'active':
    try:
        scanid = zap.ascan.scan(target)
        while (int(zap.ascan.status(scanid)) < 100):
            time.sleep(5)
    except:
        module.fail_json(msg='Active Scan Failed')
else:
    try:
        while (int(zap.pscan.records_to_scan) > 0):
            time.sleep(2)
    except:
        module.fail_json(msg='Passive Scan Failed')
```

If scantype is set and the value is active, only then does it go ahead and do an active scan. This improvement makes our module more flexible:

```
Using the new and improved module in our playbook
- name: Testing OWASP ZAP Test Module
  connection: local
  hosts: localhost
  tasks:
  - name: Scan a website
    owasp_zap_test_module:
      host: "http://172.16.1.102:8080"
      target: "http://testphp.vulnweb.com"
      scantype: passive
    register: output
  - name: Print version
    debug:
      msg: "Scan Report: {{ output }}"
```

Using Ansible as a Python module

Using Ansible directly in your Python code is a powerful way of interacting with it. Please note that with Ansible 2.0 and newer, this is not the simplest of way of doing that.

 Before we proceed we should let you know what the core Ansible team thinks about using the Python API directly

From http://docs.ansible.com/ansible/latest/dev_guide/developing_api.html

Please note that while we make this API available it is not intended for direct consumption, it is here for the support of the Ansible command line tools. We try not to make breaking changes but we reserve the right to do so at any time if it makes sense for the Ansible toolset.

The following documentation is provided for those that still want to use the API directly, but be mindful this is not something the Ansible team supports.

The following code is from the Ansible Developer Guide documentation: `http://docs.ansible.com/ansible/latest/dev_guide/developing_api.html`:

```
import json
from collections import namedtuple
from ansible.parsing.dataloader import DataLoader
from ansible.vars.manager import VariableManager
from ansible.inventory.manager import InventoryManager
from ansible.playbook.play import Play
from ansible.executor.task_queue_manager import TaskQueueManager
from ansible.plugins.callback import CallbackBase
```

Once all the initial work is done, this is how a task will be executed:

```
try</span>:
    tqm = TaskQueueManager(
            inventory=inventory,
            variable_manager=variable_manager,
            loader=loader,
            options=options,
            passwords=passwords,
            stdout_callback=results_callback,  # Use our custom callback
instead of the ``default`` callback plugin
            )
    result = tqm.run(play)
```

Before Ansible 2.0, the whole process was a lot easier. But this code doesn't work anymore:

```
import ansible.runner

runner = ansible.runner.Runner(
    module_name='ping',
    module_args='',
    pattern='web*',
    forks=10
)
datastructure = runner.run()
```

Summary

In this chapter, we created a working Ansible module for security automation. We started by creating a sort of hello world module that didn't do much, but helped us understand the layout of what a module file could look like. We followed the instructions as per the Ansible developer guide on how to set up an environment for being able to do module development. We articulated our requirement from the module and picked OWASP ZAP as a possible candidate for creating the module.

Using the training wheels, such as the template from the developer docks, we created the module and we saw how to use it using Ansible CLI or a playbook. We added a couple more options to the original code so that we could make the module more useful and flexible. Now we have an OWASP ZAP Ansible module that can connect to any hosted OWASP ZAP that allows access with the API key and executes a passive or active scan on the target.

This is the penultimate chapter of the book. In the next chapter, we will look at additional references, security of our secrets using Ansible Vault, and some world-class references of security automation already enabled using Ansible.

11
Ansible Security Best Practices, References, and Further Reading

Last chapter. We have finally got here. Time to reflect on what we have learned together. Time to list where you should head from here. Most importantly, there are a few topics that will enhance your experience of working with Ansible.

Some of the topics we'll cover in this chapter are as follows:

- Working with Ansible Vault and why you should be storing all your secrets inside the vault
- Using Ansible Galaxy for sharing playbooks and roles
- Securing the master controller
- Additional references
- Looking forward to what's new and upcoming in Ansible 2.5

Working with Ansible Vault

Ansible Vault is a command line utility, by default installed along with Ansible. It allows us to encrypt secrets such as keys, credentials, passwords, and so on to include in our playbooks. By doing this, we can also use these encrypted files to share with others as they contain password protection to access the encrypted data. We can use this feature to encrypt our variables, templates, and files inside our playbooks.

Ansible version 2.3 supports encrypting single variables using an Ansible single encrypted variable with the `!vault` tag. We will see some examples of how we will use this in our playbooks in next section.

 Read more about Ansible Vault at `https://docs.ansible.com/ansible/latest/vault.html`.

As this is a very simple and powerful way to store and manage secret data, it's really important to use Ansible Vault to store all the secret information in our playbooks.

Some of the really good use cases include how we can use these playbooks without changing our version control systems, CI/CD integration pipelines, and so on.

How to use Ansible Vault with variables and files

The following examples demonstrate how we can use secrets in our playbook variable files.

Let's take an example of installing MySQL server in an Ubuntu operating system using the following playbook. As per the Ansible documentation, it's easy and better to store Vault variables and normal variables differently.

The following code snippet is the high-level file structure for installing MySQL server with the root password:

```
├──── group_vars
│     └──── mysql.yml # contains vault secret values
├──── hosts
├──── main.yml
└──── roles
      └──── mysqlsetup
            └──── tasks
                  └──── main.yml
```

Now we can see that the `mysqlsetup` role contains the following tasks that require the `mysql_root_password` variable, which contains the root password for the MySQL server:

```
- name: set mysql root password
  debconf:
    name: mysql-server
    question: mysql-server/root_password
    value: "{{ mysql_root_password | quote }}"
```

```
      vtype: password

- name: confirm mysql root password
  debconf:
    name: mysql-server
    question: mysql-server/root_password_again
    value: "{{ mysql_root_password | quote }}"
    vtype: password

- name: install mysqlserver
  apt:
    name: "{{ item }}"
    state: present
    update_cache: yes
  with_items:
   - mysql-server
   - mysql-client
```

Now, if we see the group_vars/main.yml file, the content looks as shown in the codeblock. It contains the secrets variable to use in the playbook, called mysql_root_password:

```
mysql_root_password: supersecretpassword
```

To encrypt the vault file, we will use the following command and it then prompts for the password to protect:

```
$ ansible-vault encrypt group_vars/mysql.yml

New Vault password:
Confirm New Vault password:
Encryption successful
```

Now, if we see the vault content it looks like the following, with AES256 encryption using the given password:

```
$ cat group_vars/main.yml
```

```
$ANSIBLE_VAULT;1.1;AES256
30356164636532373531656663666633031633037376432393865346237663065303838865313
03362
36316233306639396662353266383431643935643036303020a383338613635623533832366
13339
653331646632626265653323134386161376438323836313633363964363735343396238323
56263
303834383030373137650a633261653037306432386330303261653564366238323862303730303
26131
```

```
34353534313337616561643333613435396636363836396239306139383330335396531383
43231
64306566386261623064633337366665363361396436373376636
```

Now, to execute the playbook run the following command, it will prompt for the vault password:

```
$ ansible-playbook --ask-vault-pass -i hosts main.yml
```

The following screenshot shows that we provided the Vault password while executing the Ansible Playbook

```
$ ansible-playbook --ask-vault -i hosts main.yml
Vault password:

PLAY [Installing MySQL server] ****************************************

TASK [mysqlsetup : set mysql root password] **************************
changed: [192.168.33.22]

TASK [mysqlsetup : confirm mysql root password] *********************
changed: [192.168.33.22]

TASK [mysqlsetup : install mysqlserver] ****************************
changed: [192.168.33.22] => (item=[u'mysql-server', u'mysql-client'])

PLAY RECAP ********************************************************
192.168.33.22              : ok=3     changed=3    unreachable=0    failed=0
```

- We can also pass the `ansible-vault` password file with playbook execution by specifying flag, it helps in our continuous integration and pipeline platforms.
- The following file contains the password which used to encrypt the `mysql.yml` file:

```
$ cat ~/.vaultpassword
```

```
thisisvaultpassword
```

Make sure to give proper permissions for this file, so others cannot access this file using `chmod`. Also, it's good practice to add this file to your `.gitignore`, so it will not be version controlled when pushing playbooks.

Vault password file can be an executable script, which can retrieve data stored somewhere securely rather than having to keep the key in plain text on disk and relying on file permissions to keep it safe.

To pass the vault password file through the command line, use the following command when executing playbooks:

```
$ ansible-playbook --vault-password-file ~/.vaultpassword -i hosts main.yml
```

We can also use system environment variables such as ANSIBLE_VAULT_PASSWORD_FILE=~/.vaultpassword and Ansible will use this while executing playbooks.

We can use ansible-vault for multiple operations, such as creating a file using create argument. This encrypts the content of the file by default. It will also open the default text editor to edit the file as well:

```
$ ansbile-vault create vault.yml

New Vault password:
Confirm New Vault password:
```

We can use view command to see the vault encrypted information in plain text.

```
$ ansible-vault view vault.yml
Vault password:
API_KEY: KANGEG4TNG434G43HG43H9GH344FEGEW
```

To change the content, we can use the edit sub command in ansible-vault:

```
$ ansible-vault edit vault.yml

Vault password:
```

We can also decrypt the secret information using the following command

```
$ ansible-vault decrypt vault.yml

Vault password:
Decryption successful
```

To change the vault password for key rotation, we can use the rekey option:

```
$ ansible-vault rekey vault.yml
Vault password:
New Vault password:
Confirm New Vault password:
Rekey successful
```

Ansible Vault single encrypted variable

This feature is available from Ansible version 2.3. It allows us to use vaulted variables with the !vault tag in YAML files; we will see a simple example and use case for this.

The following playbook is used to perform reverse IP lookups using the ViewDNS API.

We want to secure api_key as it contains sensitive information. We use the ansible-vault encrypt_string command to perform this encryption. Here, we used echo with the -n flag to remove the new line:

```
$ echo -n '53ff4ad63849e6977cb652763g7b7c64e2fa42a' | ansible-vault
encrypt_string --stdin-name 'api_key'
```

```
$ echo -n '53ff4ad63849e6977cb652763g7b7c64e2fa42a' | ansible-vault encrypt_string --stdin-name 'api_key'
New Vault password:
Confirm New Vault password:
Reading plaintext input from stdin. (ctrl-d to end input)
api_key: !vault |
          $ANSIBLE_VAULT;1.1;AES256
          3062356163323630323135306135336532613634616530366233376236373036635616131363316133
          3434393553162316532393433333313962386162626161663340a643337396333663836633634656537
          6630363366633765326664636561353333332643532356166346334336537373237325326462616233939
          3863626437393730320a663737663036663332396435323962313632343639383132393766666664439
          3366373536346466346135313831333933626462333839383633063065663530666262646466643563
          6636653639663732336333263633333386133346635626234303165
Encryption successful
```

Then we can place the variable, as shown in the following code block, inside the playbook variables and execute the playbook as normal, using ansible-playbook with the --ask-vault-pass option:

```
- name: ViewDNS domain information
  hosts: localhost
  vars:
    domain: google.com
    api_key: !vault |
          $ANSIBLE_VAULT;1.1;AES256
          36623761316238613461326466326162373764353437393733343333437616133663030333353326
          26465
          66623834353039303031643536646436393037613533664330a393365633237306530653996335
          53764
          64626237313738656530373639653739656564316161663831653431623832336635393636376
          53330
          66326635633632643400a32353735616665533389613537616132343535393730306133662663533
          76539
          37383861653239326336613837666237636463396465393662666561393132343166666633646
          53465
              62653861363861323633534336532623061646438363235383334
```

```
      output_type: json
  tasks:
    - name: "getting {{ domain }} server info"
      uri:
        url: "https://api.viewdns.info/reverseip/?host={{ domain
}}&apikey={{ api_key }}&output={{ output_type }}"
        method: GET
      register: results
    - debug:
        msg: "{{ results.json }}"
```

Then, playbook being executed will be automatically decrypted after we provide it with the given password.

The screenshot below shows the playbook executing after prompting for the vault password.

Read more about `encrypt_string` **options at** `https://docs.ansible.com/ansible/2.4/vault.html#use-encrypt-string-to-create-encrypted-variables-to-embed-in-yaml`.

Ansible Vault usage in Ansible Tower

Ansible Tower is already integrated with Ansible Vault.

The following screenshot refers to creating new credentials in Ansible Tower. Also we can add Vault Password, this enables users to use a more secure way of storing secrets and retrieving them

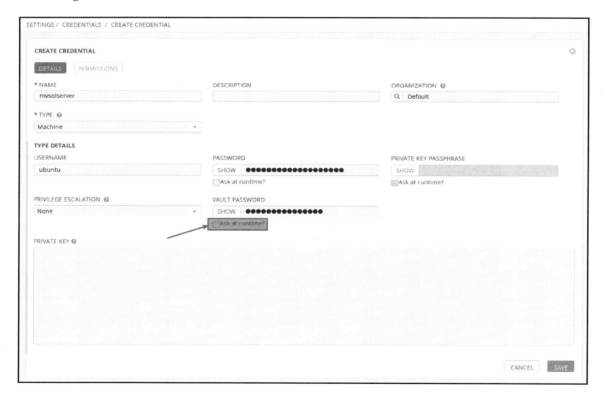

Setting up and using Ansible Galaxy

Ansible Galaxy, also known as Galaxy, is an official centralized hub for finding, sharing, and reusing Ansible roles. This allows the community to share and collaborate on Ansible playbooks, and allows new users to quickly get started with using Ansible. To share our custom-written roles with the community, we can publish them to Ansible Galaxy using GitHub authentication.

These roles can be accessed at `https://galaxy.ansible.com` as well as using a command-line tool called `ansible-galaxy`, which is installed with Ansible:

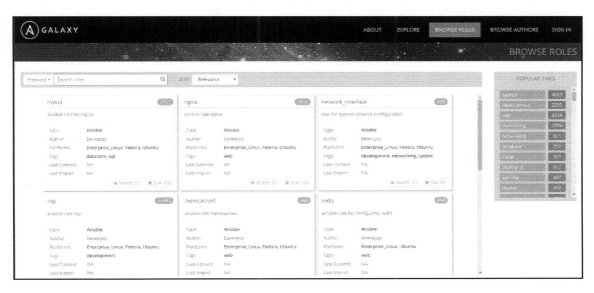

We can find roles using different parameters such as Author, Platform, Tag, and so on. This allows users to understand whether this role works for their distribution and version, which Ansible version is required, and other information.

The following screenshot shows how we can use `ansible-galaxy` CLI to perform different operations, such as searching and installing:

```
$ ansible-galaxy --help
Usage: ansible-galaxy [delete|import|info|init|install|list|login|remove|search|setup] [--help] [options] ...

Options:
  -h, --help              show this help message and exit
  -c, --ignore-certs      Ignore SSL certificate validation errors.
  -s API_SERVER, --server=API_SERVER
                          The API server destination
  -v, --verbose           verbose mode (-vvv for more, -vvvv to enable
                          connection debugging)
  --version               show program's version number and exit

See 'ansible-galaxy <command> --help' for more information on a specific
command.
```

 Read more about Ansible Galaxy from docs at `http://docs.ansible.com/ansible/latest/galaxy.html`.

Learn more about Galaxy usage at `https://galaxy.ansible.com/intro`.

Using Ansible Galaxy roles

To download a role from the Ansible Galaxy website, we can run the following command, where `username` and `role_name` are the options:

```
$ ansible-galaxy install username.role_name
```

The following command will download the `docker_ubuntu` role by user `angstwad`:

```
$ ansible-galaxy install angstwad.docker_ubuntu

- downloading role 'docker_ubuntu', owned by angstwad
- downloading role from
https://github.com/angstwad/docker.ubuntu/archive/v3.3.4.tar.gz
- extracting angstwad.docker_ubuntu to
/home/ubuntu/.ansible/roles/angstwad.docker_ubuntu
- angstwad.docker_ubuntu (v3.3.4) was installed successfully
```

To use this role to install Docker on Ubuntu is as simple as including this role in our playbook and executing it:

```
- name: Run docker.ubuntu
  hosts: docker
  become: yes

  roles:
    - angstwad.docker_ubuntu
$ ansible-playbook -i hosts main.yml
```

We can install or include roles direct from GitHub by specifying the GitHub URL. This allows the use of private version control systems as local inventories of playbook roles:

```
$ ansible-galaxy install
git+https://github.com/geerlingguy/ansible-role-composer.git
```

Publishing our role to Ansible Galaxy

To publish our own roles to Ansible Galaxy, we need to have a GitHub account, which will be used to authenticate Ansible Galaxy, and the version control repository in GitHub will be the place to store our roles.

The following steps are used to create and share a new role in Ansible Galaxy:

1. First, create a new repository in GitHub and clone it locally using the following command:

   ```
   $ git clone
   https://username@github.com/username/ansible-role-docker.git
   docker
   ```

2. Then we can create a role structure using the `ansible-galaxy` command to create the structure:

   ```
   $ ansible-galaxy init docker --force
   - docker was created successfully

   # The structure looks like below
   ├────── defaults
   │    └────── main.yml
   ├────── files
   ├────── handlers
   │    └────── main.yml
   ├────── meta
   ```

```
|       └──── main.yml
├──── README.md
├──── tasks
|       └──── main.yml
├──── templates
├──── tests
|       ├──── inventory
|       └──── test.yml
└──── vars
        └──── main.yml
```

3. Now, we can add tasks and other steps in the same way as we created them previously. The following are some good practices from Ansible Galaxy itself (https://galaxy.ansible.com/intro#good):

1. Provide clear documentation in README.md.

2. Give accurate information in meta/main.yml.

3. Include dependencies in meta/main.yml.

4. Prefix variable names with the role name.

5. Integrate your roles with Travis CI.

4. The meta file contains the information that will be used to publish the role in Ansible Galaxy; we can modify it as required. Here is an example:

```
---
galaxy_info:
  author: USERNAME
  description: Quick and easy docker installer.
  company: ORG
  license: MIT
  min_ansible_version: 1.9
  platforms:
  - name: Ubuntu
    versions:
    - xenial
    - trusty
  galaxy_tags:
    - docker
    - installer
    - ubuntu
dependencies:
  - { role: username.common, some_parameter: 3 }
```

5. Then we can push the role to GitHub and import it to Ansible Galaxy by adding a new role in the portal:

Refer to http://docs.ansible.com/ansible/latest/playbooks_reuse.html for how to write reusable roles and more details about writing community roles.

Ansible Galaxy local setup

To set up Ansible Galaxy locally, we have different methods. Most of the installations use containers behind the scenes. The following steps describe how to install an Ansible Galaxy local setup using `docker` and `docker-compose`.

Before proceeding, we need the following prerequisites:

- Ansible 2.4+
- Docker
- The `docker-py` Python module
- The `docker-compose` Python module
- GNU make
- Git

We can clone the `galaxy` repository by running the following `git` command, which will clone the entire galaxy repository maintained by Ansible:

```
$ git clone https://github.com/ansible/galaxy.git
$ cd galaxy/installer
```

Change the required variables in the galaxy playbook; by default it will assume that the installation is in localhost. Also, update the passwords and other variables inside `inventory` file:

Then execute the following command to start the Ansible playbook setup to start the local Ansible Galaxy

```
$ ansible-playbook -i inventory galaxy.yml --tags start
```

This will take a while, as it has to download multiple Docker containers locally and set up the integration between them using `docker-compose`.

Once playbook execution has completed, we can see the following output about running Docker containers. It still takes some time to do database migrations and start the web server application:

Then once the setup is completed, we can navigate to `http://localhost` to see the web interface:

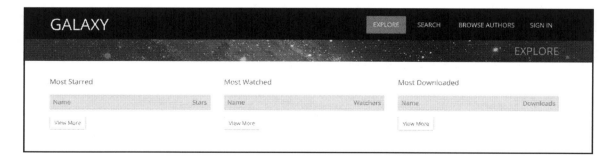

Read more about Ansible Galaxy local setup and other options for authentication and deployment at `https://github.com/ansible/galaxy/blob/develop/INSTALL.md`.

Ansible controller machine security

The controller machine for Ansible requires SSH and Python to be installed and configured. Ansible has a very low attack surface. In January 2017, multiple security issues were found by a company called Computest.

Read more about what they found at `https://www.computest.nl/advisories/CT-2017-0109_Ansible.txt`.

This vulnerability was dubbed *owning the farm*, since compromising the controller would imply that all the nodes could potentially be compromised.

The controller machine should be a hardened server and treated with all the seriousness that it deserves. In the vulnerability that was disclosed, if a node gets compromised attackers could leverage that to attack and gain access to the controller. Once they have access, the could extend their control over all the other nodes being managed by the controller.

Since the attack surface is already very limited, the best we can do is ensure that the server stays secure and hardened.

Two projects worth following and investigating are:

- https://docs.openstack.org/ansible-hardening/latest/getting-started.html#usage
- https://github.com/dev-sec/ansible-os-hardening

Explanation of Ansible OS hardening playbook

We have seen multiple playbooks and guidelines for following different standards in Chapter 7, *Security Hardening for Applications and Networks*. This can be completely customized based on your environment, but following certain guidelines will ensure it's well protected.

The following playbook is created by DevSec for Linux baselines. It covers most of the required hardening checks based on multiple standards, which includes Ubuntu Security Features, NSA Guide to Secure Configuration, ArchLinux System Hardening and other. This can be improved if required by adding more tasks (or) roles.

Ansible OS Hardening Playbook covers

- Configures package management, that is, allows only signed packages
- Removes packages with known issues
- Configures pam and the pam_limits module
- Shadow password suite configuration
- Configures system path permissions
- Disables core dumps through soft limits
- Restricts root logins to system console
- Sets SUIDs
- Configures kernel parameters through sysctl

The following command is to download the os-hardening role from Ansible Galaxy:

```
$ ansible-galaxy install dev-sec.os-hardening
```

```
$ ansible-galaxy install dev-sec.os-hardening
- downloading role 'os-hardening', owned by dev-sec
- downloading role from https://github.com/dev-sec/ansible-os-hardening/archive/4.2.0.tar.gz
- extracting dev-sec.os-hardening to /home/ubuntu/.ansible/roles/dev-sec.os-hardening
- dev-sec.os-hardening (4.2.0) was installed successfully
$
```

Then call that role in your playbook and execute it to perform the baseline hardening, and also change the variables as required. Refer to https://galaxy.ansible.com/dev-sec/os-hardening for more detailed options:

```
- hosts: localhost
  become: yes

  roles:
    - dev-sec.os-hardening
$ ansible-playbook main.yml
```

The following screenshot refers to the playbook execution, with a list of checks it is performing on the Ansible controller machine:

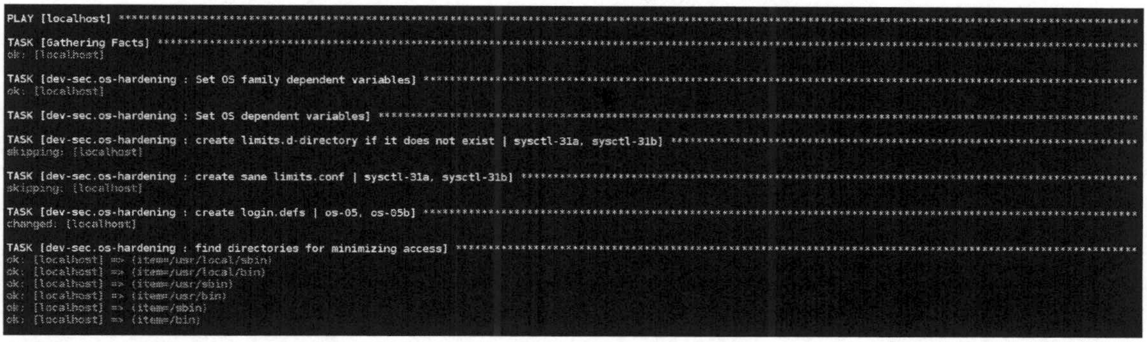

The following is the checks to minimize the system access by updating the configuration parameters in the system:

The following screenshot refers to upgrading the password hashing algorithm, updating the `suid` and guide for the superuser binaries:

```
TASK [dev-sec.os-hardening : NSA 2.3.3.5 Upgrade Password Hashing Algorithm to SHA-512] *********************************
changed: [localhost]

TASK [dev-sec.os-hardening : create profile.conf] ********************************
changed: [localhost]

TASK [dev-sec.os-hardening : create securetty] ********************************
changed: [localhost]

TASK [dev-sec.os-hardening : remove suid/sgid bit from binaries in blacklist | os-06] *********************
ok: [localhost] => (item=/usr/bin/rcp)
ok: [localhost] => (item=/usr/bin/rlogin)
ok: [localhost] => (item=/usr/bin/rsh)
ok: [localhost] => (item=/usr/libexec/openssh/ssh-keysign)
changed: [localhost] => (item=/usr/lib/openssh/ssh-keysign)
ok: [localhost] => (item=/sbin/netreport)
ok: [localhost] => (item=/usr/sbin/usernetctl)
ok: [localhost] => (item=/usr/sbin/userisdnctl)
ok: [localhost] => (item=/usr/sbin/pppd)
ok: [localhost] => (item=/usr/bin/lockfile)
ok: [localhost] => (item=/usr/bin/mail-lock)
ok: [localhost] => (item=/usr/bin/mail-unlock)
ok: [localhost] => (item=/usr/bin/mail-touchlock)
ok: [localhost] => (item=/usr/bin/dotlockfile)
ok: [localhost] => (item=/usr/bin/arping)
ok: [localhost] => (item=/usr/sbin/uuidd)
ok: [localhost] => (item=/usr/bin/mtr)
ok: [localhost] => (item=/usr/lib/evolution/camel-lock-helper-1.2)
ok: [localhost] => (item=/usr/lib/pt_chown)
changed: [localhost] => (item=/usr/lib/eject/dmcrypt-get-device)
ok: [localhost] => (item=/usr/lib/mc/cons.saver)
```

 To know more checks what this playbook executes visit `https://github.com/dev-sec/ansible-os-hardening/blob/master/tasks/main.yml`.

Best practices and reference playbook projects

Ansible is powerful and flexible. People use it in many different ways, and one of the ways we can understand how to use it for security automation is to keep track of and read playbooks created for specific use cases.

Projects such as Algo, DebOps, and OpenStack are large Ansible playbook projects that are well maintained and secure by default.

DebOps – your Debian-based data center in a box

DebOps (`https://debops.org`) is a project created by Maciej Delmanowski. It contains a collection of various Ansible playbooks that can be used for Debian and Ubuntu hosts. This project has more than 128 Ansible roles, which are customized for production use cases and work with multiple environments.

We can see a list of available playbook services at `https://github.com/debops/debops-playbooks`:

Setting up the DebOps controller

There are two different ways we can quickly get started with a DebOps setup:

- Vagrant setup
- Docker setup

Run the following command to start the Docker container created by DebOps:

```
$ docker run --name debops -it debops/debops
```

We can create and execute different roles to perform different actions using DebOps playbooks. Refer to the main documentation at `https://docs.debops.org/en/latest/index.html`.

Algo – set up a personal IPSEC VPN in the cloud

Algo from Trail of Bits provides Ansible roles and scripts to automate the installation of a personal IPSEC VPN.

By running the Ansible playbooks, you get a complete hardened VPN server, and deployments to all major cloud providers are already configured (`https://github.com/trailofbits/algo/blob/master/docs/deploy-from-ansible.md`).

OpenStack-Ansible

OpenStack-Ansible is the official project for deploying and configuring OpenStack using Ansible playbooks.

Start here for OpenStack-Ansible: `https://github.com/openstack/openstack-ansible`.

Not only does this project use Ansible playbooks extensively, but their security documentation is also worth reading and emulating. The best part is that all of the security configuration is declarative security codified in Ansible playbooks.

Documentation on this project is available at `https://docs.openstack.org/project-deploy-guide/openstack-ansible/latest/app-security.html`.

Additional references

Some good online references and links for Ansible that we found during our research for this book are:

- **Streisand**: Automated installation and configuration of anti-censorship software
- **Sovereign**: Maintain your own private cloud using Ansible playbooks
- **AWX**: Open source version of Ansible Tower

Streisand – automated installation and configuration of anti-censorship software

Using Ansible playbooks, Streisand can set up a cloud server full of software to bypass internet restrictions and online censorship. Tools that are set up include IPSEC-based VPN, OpenVPN, OpenConnect, Tor, and WireGuard.

Get started with Streisand at `https://github.com/StreisandEffect/streisand`.

Sovereign – maintain your own private cloud using Ansible playbooks

Using Ansible playbooks, Sovereign sets up your own private cloud with open source software. This puts you in control of your data with services including email, calendar, file sync, RSS reader, Git hosting, read it later, and chat.

Get started with Sovereign at `https://github.com/sovereign/sovereign`.

AWX – open source version of Ansible Tower

AWX provides a web-based user interface, REST API, and task engine built on top of Ansible. AWX can be used with the tower-CLI tool and client library.

Get started with AWX here: `https://github.com/ansible/awx`.

Get started with tower-cli here: `https://github.com/ansible/tower-cli/`
.

Coming soon to Ansible 2.5

Ansible version 2.5 is expected to be released in March 2018. There are no major changes from the current stable release of 2.4.2. Since the software world is always a moving target, a good place to keep track of what may or may not change is to follow the roadmap and porting guide:

- **Ansible 2.5 Porting Guide**
  (https://docs.ansible.com/ansible/devel/porting_guide_2.5.html)
- **Ansible 2.5 roadmap**
  (https://github.com/ansible/ansible/blob/devel/CHANGELOG.md#2.5)

Summary

In this chapter, we covered how to work with Ansible Vault, using the hosted Ansible Galaxy site and even self-hosting it. We also discussed on a need for keeping the controller node safe and secure.

Apart from these topics, we also looked at some of the most comprehensive software projects that use Ansible in a variety of ways. In all these projects, Ansible is the centrepiece of their orchestration and provisioning of software and related services. The main idea of highlighting all these projects was to expand on the theme of the book and also make you aware of the sheer number of ways Ansible is being used for automation, especially around security workloads. We also looked at what is coming in the next year in terms of Ansible 2.5, and concluded that so far nothing we have covered will break when it does become stable.

We are looking forward to seeing what kinds of security automation workflows all of you are going to build after taking this journey with us.

Index